Acknowledgement
The publishers wish to thank Jones & Brother, who kindly provided
a Hi-Speed Cooker for recipe development, testing, and
preparation for photography. The advanced MF2100 combination
cooker proved invaluable in the compilation of this book.

Compiled and Edited by Judith Ferguson
Designed by Philip Clucas
Photography by Peter Barry
Produced by Ted Smart,
David Gibbon and Gerald Hughes

THE
MICROWAVE
COOKBOOK

JUDITH FERGUSON

CONTENTS

Microwave

INTRODUCTION

Microwave ovens, whatever the make or model, have certain things in common. The energy that makes fast cooking possible is comprised of electromagnetic waves converted from electricity. These waves are a type of high frequency radio wave and are of short length, hence the name microwave.

Inside the oven is a magnetron, which converts ordinary electricity into microwaves. A wave guide channels the microwaves into the oven cavity and a stirrer fan circulates them evenly. Microwaves are attracted to the particles of moisture that form part of any food. As the microwaves are absorbed, to a depth of about 4-5cm/1½-2 inches, they cause the water molecules in the food to vibrate about 2000 million times per second. This generates the heat that cooks the food. The heat reaches the center of the food by conduction, just as in ordinary cooking, but this is accomplished much faster than in conventional cooking because no heat is generated until the microwaves are absorbed by the food. All the energy is concentrated on cooking the food rather than being wasted on heating the baking dishes or the oven itself. Standing time is often necessary to allow the food to continue cooking after it has been removed from the oven.

Microwave ovens have safety features built into them and are rigorously tested by their manufacturers and by independent agencies. The majority of microwave ovens are lined with metal, through which microwaves cannot pass. The doors have special seals to prevent the escape of microwaves, and have cut-out devices to cut off microwave energy immediately the door is opened. There are no pans to upset and no open flames or hot elements, the interior of the oven staying cool enough to touch. Although microwave ovens don't heat baking dishes, the heat generated by the cooking food does, so it is a good idea to use oven gloves or potholders to remove dishes from the oven.

Microwave ovens are cleaner and more hygienic to cook with than conventional gas or electric ovens. Foods do not spatter as much, and spills do not burn, so cleaning up is faster. Faster cooking times and lower electricity consumption combine to make microwave ovens cheaper to run, especially for cooking one or two portions of food. They also take up less space and are certainly more portable than conventional ovens.

Combination ovens seem to be the answer to the problem of browning in a microwave oven. While the power settings go by different names in different oven models, there is generally a setting for microwave cooking alone, a convection setting with conventional electric heat and a setting which combines the two, giving almost the speed of microwave cooking with the browning ability of convection heat. However, the wattage is usually lower than in standard microwave ovens, so cooking times will be slightly longer. On combination settings, use recipes developed for microwave ovens, but follow the instructions for your particular oven for times and settings.

Safe, clean and versatile, your microwave oven will do much to speed up the cooking process and widen the scope of cooking available to you within the busy schedule of a full life. Once you understand your oven and its potential, the fun of cooking begins.

Microwave

SOUPS AND APPETIZERS

Microwave
SOUPS AND APPETIZERS

Soups and starters or appetizers are the beginnings of a great meal. To make a memorable start, carefully consider how the soup or starter will co-ordinate with the rest of the meal. Consider color, texture and variety of ingredients.

Are soup and starters reserved only for the beginning of a meal? Absolutely not. They can be meals in themselves: soups, accompanied by salads and good bread, make wonderful cold weather lunches and dinners, while starters can double as light meals anytime. Microwave cooking makes light work of a light meal.

Soups can easily be made in small quantities in a microwave oven. Depending on your oven and your own preference, you may want to add 1½ times the flour quantity when adapting soup recipes for microwave cooking. Liquids do not evaporate as fast in microwave cooking as they do in conventional cooking and so more thickening may be required. The soup recipes in this book have been designed to include standing time, but always allow 1 to 2 minutes when adapting any soup recipe for your microwave oven.

Sauce recipes may need more flour, too, depending on your oven. These recipes were tested in a 700 watt maximum oven, but ovens with a lower maximum wattage may require a recipe with more flour.

Soufflés wait for no one, and those made in a microwave oven are no exception. I've included one, though, because they cook in a matter of minutes and are great fun to watch. Beware of over-cooking, though.

Pâtés are one food the microwave oven cooks excellently, and in a fraction of the time taken in a conventional oven. A custard cup of water in the oven with the pâté or terrine keeps the mixture moist.

A microwave oven can be a great boon when giving a dinner party. Preparations can be made ahead of time and then your first course can be reheated in a matter of minutes while you relax with your guests. Better still, soups and starters can be cooked and reheated in their serving dishes, providing they are safe for the microwave oven. Think of the advantage that will give when the time comes to washing the dishes!

Microwave
SOUPS AND APPETIZERS

CREAM AND PURÉE SOUPS

Crab Bisque

PREPARATION TIME: 15 minutes

MICROWAVE COOKING TIME:
17 minutes

SERVES: 4 people

SOUP
450g/1lb crabmeat, fresh or frozen
45g/1½ oz/3 tbsps butter or margarine
45g/1½ oz/3 tbsps flour/plain flour
1 shallot finely chopped
570ml/1 pint/2 cups milk
140ml/¼ pint/½ cup cream
280ml/½ pint/1 cup fish or chicken stock
1 bay leaf
Salt
Pepper
Tabasco
30ml/2 tbsps dry sherry

CROÛTONS
30g/1oz/2 tbsps butter or margarine
2 slices bread, crusts removed
Salt
Pepper
Paprika

Put butter and shallot into a
casserole. Cover and cook for
3 minutes on HIGH, stirring
occasionally. Stir in the flour and
cook for 2 minutes on HIGH. Stir in
the milk, stock, seasonings, bay leaf
and a few drops of tabasco and cover
and cook on HIGH for 5 minutes,
stirring frequently. Blend in the
crabmeat and sherry. Cook on
MEDIUM for 3-4 minutes. To
prepare croûtons, place butter in a
small bowl and cook on LOW for
15-20 seconds or until softened. Cut
each slice of bread into 12-16 squares,
depending on the size and thickness
of the slices. Toss the cubes of bread
in the melted butter with salt and
pepper. Spread the bread out on a
flat plate. Sprinkle the bread with
paprika and cook on HIGH for 1½-2
minutes or until the croûtons are
firm but not crisp. Stir and turn the
croûtons several times during

**This page: Crab Bisque (top) and
Cream of Chicken Soup (bottom).
Facing page: Cream of Cucumber
Soup (top) and Leek and Potato
Soup (bottom).**

cooking. Let them stand for 5 minutes before serving. Re-heat the soup on HIGH for 1 minute. Stir in the cream just before serving, top with the croûtons and dust with more paprika.

Leek and Potato Soup

PREPARATION TIME: 10 minutes

MICROWAVE COOKING TIME: 20 minutes

SERVES: 4 people

3 leeks, washed and sliced thinly
550g/1½lbs/3½ cups potatoes, diced
45g/1½ oz/3 tbsps butter or margarine
570ml/1 pint/2 cups milk
430ml/¾ pint/1½ cups chicken or
    vegetable stock
1 bay leaf
1.25ml/¼ tsp thyme
Salt
Pepper

GARNISH
1 bunch chives, chopped
120ml/¼ pint/½ cup sour cream

Put leeks, potatoes and butter into a large bowl. Cover with plastic wrap and pierce several times. Cook on HIGH for 10 minutes. Add milk, stock, thyme, bay leaf and seasoning, and cook for 7 minutes on HIGH. Leave standing, covered, for 1 minute. Uncover and allow to cool slightly. Remove bay leaf, pour soup into a food processor, and purée until smooth. Check seasoning and heat through for 3 minutes on HIGH. Serve with a spoonful of sour cream and chopped chives for each individual portion.

Cream of Chicken Soup

PREPARATION TIME: 15 minutes

MICROWAVE COOKING TIME: 31 minutes

SERVES: 4 people

450g/1lb chicken breasts
430ml/¾ pint/1½ cups water
570ml/1 pint/2 cups milk
1 chicken bouillon cube
30g/1oz/2 tbsps butter
30g/1oz/2 tbsps flour/plain flour
60ml/2 fl oz/¼ cup heavy/double cream
1 bay leaf
1 sprig thyme
1.25ml/¼ tsp sage, fresh or dried
Salt
Pepper

GARNISH
1 bunch chives, chopped

Put the chicken into a large bowl with the water. Cover with plastic wrap, pierce several times, and cook for 15 minutes on HIGH. Remove chicken from bowl and leave to cool. Strain the liquid from the chicken and set it aside. Put butter and flour into the bowl and cook for 1 minute on HIGH. Gradually stir in the liquid from the chicken and the milk. Add bay leaf, thyme and seasoning, and cook for 4 minutes on HIGH, stirring occasionally. Remove skin and bone from chicken, and cut into small pieces. Crumble the stock cube and add to the bowl along with the chicken and sage. Cook, uncovered, for 10 minutes on HIGH. Add cream and cook for 1 minute on HIGH. Serve garnished with chopped chives.

Lentil Soup with Smoked Sausage

PREPARATION TIME: 10 minutes

MICROWAVE COOKING TIME: 60-70 minutes

SERVES: 4 people

225g/½lb smoked sausage
255g/9oz/1½ cups brown lentils, washed
1 medium onion, chopped
1 bay leaf
1.25ml/¼ tsp thyme
15ml/1 tbsp Worcester sauce
Powdered cloves
1 litre/1¾ pints/4 cups chicken or
    vegetable stock

GARNISH
45g/1½ oz/⅓ cup Parmesan cheese,
    grated

Put onion into a large bowl. Cover with plastic wrap and pierce in several places. Cook for 8 minutes on HIGH, or until onion is softened. Add lentils, herbs, Worcester sauce, pinch of powdered cloves and the stock. Re-cover bowl and cook on HIGH for about 20 minutes, stirring well. Reduce setting to MEDIUM and cook for about 20 minutes, stirring well. Remove skin from smoked sausage if desired. Add sausage to the bowl, and continue to cook for another 20-30 minutes, or until lentils are soft. Remove the bay leaf and the sausage. Purée the soup if desired. Slice the sausage into thin rounds and add to the soup. Stir soup well and adjust seasoning. Serve garnished with Parmesan cheese.

Creamy Spinach Soup

PREPARATION TIME: 15 minutes

MICROWAVE COOKING TIME: 16 minutes

SERVES: 4 people

900g/2lbs fresh spinach, washed and
    stems removed
30g/1oz/2 tbsps butter or margarine
30g/1oz/2 tbsps flour/plain flour
1 shallot, finely chopped
430ml/¾ pint/1½ cups milk
430ml/¾ pint/1½ cups chicken or
    vegetable stock
140ml/¼ pint/½ cup cream
1.25ml/¼ tsp marjoram
Squeeze of lemon juice
Grated nutmeg
Salt
Pepper

GARNISH
1 hard-boiled egg, chopped

Put washed spinach into a roasting bag and tie loosely. Stand the bag upright in the oven and cook for 2 minutes on HIGH, or until spinach

Facing page: Creamy Spinach Soup (top) and Lentil Soup with Smoked Sausage (bottom).

has wilted. (It can also be cooked in a bowl covered with pierced plastic wrap.) Put shallot and butter into a large bowl, cover and cook for 5 minutes on HIGH. Add flour, and cook for 2 minutes on HIGH. Stir in the milk and stock, and add marjoram, bay leaf and grated nutmeg. Cook for 2 minutes on HIGH, stirring occasionally. Add spinach, salt, pepper and lemon juice, and cook for 3 minutes on HIGH. Pour soup into a food processor and purée until smooth. Add cream, and adjust seasoning. Heat through for 2 minutes on HIGH. Serve garnished with egg.

Bouillabaisse

PREPARATION TIME: 15 minutes

MICROWAVE COOKING TIME: 10 minutes

SERVES: 4 people

450g/1lb assorted fish (eg monkfish, red snapper, cod, white fish, rock salmon)
225g/½lb assorted cooked shellfish (shrimp, lobster, crab)
2 leeks, cleaned and thinly sliced
1 small bulb Florentine fennel, sliced
30ml/2 tbsps olive oil
4 tomatoes, skinned, seeded and roughly chopped
15ml/1 tbsp tomato paste
850ml/1½ pints/3 cups water
150ml/6 fl oz/⅔ cup white wine
1 clove garlic, crushed
1 strip orange rind
2.5ml/½ tsp saffron
1 bay leaf
5ml/1 tsp lemon juice
15ml/1 tbsp chopped parsley
Salt
Pepper

GARNISH
4 slices French bread, toasted
60ml/2 fl oz/¼ cup prepared mayonnaise, mixed with 1 clove garlic, crushed, and a pinch of Cayenne pepper

Cut fish into 5cm (2") pieces. Remove shells from shellfish and cut crab and lobster into small pieces. Put leeks, fennel, garlic and olive oil

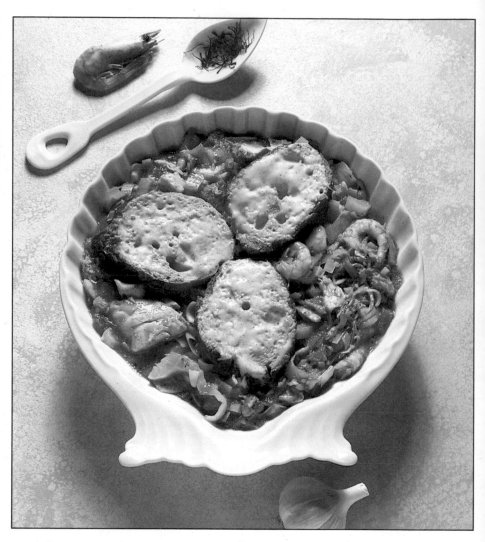

into a large casserole. Cover and cook for 3 minutes on HIGH. Add orange rind, saffron, bay leaf, lemon juice, water and wine. Stir in the tomato paste and seasoning, and mix well. Add fish and tomatoes and cook for 5 minutes, covered, on HIGH. Add shellfish and parsley, and cook for 2 minutes on HIGH. Mix the mayonnaise, garlic and Cayenne pepper and spread on the pieces of toasted French bread. Place bread in the bottom of the serving dish and spoon over the soup.

Cream of Celery Soup

PREPARATION TIME: 10 minutes

MICROWAVE COOKING TIME: 32 minutes

SERVES: 4 people

1 large head/4 cups chopped celery, leaves reserved
1 shallot, finely chopped
30g/1oz/2 tbsps butter
30g/1oz/2 tbsps flour
280ml/½ pint/1 cup chicken or vegetable stock
430ml/¾ pint/1½ cups milk
140ml/¼ pint/½ cup heavy/double cream
15ml/1 tbsp celery seeds (optional)
1 bay leaf
1 sprig thyme
Salt
Pepper

This page: Bouillabaisse.
Facing page: Cheddar Cheese Soup (top) and Cream of Celery Soup (bottom).

Put butter into a large casserole and heat for 1 minute on HIGH. Add celery and shallot, then cover and cook for 10 minutes on HIGH, stirring frequently, or until celery and shallot are soft. Stir in the flour and cook for 1 minute on HIGH. Add stock, milk, bay leaf, thyme and seasoning. Cover and cook for 18 minutes on HIGH, stirring frequently. Allow the soup to cool slightly. Remove bay leaf and thyme, and pour soup into a food processor. Purée until smooth, and return the soup to the bowl. Add celery seeds and re-heat for 2 minutes on HIGH. Just before serving, stir in the cream, and garnish with reserved celery leaves.

Cheddar Cheese Soup

PREPARATION TIME: 10 minutes

MICROWAVE COOKING TIME: 22 minutes

SERVES: 4 people

225g/8oz/2 cups mature Cheddar
    cheese and Red Leicester/Colby cheese,
    grated and mixed
1 carrot, peeled and diced
2 sticks celery, diced
45g/1½ oz/3 tbsps butter
30g/1oz/¼ cup flour/plain flour
570ml/1 pint/2 cups milk
430ml/¾ pint/1½ cups chicken or
    vegetable stock
1 bay leaf
1.25ml/¼ tsp thyme

GARNISH
Chopped parsley

Put butter, celery and carrot into a bowl. Cover with plastic wrap and pierce several times. Cook for 5 minutes on HIGH. Stir in the flour, and add the stock gradually, mixing well. Add thyme and bay leaf, and cook for 10 minutes on HIGH, uncovered. Add milk and cook for 5 minutes on HIGH. Put cheese into a bowl and stir in 140ml/¼ pint/½ cup of the liquid from the soup. Return cheese mixture to soup and cook, uncovered, for 2 minutes on HIGH. Serve with a garnish of chopped parsley.

Cream of Cucumber Soup

PREPARATION TIME: 10 minutes

MICROWAVE COOKING TIME: 22 minutes

SERVES: 4 people

1 large cucumber
1 shallot, finely chopped
30g/1oz/2 tbsps butter
30g/1oz/2 tbsps flour/plain flour
280ml/½ pint/1 cup chicken or vegetable
    stock
570ml/1 pint/2 cups milk
140ml/¼ pint/½ cup light/single cream
15ml/1 tbsp chopped parsley
1 small clove garlic, crushed
1 bunch dill, finely chopped
Grated nutmeg
Salt
Pepper

Put butter, shallot and garlic into a large bowl. Cover with plastic wrap and pierce several times. Cook for 3 minutes on HIGH. Add flour and blend thoroughly. Wash cucumber, reserve 4 slices for garnish, and grate the rest. Add it to the bowl and cook for 5 minutes on HIGH, until cucumber is slightly softened. Stir in the stock, parsley, nutmeg, chopped dill and seasoning. Re-cover bowl and cook for 7 minutes on HIGH. Stir in the milk and cream and pour into a food processor. Purée until smooth and return to the bowl. Heat through for 3 minutes on HIGH and serve garnished with the cucumber slices. Serve hot or cold.

Clam Chowder

PREPARATION TIME: 15 minutes

MICROWAVE COOKING TIME: 16 minutes

SERVES: 4 people

1 litre/1 quart clams
280ml/½ pint/1 cup water, mixed with
    5ml/1 tsp lemon juice
1 shallot, roughly chopped
4 strips green streaky bacon (rindless and
    boneless)
340g/12oz/2 cups diced potatoes
1 onion, finely sliced

1 litre/1¾ pints/3¼ cups milk
30g/1oz/2 tbsps butter
30g/1oz/2 tbsps flour/plain flour
Light/single cream as necessary
1 bay leaf
1.25ml/¼ tsp thyme
30ml/2 tbsps chopped parsley
Salt and pepper

GARNISH
Paprika

Scrub clams well and discard any that are open or broken. Put into a large bowl with the water, shallot and bay leaf. Cover with pierced plastic wrap and cook for 2 minutes on HIGH. Drain through a fine strainer and reserve. Remove clams from shells and set aside. Put butter, sliced onion and diced bacon into the rinsed-out bowl, cover, and cook on HIGH for 3 minutes. Stir in flour and cook a further 2 minutes on HIGH, stirring frequently. Add potatoes, milk, reserved clam liquid, thyme and seasoning. Cook for 10 minutes on HIGH, stirring occasionally. Add parsley and clams and, if soup is very thick, some cream to thin it down. Cook for 1 minute on HIGH. Serve sprinkled lightly with paprika.

Vichyssoise

PREPARATION TIME: 10-12 minutes

MICROWAVE COOKING TIME: 25 minutes

SERVES: 4 people

45g/1½ oz/3 tbsps butter or margarine
3 leeks
2-3 medium potatoes, peeled and sliced
850ml/1½ pints/3 cups chicken or
    vegetable stock
90ml/3 tbsps/⅓ cup sour cream
140ml/¼ pint/½ cup milk
Salt and pepper

Facing page: Clam Chowder (top) and Vichyssoise (bottom).

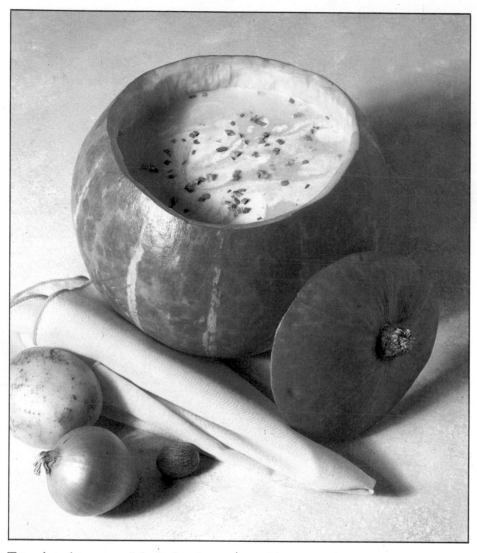

1 sprig fresh rosemary
Salt
Pepper

GARNISH
Parsley leaves

Put leeks, potatoes, carrots and butter into a large bowl. Cover with plastic wrap, and pierce several times. Cook for 10 minutes on HIGH. Add milk, stock, bay leaf, sprig of rosemary and seasoning. Re-cover and cook for 7 minutes on HIGH. Leave standing, covered, for 1 minute. Put parsley leaves and 15ml/1 tbsp water into a small dish. Cover with plastic wrap and pierce several times. Cook on HIGH for 1 minute. Uncover the soup and allow it to cool slightly. Remove bay leaf and rosemary, pour soup into a food processor, and purée until smooth. Check seasoning and heat through for 3 minutes on HIGH. Serve with a garnish of parsley leaves.

Pumpkin Soup

PREPARATION TIME: 20 minutes
MICROWAVE COOKING TIME: 25 minutes
SERVES: 4-6 people

1 whole pumpkin, weighing about 1kg/ 2lbs
2 medium potatoes, peeled and sliced
2 small onions, finely chopped
30g/1oz/2 tbsps butter
850ml/1½ pints/3 cups chicken stock
280ml/½ pint/1 cup milk
140ml/¼ pint/½ cup heavy/double cream
2.5ml/½ tsp tarragon
2.5ml/½ tsp chopped parsley
Nutmeg
Salt
Pepper

GARNISH
1 small bunch chives

Trim the white part of the leeks, slice thinly and wash well. Shred the green part finely, wash well and set aside. Put butter into a large bowl and cook, uncovered, for about 1½ minutes on HIGH. Add potatoes and white part of leeks to the butter. Cover with plastic wrap and pierce several times. Cook for 5 minutes on HIGH, stirring frequently. Add half the stock, re-cover and cook on HIGH for about 14 minutes or until the vegetables are very soft. Cool slightly, pour into a food processor, and purée until smooth. Add remaining stock and milk, and adjust the seasoning. Put reserved green part of the leeks into a small bowl with 2-3 tbsps of water. Cover the bowl with plastic wrap and pierce several times. Cook for about 2 minutes on HIGH. Re-heat soup on HIGH for 3 minutes.

Add more milk if the soup is too thick. To serve, top with the soured cream and the thinly shredded green part of leeks. Serve hot or cold.

French Country Soup

PREPARATION TIME: 10 minutes
MICROWAVE COOKING TIME: 21 minutes
SERVES: 4 people

3 leeks, washed and sliced thinly
180g/6oz/1 cup chopped carrots
350g/12oz/2 cups diced potatoes
570ml/1 pint/2 cups milk
570ml/1 pint/2 cups chicken or vegetable stock
45g/1½ oz/3 tbsps butter or margarine
1 bay leaf

This page: Pumpkin Soup.
Facing page: French Country Soup.

Cut top off pumpkin and scoop out pulp and discard seeds. Push as much of the pulp as possible through a sieve. Using a small, sharp knife or tablespoon, remove pumpkin flesh from inside shell, leaving a 1cm (½") lining of flesh. Put flesh, pulp, potatoes and onions into a large bowl with the butter. Cover with plastic wrap and pierce several times. Cook on HIGH for 10 minutes. Add stock, milk, thyme, parsley, nutmeg, and salt and pepper. Re-cover the bowl and cook on HIGH for 10 minutes. Pour the soup into a food processor and purée until smooth. Add double cream and mix in well. Wash pumpkin shell and top, and dry well. Return soup to the bowl and re-heat for 5 minutes on HIGH. Pour soup into cleaned pumpkin shell to serve, and garnish with chopped chives.

Watercress and Potato Soup

PREPARATION TIME: 10 minutes

MICROWAVE COOKING TIME: 22 minutes

SERVES: 4 people

1 bunch (about 2 cups) watercress
675g/1½lbs/3 cups diced potatoes
430ml/¾ pint/1½ cups chicken or
    vegetable stock
430ml/¾ pint/1½ cups light/single
    cream, or milk
1 shallot, finely chopped
45g/1½ oz/3 tbsps butter or margarine
Nutmeg
Lemon juice
Salt and pepper

Put the butter, shallot and potatoes into a large bowl. Cover with plastic wrap and pierce several times. Cook for about 2 minutes on HIGH. Add stock, salt and pepper, and pinch of nutmeg. Re-cover the bowl and cook on HIGH for about 10 minutes or until the vegetables are soft. Chop the watercress leaves, reserving 4 sprigs for garnish. Add the chopped leaves to the other ingredients in the bowl, re-cover and cook for another

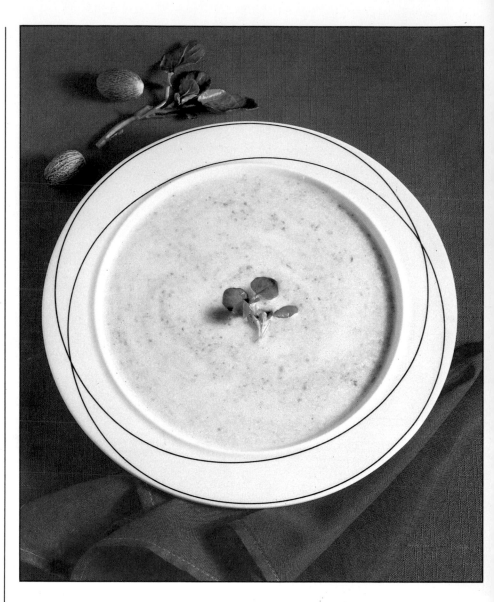

2 minutes on HIGH. Put into a food processor and purée until smooth. Return to the bowl. Stir in the cream and cook for 3-4 minutes on LOW until heated through. Do not allow the soup to boil. Stir in the lemon juice to taste, and adjust the seasoning. Serve the soup garnished with sprigs of watercress. Serve hot or cold.

Bean and Bacon Soup

PREPARATION TIME: 10 minutes

MICROWAVE COOKING TIME: 1 hour 35 minutes and 10 minutes standing time

SERVES: 4 people

225g/½lb navy/haricot beans, picked
    over and washed
225g/½lb smoked streaky bacon
1 large onion, finely chopped
1 stalk celery, finely chopped
1 bay leaf
1.25ml/¼ tsp thyme
Pinch of sage
½ clove garlic, crushed
15ml/1 tbsp chopped parsley
Salt
Pepper

**This page: Watercress and Potato Soup.
Facing page: Bean and Bacon Soup (top) and Cream of Onion Soup (bottom).**

Put beans into a large casserole and add 1150ml/2 pints/4 cups water. Cover and cook for 10 minutes on HIGH, or until boiling. Allow to boil for 2 minutes, then set aside, covered, for 1 hour. Heat a browning dish for 5 minutes on HIGH and brown the bacon for 2 minutes. Crumble and set aside, reserving the fat. Put onion, celery, garlic and bacon fat into a large casserole and cook on HIGH for 2 minutes. Drain beans, and add to the casserole along with the thyme, sage and bay leaf. Pour on 1150ml/2 pints/4 cups of fresh water, cover, and cook for 45-55 minutes on HIGH. Then stir in the bacon, reserving 4 tbsps for garnish. Re-cover dish and cook a further 25-35 minutes on HIGH, or until beans are soft but not breaking apart. Add water as necessary during cooking. Allow to stand, covered, for 10 minutes. Remove the bay leaf and serve garnished with the reserved bacon.

Mulligatawny Soup

PREPARATION TIME: 12 minutes

MICROWAVE COOKING TIME: 36-38 minutes

SERVES: 4 people

180g/6oz/1 cup onions, thinly sliced
2 apples, peeled and grated
60g/2oz/4 tbsps butter
60g/2oz/4 tbsps flour/plain flour
1 tbsp tomato paste
10ml/2 tsps curry powder
15ml/1 tbsp mango chutney
60g/2oz/⅓ cup quick-cooking rice
1150ml/2 pints/4 cups beef or chicken stock
1 small bunch fresh coriander leaves
1 bay leaf
1 clove garlic, crushed
Salt
Pepper

GARNISH
90ml/3 fl oz/⅓ cup plain yogurt

Reserve 4 sprigs of coriander for garnish and chop 1 tbsp of the remainder. Put butter, onion and garlic into a large casserole. Cover

and cook for 5 minutes on HIGH. Blend in the flour and curry powder, then cover and cook for 2 minutes on HIGH. Add tomato paste, stock and 1 tbsp coriander, and cook for 5 minutes on HIGH until boiling. Add apple, chutney, rice and seasoning, and cook for 10 minutes on MEDIUM, or until rice is tender. Cook an additional 2 minutes on HIGH if necessary. Serve topped with yogurt and reserved coriander leaves.

Cream of Mushroom Soup

PREPARATION TIME: 10 minutes

MICROWAVE COOKING TIME: 17 minutes

SERVES: 4 people

340g/¾lb mushrooms
1 shallot, finely chopped
570ml/1 pint/2 cups chicken or vegetable stock
430ml/¾ pint/1½ cups milk
30g/1oz/2 tbsps butter or margarine
45g/1½ oz/3 tbsps flour/plain flour
1.25ml/¼ tsp thyme
30ml/2 tbsps dry sherry
90ml/3 fl oz/⅓ cup heavy/double cream
Salt
Pepper

Reserve 4 mushrooms to use as garnish, and chop the rest finely. Put them with the butter and shallot into a large glass bowl. Cover with plastic wrap and pierce several times. Cook for 4 minutes on HIGH or until mushrooms are soft. Stir occasionally. Add flour and stir well. Gradually add the stock, re-cover, and cook for 5 minutes on HIGH. Stir the mixture several times while cooking. Add milk, thyme and sherry, and cook on HIGH for 6 minutes, or until boiling. Stir several times during cooking. Allow the soup to stand for 1-2 minutes, covered. Slice remaining mushrooms thinly. Put them in a small bowl with 1 tbsp of water and a squeeze of lemon juice. Cover bowl with plastic wrap and pierce several times, and cook for 1 minute on HIGH. Add cream to the soup and

cook for 2 minutes on HIGH. Serve the soup garnished with the slices of mushroom.

Cream of Broccoli Soup

PREPARATION TIME: 10 minutes

MICROWAVE COOKING TIME: 20 minutes

SERVES: 4 people

450g/1lb broccoli spears, fresh or frozen
30g/1oz/2 tbsps butter
30g/1oz/2 tbsps flour/plain flour
430ml/¾ pint/1½ cups chicken or vegetable stock
570ml/1 pint/2 cups milk
1 bay leaf
1.25ml/¼ tsp thyme
15ml/1 tbsp chopped parsley
140ml/¼ pint/½ cup heavy/double cream
Salt
Pepper

Chop broccoli roughly, reserving 4-8 small flowerets for garnish. Put chopped broccoli into a loosely tied roasting bag with 2 tbsps water. Cook on HIGH for 5 minutes. (The broccoli may also be cooked in a bowl covered with pierced plastic wrap.) Put butter into a large bowl and cook for 1 minute on HIGH. Stir in the flour, and add the milk, stock, thyme, parsley, bay leaf and seasoning. Cook for 7 minutes on HIGH, stirring several times. Add broccoli and cook a further 3 minutes on HIGH. Pour the soup into a food processor and purée until smooth. Put reserved flowerets of broccoli into a small bowl with 1 tbsp of water. Cover with pierced plastic wrap and cook for 2 minutes on HIGH. Set aside. Add cream and re-heat the soup for 2 minutes on HIGH. Serve with a garnish of broccoli florets.

Facing page: Cream of Mushroom Soup (top) and Mulligatawny Soup (bottom).

140ml/¼ pint/½ cup cream
650ml/1½ pints/3 cups beef stock
60ml/4 tbsps/¼ cup white wine
1 bunch dill
1 bay leaf
Salt
Pepper

GARNISH
140ml/¼ pint/½ cup sour cream

Reserve 4 sprigs of dill for garnish and chop the rest. Put the dill, carrot, onion, potatoes, cabbage, garlic, bay leaf, seasoning, and half the stock into a large casserole. Cover and cook on HIGH for 15 minutes or until vegetables soften. Add the remaining stock, beets, wine and tomato paste, and cover and cook on HIGH for 10 minutes. Stir occasionally. Remove bay leaf. Pour soup into a food processor and purée until smooth. Add cream and blend thoroughly. Return soup to bowl and re-heat for 2 minutes on HIGH. Serve topped with sour cream and sprigs of dill.

Stilton Cheese and Walnut Soup

PREPARATION TIME: 10 minutes

MICROWAVE COOKING TIME: 18 minutes

SERVES: 4 people

225g/8oz/2 cups Stilton cheese, crumbled (half Cheddar and half blue cheese may be substituted)
1 large onion, finely chopped
45g/1½ oz/3 tbsps butter
30g/1oz/2 tbsps flour/plain flour
430ml/¾ pint/1½ cups chicken stock
430ml/¾ pint/1½ cups milk
60ml/4 tbsps/¼ cup cream
90g/3oz/½ cup walnuts, finely chopped
1 bay leaf
1 sprig thyme
Salt and pepper

Cream of Onion Soup

PREPARATION TIME: 10 minutes

MICROWAVE COOKING TIME: 18 minutes

SERVES: 4 people

675g/1½lbs onions, finely chopped
30g/1oz/2 tbsps butter
30g/1oz/2 tbsps flour
570ml/1 pint/2 cups beef or chicken stock
430ml/¾ pint/1½ cups milk
15ml/1 tbsp Madeira
140ml/¼ pint/½ cup cream

GARNISH
4 green onions, sliced

Put the butter into a large bowl and cook for 1 minute on HIGH. Add onions, and cook for 5 minutes on HIGH, stirring occasionally until light brown. Stir in the flour, stock, bay leaf, and salt and pepper. Cook for 10 minutes on HIGH. Pour the soup into a food processor and purée until smooth. Pour milk into a small bowl and heat for 2 minutes on HIGH. Pour the soup back into a bowl, add the milk, and stir well. Re-heat on HIGH for 2 minutes and add the Madeira. Stir in the cream before serving and garnish with the sliced green onions.

Creamy Borscht

PREPARATION TIME: 15 minutes

MICROWAVE COOKING TIME: 27 minutes

SERVES: 4 people

3 beetroots, grated
255g/9oz/1½ cups cabbage, shredded
1 medium carrot, thinly sliced
2 medium potatoes, peeled and thinly sliced
1 medium onion, finely chopped
1 small clove garlic, crushed
1 teaspoon tomato paste

**This page: Creamy Borscht.
Facing page: Cream of Broccoli Soup (top) and Stilton Cheese and Walnut Soup (bottom).**

Jerusalem Artichoke and Almond Soup

PREPARATION TIME: 15 minutes

MICROWAVE COOKING TIME: 33-38 minutes

CONVENTIONAL OVEN TEMPERATURE: 180°C, 350°F, Gas Mark 4

SERVES: 4 people

1kg/2½lbs Jerusalem artichoke
2 shallots, finely chopped
30g/1oz/¼ cup blanched almonds
30g/1oz/2 tbsps butter or margarine
280ml/½ pint/1 cup chicken stock
430ml/¾ pint/1½ cups milk
140ml/¼ pint/½ cup heavy/double cream
60ml/2 fl oz/¼ cup white wine
1 bay leaf
Grated nutmeg
Lemon juice
Salt
Pepper

GARNISH
30g/1oz/¼ cup sliced almonds, browned

Peel artichokes and keep in a bowl of cold water and lemon juice. Thinly slice them and put them into a bowl with shallots, butter and almonds. Cover with plastic wrap and pierce several times, and cook for 4 minutes on HIGH. Pour in the stock and wine, add the bay leaf, grated nutmeg and seasoning, and cook, uncovered, for 10 minutes on HIGH. Remove bay leaf, add cream and milk, and pour into a food processor. Purée until smooth and adjust seasoning. Meanwhile, brown almonds for garnish in a conventional oven for 15 minutes or in a microwave-convection oven on Combination for 7 minutes, stirring often. Re-heat soup for 2 minutes on HIGH, and serve garnished with the browned almonds and more grated nutmeg.

This page: Jerusalem Artichoke and Almond Soup (top) and Cream of Carrot and Orange Soup (bottom). Facing page: Spiced Tomato Soup (top) and Green Pea Soup (bottom).

Put onion and butter into a large bowl. Cover with plastic wrap and pierce several times. Cook for 6 minutes on HIGH. Stir in flour, add the stock gradually and mix well. Add bay leaf, thyme, salt and pepper, and cook, uncovered, for 10 minutes on HIGH. Remove the herbs. Crumble the cheese into a bowl and add 140ml/¼ pint/½ cup of the soup to the cheese. Stir in well. Return cheese mixture to the rest of the soup and add cream. Cook 1 minute, uncovered, on HIGH. Add the walnuts to the bowl, reserving about 2 tbsps for garnish. Cook on HIGH for 1 minute. Serve garnished with the reserved walnuts.

Green Pea Soup

PREPARATION TIME: 10 minutes

MICROWAVE COOKING TIME:
12 minutes

SERVES: 4 people

450g/1lb frozen peas
30g/1oz/2 tbsps butter
30g/1oz/2 tbsps flour
280ml/½ pint/1 cup chicken or vegetable
  stock
430ml/¾ pint/1½ cups milk
140ml/¼ pint/½ cup light/single cream
1 shallot, finely chopped
1 small bunch fresh mint
1.25ml/¼ tsp marjoram
15ml/1 tbsp chopped parsley
Salt
Pepper

Put butter and shallot into a large bowl and cover with pierced plastic wrap. Cook for 5 minutes on HIGH, then add the peas to the bowl, reserving 90g/3oz/½ cup. Add the stock, milk, marjoram, parsley and seasoning. Cook for 5 minutes on HIGH. Pour into a food processor and purée until smooth. Chop the mint, reserving 4-8 leaves for garnish, if desired. Return soup to the bowl, and add chopped mint, cream and reserved peas. Re-heat soup for 2 minutes on HIGH. Garnish with the mint leaves.

Cream of Lettuce Soup

PREPARATION TIME: 10 minutes

MICROWAVE COOKING TIME:
18 minutes

SERVES: 4 people

2-3 potatoes, peeled and diced
1 onion, finely chopped
1 head romaine/cos lettuce
280ml/½ pint/1 cup chicken stock
570ml/1 pint/2 cups milk
30g/1oz/2 tbsps butter or margarine
140ml/¼ pint/½ cup cream
Ground nutmeg
1.25ml/¼ tsp thyme
15ml/1 tsp chopped parsley
Salt
Pepper

Put potatoes and onion into a large bowl with the butter and stock. Cover with plastic wrap and pierce several times. Cook on HIGH for 10 minutes. Wash lettuce well and shred leaves finely, reserving a small amount for garnish. Add to the bowl with the seasoning, thyme and ground nutmeg, and cook for 1 minute on HIGH. Add the milk and pour the soup into a food processor, and purée until smooth. Add the cream. Return to the bowl and re-heat for 7 minutes on HIGH. Serve soup garnished with reserved shredded lettuce. Serve hot or cold.

Spiced Tomato Soup

PREPARATION TIME: 10 minutes

MICROWAVE COOKING TIME:
22 minutes

SERVES: 4 people

800g/28oz can tomatoes
2 onions, finely chopped
570ml/1 pint/2 cups beef stock
15ml/1 tbsp cornflour/cornstarch
1 tbsp tomato paste
60ml/2 fl oz/¼ cup port or brandy
5ml/1 tsp thyme
½ stick cinnamon
2 whole cloves
3 black peppercorns
3 allspice berries
1 bay leaf
Salt
Sugar

GARNISH
2 tomatoes
60ml/4 tbsps heavy/double cream

Put tomatoes and their juice, stock, onion, herbs, spices and salt into a large bowl. Cook, uncovered, for 20 minutes on HIGH. Add a pinch of sugar if necessary, to bring out the tomato flavor. Sieve tomatoes, extracting as much pulp as possible. Blend cornstarch and port and stir into the soup. Put tomatoes for garnish into a bowl of water and cook on HIGH for 1 minute. Drain and put into cold water. Peel, remove seeds, cut into thin shreds and set aside. Return soup to oven and cook, uncovered, for 2 minutes on HIGH, stirring often. Adjust seasoning, and serve soup garnished with a swirl of double cream and the shreds of tomato.

Cream of Carrot and Orange Soup

PREPARATION TIME: 10 minutes

MICROWAVE COOKING TIME:
18 minutes

SERVES: 4 people

450g/1lb/3 cups grated carrots
1 shallot, finely chopped
30g/1oz/2 tbsps butter or margarine
280ml/½ pint/1 cup chicken or vegetable
  stock
570ml/1 pint/2 cups milk
100ml/6 tbsps/⅓ cup heavy/double
  cream
Juice and rind of 1 orange
1 bay leaf
1 sprig of thyme
1 small bunch chives, chopped
Salt
Pepper

Pare the rind from the orange and squeeze the juice. Put butter into a large bowl and heat for 1 minute on HIGH. Add onion and cook for 5 minutes on HIGH. Add carrots, stock, bay leaf, thyme, and salt and pepper. Cover with pierced plastic wrap and cook for 10 minutes on HIGH. Add milk, orange juice and orange rind and cook for 1 minute on HIGH. Remove bay leaf, thyme, and orange rind, and pour into a food processor. Purée until smooth. Return soup to bowl, and heat through for 2 minutes on HIGH. Stir in the chives and the cream before serving. Serve hot or cold.

Facing page: Cream of Lettuce Soup.

VEGETABLE AND PASTA SOUPS

Chicken Vegetable Soup

PREPARATION TIME: 15 minutes

MICROWAVE COOKING TIME:
23 minutes

SERVES: 4 people

450g/1lb chicken parts
1150ml/2 pints/4 cups water
1 chicken bouillon cube
1 small turnip, diced
1 onion, finely chopped
3 sticks celery, sliced
2 medium carrots, diced
60g/2oz/¼ cup frozen peas
60g/2oz/¼ cup fresh or frozen sliced
   green beans
60g/2oz/½ cup mushrooms, quartered
1.25ml/¼ tsp thyme
1 bay leaf
15ml/1 tbsp chopped parsley

Put the chicken parts and the water into a large casserole with the thyme, bay leaf and seasoning. Cover and cook on HIGH for 15 minutes. Remove chicken and leave to cool. Remove the skin and bones and cut the chicken into small pieces. Set aside. Strain stock. Return stock to casserole and skim any fat from the surface. Taste and, if necessary, add the stock cube. Add the carrot, onion, celery and turnip; cover and cook for 10 minutes on HIGH. At this stage, if using fresh beans, cut into even sized lengths and add to the stock with the mushrooms. Cover and cook for 4 minutes on HIGH. Add frozen peas and parsley and cook a further 1 minute on HIGH. (If using frozen beans, add with the peas.) Add chicken. Adjust seasoning, and heat through for 3 minutes on HIGH. Serve.

Greek Lemon Soup

PREPARATION TIME: 8 minutes

MICROWAVE COOKING TIME:
17 minutes

SERVES: 4 people

3 lemons
1 onion, finely chopped
45g/1½ oz/3 tbsps butter or margarine
30g/1oz/2 tbsps flour/plain flour
90g/3oz/1 cup quick-cooking rice
1 litre/1¾ pints/4 cups chicken stock
1.25ml/¼ tsp powdered oregano
Nutmeg
Salt
Pepper

Put butter and onion into a bowl. Cover with plastic wrap and pierce several times. Cook on HIGH for about 3 minutes. Add flour to bowl and cook on HIGH for an additional 1½-2 minutes. Gradually stir in the stock. Grate rind and squeeze juice from 2 lemons, and add to the bowl with the bay leaf, pinch of nutmeg, oregano, salt and pepper. Cook on HIGH for 5 minutes. Add rice, re-cover the bowl, and cook for 5 minutes on HIGH, stirring frequently. Additional cooking time may be needed if the rice is not tender. Leave to stand, covered, about 2 minutes. Slice remaining lemon thinly and garnish each serving of soup with a slice of lemon.

Minestrone

PREPARATION TIME: 15 minutes

MICROWAVE COOKING TIME:
26 minutes

SERVES: 4 people

2 small leeks, washed and cut into thin
   strips
30ml/2 tbsps oil
225g/8oz/1½ cups canned tomatoes
1 green pepper, sliced
215g/7oz can canellini, or haricot, beans
1 carrot, cut into 2.5cm (1") strips
2 sticks celery, cut into 2.5cm (1") strips
1 zucchini/courgette, cut into 2.5cm (1")
   strips
1 clove garlic, crushed
120g/¼lb ham, cut into thin strips
1150ml/2 pints/4 cups stock (preferably
   ham)
30g/1oz/⅓ cup macaroni
1 bay leaf
2.5ml/½ tsp basil
2.5ml/½ tsp oregano
2.5ml/½ tsp fennel seed
Salt and pepper
Sugar

GARNISH
90g/3oz/½ cup Parmesan cheese, grated

Put oil, leeks, carrot, celery, garlic and herbs in a large casserole. Cover and cook 6 minutes on HIGH. Add macaroni, tomatoes and their juice, stock, ham, drained beans, salt, pepper and a pinch of sugar, and cook, covered, on HIGH for 6 minutes. Add zucchini/courgette, green pepper and parsley, and cook 5 minutes on HIGH, or until pasta is tender. Serve with grated Parmesan cheese.

Facing page: Minestrone.

Cream of Asparagus Soup

PREPARATION TIME: 10 minutes
MICROWAVE COOKING TIME: 32 minutes
SERVES: 4 people

450g/1lb asparagus, fresh or frozen
45g/1½ oz/3 tbsps butter or margarine
45g/1½ oz/3 tbsps flour/plain flour
1 shallot, finely chopped
850ml/1½ pints/3 cups chicken stock
140ml/¼ pint/½ cup cream
1 bay leaf
1.25ml/¼ tsp thyme
Salt
Pepper
Nutmeg

Place butter and shallot into a large casserole. Cover and cook on HIGH for 6 minutes. Stir in the flour and cook a further 1 minute on HIGH. Stir in the stock and cook for 15 minutes on HIGH, until boiling. Chop asparagus roughly and, if using fresh, reserve 4 tips for garnish. Add asparagus, bay leaf, seasoning, and a pinch of grated nutmeg, and cook for 10 minutes on MEDIUM. Remove the bay leaf, and pour the soup into a food processor and purée until smooth. Put reserved asparagus tips into a small bowl with 1 tbsp of water. Cover with plastic wrap and pierce several times. Cook for 1 minute on HIGH and set aside. Add the cream to the soup, cover, and re-heat for 2-3 minutes. Serve garnished with the reserved asparagus tips and more grated nutmeg.

French Onion Soup

PREPARATION TIME: 10 minutes
MICROWAVE COOKING TIME: 27 minutes
SERVES: 4 people

675g/1½lbs onions, thinly sliced
60g/2oz/4 tbsps butter or margarine
30g/1oz/2 tbsps flour/plain flour
140ml/¼ pint/½ cup dry cider or white wine
30ml/2 tbsps Calvados or brandy

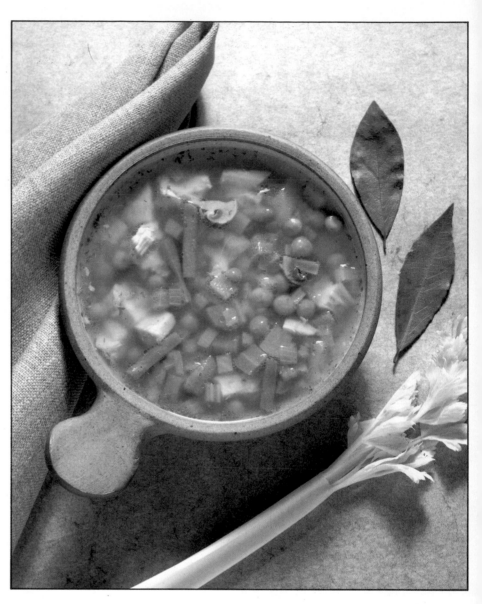

1150ml/2 pints/4 cups beef stock
1.25ml/¼ tbsp thyme
1 bay leaf
4 slices French bread, toasted and buttered
60g/2oz/½ cup Gruyère or Swiss cheese
Salt
Pepper

Place onions, butter, salt and pepper into a large bowl and cook on HIGH for 8 minutes. Stir occasionally. Stir in the flour, add the stock, cider, Calvados, thyme and bay leaf. Cover bowl with plastic wrap and pierce several times. Cook on HIGH for 10 minutes. Uncover and stir occasionally. Reduce the setting to LOW and cook a further 8 minutes.

Leave the bowl to stand covered for 1-2 minutes. Put slices of toast on a plate, and sprinkle over the grated cheese thickly. Cook on LOW until cheese starts to melt, and then grill/broil conventionally until lightly browned. Spoon the soup into individual micro-proof bowls. Top each with the cheese toast and heat through for 1 minute on HIGH. Serve immediately.

This page: Chicken Vegetable Soup. Facing page: Cream of Asparagus Soup (top) and French Onion Soup (bottom).

Chinese Chicken and Mushroom Soup

PREPARATION TIME: 8 minutes

MICROWAVE COOKING TIME:
36 minutes

SERVES: 4 people

6 dried Chinese mushrooms
2 chicken breasts
280ml/½ pint/1 cup water
1 small can water chestnuts, sliced
1 small can bamboo shoots, sliced
1 bunch spring/green onions, sliced
* diagonally*
120g/¼lb fine Chinese egg noodles
120g/¼lb pea pods/mangetout
15ml/1 tbsp (light) soy sauce
30ml/2 tbsps dry sherry
5ml/1 tsp sesame seed oil
15ml/1 tbsp cornstarch/cornflour
850ml/1½ pints/3 cups chicken stock
Salt and pepper

Put mushrooms into a small bowl and cover with cold water. Cover bowl with plastic wrap and pierce several times. Heat on HIGH for 2 minutes and leave to stand. Put chicken breasts into a bowl with 280ml/½ pint/1 cup water. Cover with pierced plastic wrap and cook for 15 minutes on HIGH. Put noodles into a bowl with 1150ml/ 2 pints water. Cover with pierced plastic wrap and cook for 3 minutes on HIGH. Leave standing, covered, for 5 minutes. Drain and slice mushrooms, and put into a large bowl with the stock. Cover with pierced plastic wrap and cook for 1 minute on HIGH. Skin, bone and shred chicken and add to bowl with spring onions, pea pods/mangetout, water chestnuts and bamboo shoots and cook for 1 minute on HIGH. Mix cornflour/cornstarch, soy sauce and sherry with a tbsp of the hot liquid. Pour into the bowl with the rest of the soup and cook, stirring several times, for 5 minutes on HIGH. Drain noodles and add them to the bowl with the sesame seed oil. Heat soup through for 2 minutes on HIGH. Serve garnished with more chopped spring onion if desired.

Potato Soup

PREPARATION TIME: 10 minutes

MICROWAVE COOKING TIME:
21 minutes

SERVES: 4 people

675g/1½lbs/4 cups diced potatoes
45g/1½oz/3 tbsps butter or margarine
1 onion, thinly sliced
280ml/½ pint/1 cup water
850ml/1½ pints/3 cups milk
1 bay leaf
1 sprig of thyme
Salt
Pepper
Nutmeg

GARNISH
60g/2oz/½ cup Red Leicester/Colby
* cheese, grated*

Put potatoes, onions and butter into a large bowl. Cover with plastic wrap and pierce several times. Cook for 10 minutes on HIGH. Add milk, water, thyme, bay leaf, seasoning and grated nutmeg, and cook for 7 minutes on HIGH. Leave standing, covered, for 1 minute. Uncover and allow to cool slightly. Remove bay leaf and thyme, pour soup into a food processor, and purée until smooth. Check seasoning and consistency. If too thick, add more milk. Cover and heat through for 3 minutes on HIGH. Serve garnished with the grated cheese.

**This page: Potato Soup (top) and Greek Lemon Soup (bottom).
Facing page: Chinese Chicken and Mushroom Soup.**

Chili Corn Chowder

PREPARATION TIME: 15 minutes

MICROWAVE COOKING TIME:
24 minutes

SERVES: 4 people

45g/1½ oz/3 tbsps butter or margarine
1 shallot, finely chopped
4 strips/rashers smoked streaky bacon
   (rindless and boneless)
45g/1½ oz/3 tbsps flour/plain flour
570ml/1 pint/2 cups chicken stock
430ml/¾ pint/1½ cups milk
2 medium potatoes, peeled and cut into
   1cm (½") dice
1 red pepper, diced
1 green chili pepper, finely chopped
280g/10oz/1½ cups corn/sweetcorn,
   frozen
140g/¼ pint/½ cup light/single cream
15ml/1 tbsp chopped parsley
1.25ml/¼ tsp ground cumin
1 bay leaf

GARNISH
4 green onions

Put butter into a bowl and cook for 1 minute on HIGH. Dice bacon and add it with the shallot to the butter. Cover with pierced plastic wrap and cook for 5 minutes on HIGH until onions are softened. Stir in the flour and cumin, and cook for 1 minute on HIGH. Gradually stir in the stock and milk, and add potatoes and bay leaf. Cook for 6 minutes on HIGH or until boiling. Add red pepper and as much of the chili pepper as desired. Cook for 10 minutes or until potatoes soften. Remove bay leaf, add corn, cream, parsley and seasoning, and cook for 3 minutes on HIGH. Serve garnished with chopped green onion.

Italian Onion Soup

PREPARATION TIME: 10 minutes

MICROWAVE COOKING TIME:
16-23 minutes and 1-2 minutes
standing time

SERVES: 4 people

675g/1½lbs onions, thinly sliced
450g/16oz can plum tomatoes

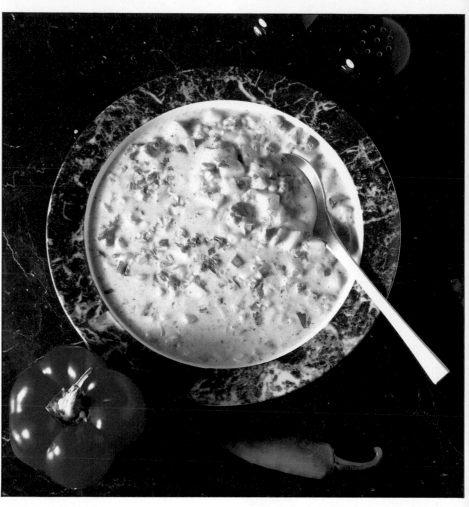

45g/1½ oz/3 tbsps butter or margarine
30g/1oz/2 tbsps flour/plain flour
140ml/¼ pint/½ cup red wine
430ml/¾ pint/1½ cups beef stock
1.25ml/¼ tsp basil
1.25ml/¼ tsp oregano
1 bay leaf
Salt
Pepper
Tomato paste
4 slices French bread, toasted and
   buttered
60g/2oz/2 tbsps Parmesan cheese, grated
60g/2oz/2 tbsps Cheddar cheese, grated

Place onions, butter, salt and pepper into a large bowl and cook on HIGH for 6 minutes. Stir occasionally. Stir in flour, add the stock, tomatoes, red wine, basil, oregano and bay leaf. Cover the bowl with plastic wrap and pierce several times. Cook on HIGH for 8 minutes. Uncover and stir occasionally. Reduce setting to LOW and cook for a further 4 minutes. Leave the bowl to stand covered for 1-2 minutes. Adjust seasoning and add tomato paste, if necessary, for color and flavor. Mix the cheeses together, put the slices of toast on a plate, and sprinkle over the grated cheese. Cook on LOW until cheese starts to melt, and then grill/broil conventionally until lightly browned. Use the Combination setting on convection microwave oven for 7 minutes. Spoon the soup into individual micro-proof bowls. Top each with the cheese toast and heat through for 1 minute on HIGH.

**This page: Chili Corn Chowder.
Facing page: Curried Cauliflower
Soup (top) and Italian Onion Soup
(bottom).**

Curried Cauliflower Soup

PREPARATION TIME: 10 minutes

MICROWAVE COOKING TIME: 15 minutes

SERVES: 4 people

4 cups cauliflowerets, or 1 small
   cauliflower cut into flowerets
2 shallots finely chopped
30g/1oz/2 tbsps butter or margarine
30g/1oz/2 tbsps flour/plain flour
10ml/2 tsps curry powder
430ml/¾ pint/1½ cups chicken or
   vegetable stock
570ml/1 pint/2 cups milk
Salt
Pepper

GARNISH
60g/2oz/⅓ cup sliced almonds, browned

Put cauliflowerets into a roasting bag
with the shallot and bay leaf. Tie bag
loosely and cook for 8 minutes on
HIGH. (Cauliflower may also be
cooked in a bowl covered with
pierced plastic wrap.) Put butter into
a large bowl and cook for 1 minute
on HIGH until melted. Stir in the
curry powder and flour, and cook for
1 minute on HIGH. Add milk and
cook for 3 minutes on HIGH, stirring
occasionally. Pour the soup into a
food processor, add the cauliflower,
and purée until smooth. Return the
soup to the oven to heat through for
2 minutes on HIGH. Serve garnished
with the browned sliced almonds.

Vegetable Soup

PREPARATION TIME: 10 minutes

MICROWAVE COOKING TIME: 21 minutes

SERVES: 4 people

1 large carrot, peeled and diced
1 large turnip, peeled and diced
2 leeks, washed and sliced thinly
2 potatoes, peeled and diced
60g/2oz/¼ cup frozen peas
60g/2oz/¼ cup frozen corn/sweetcorn
90g/3oz/½ cup fresh or frozen sliced
   green beans
120g/¼lb okra (optional)

450g/16oz can plum tomatoes
570ml/1 pint/2 cups chicken or
   vegetable stock
60g/2oz/⅓ cup soup pasta
1 bay leaf
1.25ml/¼ tsp marjoram or savory
15ml/1 tbsp chopped parsley
Pepper

Put butter into a large bowl and cook
for 45 seconds on HIGH until it
melts. Add carrots, turnips, leeks and
potatoes and mix together. Cover
with plastic wrap and pierce several
times. Cook on HIGH for 10 minutes
or until vegetables begin to soften.
Stir occasionally. Add stock,
tomatoes, bay leaf, marjoram, pasta,
salt and pepper. Cover and cook for
7 minutes on HIGH. Slice beans (if
fresh), trim okra, and slice into
rounds, and add to bowl. Re-cover
bowl and cook for 2 minutes on
HIGH. Add corn, peas and parsley.
Cook for 1 minute on HIGH or until
pasta is tender. Sprinkle with more
chopped parsley, if desired, before
serving.

**This page: Vegetable Soup.
Facing page: Jellied Vegetable
Terrine with Tomato Dressing.**

TARTS, TERRINES AND PÂTÉS

Jellied Vegetable Terrine with Tomato Dressing

PREPARATION TIME: 15 minutes

MICROWAVE COOKING TIME: 11 minutes

SERVES: 4 people

TERRINE
1 tbsp gelatine
1 chicken bouillon cube
570ml/1 pint/2 cups boiling water (less 2 tbsps)
30ml/2 tbsps dry sherry
225g/8oz green beans, ends trimmed
1 large carrot, peeled
1-2 Jerusalem artichokes, peeled
120g/4oz mushrooms, cleaned
120g/4oz/½ cup frozen peas

DRESSING
400g/14oz can tomato sauce
1 tsp tomato paste
Juice and grate rind of half a lemon
1.25ml/¼ tsp chives, snipped
1.25ml/¼ tsp parsley, chopped
1.25ml/¼ tsp thyme, chopped
1.25ml/¼ tsp basil, chopped
45-60ml/3-4 tbsps olive oil
30ml/2 tbsps red wine vinegar
¼ tsp Dijon mustard
1 bay leaf
Sugar
Salt
Pepper

GARNISH
1 bunch watercress

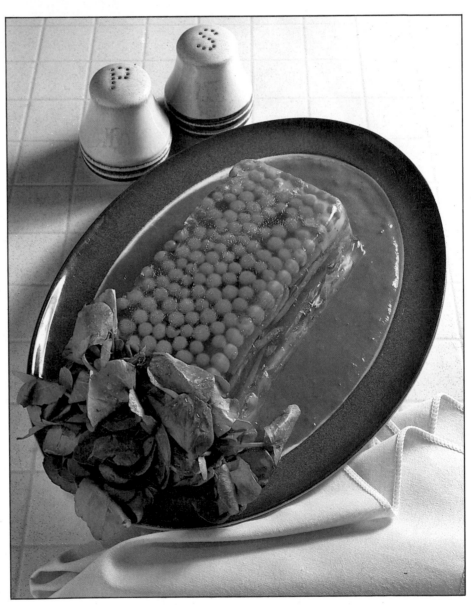

Heat water in a glass measuring jug/cup for 3-4 minutes on HIGH until boiling. Add sherry and stir in the gelatine and bouillon cube. Leave to cool at room temperature, then put into a bowl of cold water. The aspic must be cold but liquid. If it sets too quickly in the cup, melt again for 1-2 minutes on HIGH. Then chill again in the cold water, and repeat the process again when necessary. Leave green beans whole and cook for 8 minutes on HIGH with 2 tbsps water in a small, shallow dish covered with pierced plastic wrap. Cut carrots lengthways into 0.5cm (¼") sticks and cook for 10 minutes in the same way as the beans. Cut artichokes into

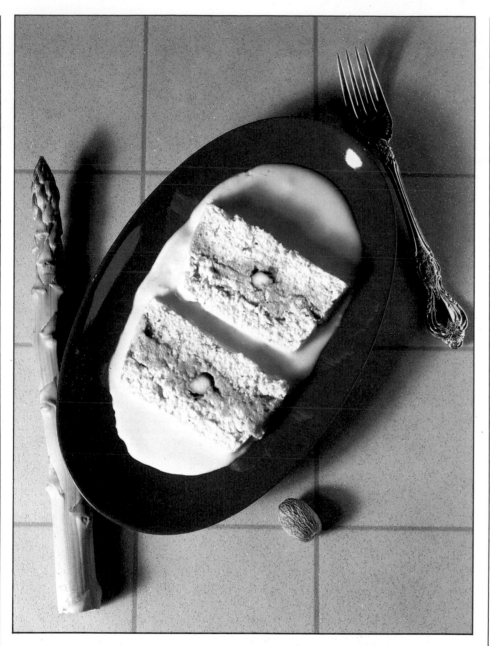

Chicken and Asparagus Terrine with Lemon Mousseline Sauce

PREPARATION TIME: 15 minutes

MICROWAVE COOKING TIME: 33 minutes

SERVES: 4-6 people

TERRINE
450g/1lb chicken breasts
430ml/¾ pint/1½ cups cream
340g/12oz low-fat cheese
30ml/2 tbsps white wine
140ml/¼ pint/½ cup water
3 eggs
450g/1lb asparagus spears, fresh or frozen
Salt
Pepper
Nutmeg
1 bay leaf

SAUCE
60g/2oz/½ cup butter
3 egg yolks
Rind and juice of 1 lemon
60ml/4 tbsps/¼ cup whipping cream
1 bay leaf
1 blade mace
Salt
Pepper

Cut tips off asparagus spears, trim stalk ends, and cook on HIGH for 6 minutes with 2 tbsps water in a shallow dish covered with pierced plastic wrap. Leave to cool. Put chicken breasts into a bowl with the white wine, water and bay leaf. Cover with pierced plastic wrap and cook for 15 minutes on HIGH. Cool and remove skin and bones. Put chicken, cheese, seasoning, nutmeg and 2 eggs into a food processor, and purée until smooth. In a clean bowl, purée the asparagus spears with 1 egg, salt and pepper. Put half the chicken mixture into a loaf pan and smooth evenly. Cover with half the asparagus mixture and layer on the reserved asparagus tips. Cover with remaining

This page: Chicken and Asparagus Terrine with Lemon Mousseline Sauce.
Facing page: Tomato Tarts Niçoise (top) and Cheese and Mushroom Tarts (bottom).

thin rounds and cook for 8 minutes. Remove stalks from mushrooms and slice caps thinly. Cook them for 3 minutes on HIGH, then the frozen peas for 1 minute on HIGH. Dampen a 450g/1lb loaf pan with water and pour in a 0.5cm (¼") layer of cool aspic. Chill until set. Arrange a layer of peas on top and pour over a thin layer of aspic to set the peas in place. Chill until set, then add more aspic to just cover the peas. Chill again until set. Repeat the process with a layer of artichokes, green beans, carrots and mushrooms. Fill the pan to the top with aspic and chill for

1-2 hours until firm. Meanwhile, put tomato sauce, paste, garlic, bay leaf, seasoning and sugar into a bowl. Cover with pierced plastic wrap and cook for 10 minutes on HIGH, stirring frequently. Allow sauce to cool completely. Whisk oil, vinegar and mustard together until thick. Whisk in the tomato sauce, add chopped herbs, and adjust seasoning. Unmould the terrine and cut into 1cm (½") slices. Serve with tomato dressing and small bouquets of watercress or parsley.

asparagus mixture, then the remaining chicken mixture. Cover the dish with plastic wrap and cook for 10 minutes on HIGH. Cover and weight down the top, leaving to stand for 5 minutes. Serve hot with the lemon mousseline sauce.
To make sauce: Put the butter into a glass measuring jug/cup or a small, deep bowl and cook for 1 minute on HIGH to melt. Put lemon juice, bay leaf and mace into another bowl and heat for 1 minute on HIGH. Beat egg yolks, lemon rind and seasoning, and strain on the juice. Pour egg yolk mixture into the butter and stir well. Have a bowl of ice water ready. Put the sauce mixture into the oven and cook for 15 seconds on HIGH. Remove and stir, repeating the process until sauce has thickened – approximately 2 minutes. Put the jug immediately into the ice water to stop the cooking. Whip cream, fold into the sauce and serve at once with the terrine.

Country Pâté

PREPARATION TIME: 10 minutes

MICROWAVE COOKING TIME: 15 minutes

SERVES: 6-8 people

225g/½ lb minced/ground pork
225g/½ lb minced/ground veal
120g/¼ lb ham, minced
120g/¼ lb pigs'/pork liver
90g/3oz minced pork fat
1 clove garlic, crushed
60ml/4 tbsps brandy
Ground allspice
Thyme
1 bay leaf
2 tsps green peppercorns in brine, rinsed
8 slices (streaky) bacon, bones and rind removed
Salt
Pepper

Line a 1lb glass loaf dish with the bacon. Remove skin and ducts from liver, mince in a food processor, and mix with the minced/ground meats, garlic, herbs, spices, brandy, peppercorns and seasoning. Press meat mixture into the dish on top of

bacon. Place bay leaf on top. Fold edges of bacon over the top and cover with plastic wrap. Put a ramekin dish of water into the oven with the pâté, and cook on MEDIUM for 6 minutes. Leave to stand for 5 minutes and cook for a further 10 minutes on MEDIUM. Cover with foil, press down and weight. Leave to chill 2-4 hours. Remove the bay leaf, and cut mixture into thin slices (about 18) to serve.

Asparagus with Orange Hollandaise

PREPARATION TIME: 10 minutes

MICROWAVE COOKING TIME: 11 minutes

SERVES: 4 people

900g/2lbs asparagus spears
60g/2oz/½ cup butter
3 egg yolks
Juice of half a lemon
Grated rind and juice of ½ an orange
1 small bay leaf
1 blade mace
Salt
Pepper

Trim any thick ends from the asparagus spears and rinse them well. Put into a shallow casserole with 45-60g/3-4 tbsps water. Cover and cook for 7 minutes until just tender. Leave covered while preparing sauce. Put the butter in a glass measuring cup or jug, or small, deep bowl and cook for 1 minute on HIGH to melt. Put orange juice, lemon juice, bay leaf and mace into another bowl and heat for 1 minute on HIGH. Beat egg yolks, orange rind and seasoning together, and strain on the juice. Pour egg yolk mixture into the butter and stir well to mix. Have a bowl of ice water on hand. Put the sauce mixture into the oven and cook for 15 seconds on HIGH. Remove and stir well, and repeat the process until sauce is thickened. It should take about 2 minutes. Put the jug immediately into the ice water to prevent sauce from cooking further. Serve at once with the asparagus.

Cheese and Mushroom Tarts

PREPARATION TIME: 10 minutes

MICROWAVE COOKING TIME: 11 minutes

SERVES: 4 people

60g/2oz/1½ cups wholewheat biscuits/crackers
60g/2oz/½ cup butter or margarine
60g/2oz/½ cup Cheddar cheese, grated
225g/½lb mushrooms, roughly chopped
60ml/4 tbsps chopped chives
15g/½ oz/1 tbsp flour
15g/½ oz/1 tbsp butter
90ml/5 tbsps/⅓ cup chicken or vegetable stock
1 egg, beaten
30ml/2 tbsps light/single cream
60g/2oz/½ cup Red Leicester/Colby cheese, grated
Cayenne pepper
Salt
Pepper

Crush the crackers/biscuits into a food processor and grate in the cheese. Melt 45g/1½ oz/⅓ cup of the butter on HIGH for 1 minute and pour into the crumbs and cheese. Process to mix. Press the mixture firmly into 8 individual tart pans or a muffin pan. Cook for 2 minutes on HIGH, and cool. Melt the remaining butter on HIGH. Mix in flour, chives, seasoning and stock, and cook for 2 minutes on HIGH, or until sauce has thickened. Fill the tart shells with the mushrooms. Beat egg, cream, Cayenne pepper and seasonings together until frothy. fold in the Red Leicester/Colby cheese. Pour on top of the mushroom filling and cook for 2 minutes on HIGH until the cheese custard sets. Tops may be browned under a grill/broiler if desired, or cooked for 5 minutes on the Combination setting in a microwave convection oven. Serve immediately.

Facing page: Country Pâté (top) and Asparagus with Orange Hollandaise (bottom).

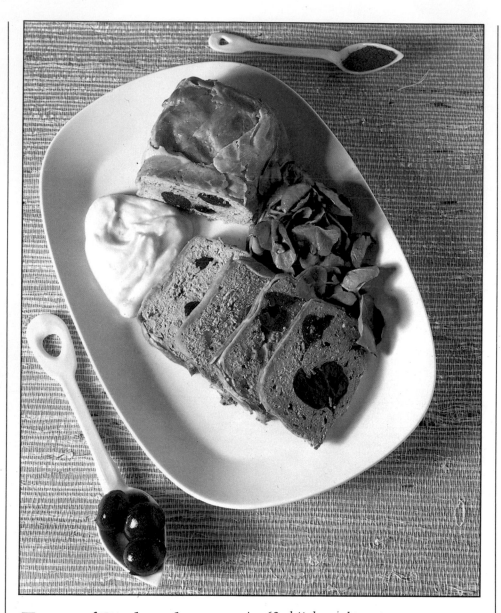

1lb glass loaf dish with the ham slices. Press mixture firmly onto the ham. Cover with plastic wrap and cook for 6 minutes on MEDIUM. Leave to stand for 5 minutes, then cook for a further 7 minutes on MEDIUM. Cover with foil and weight down the top. Leave to chill for 4-5 hours, and serve with tarragon sauce.

To make sauce: Have ready a bowl of ice water. Beat egg and sugar in a small glass bowl until creamy. Add vinegar and cook on HIGH for 30 seconds. Remove and stir. Repeat the process until sauce thickens (approximately 2 minutes). Put immediately into ice water to stop the cooking, and leave to go cold, stirring occasionally. Whip the cream and fold into the sauce with the chopped tarragon.

Tomato Tarts Niçoise

PREPARATION TIME: 20 minutes

MICROWAVE COOKING TIME: 10 minutes

SERVES: 4 people

PASTRY
150g/5oz/1 cup flour/plain flour
20g/¾ oz/1½ tbsps butter or margarine
20g/¾ oz/1½ tbsps baking powder
90ml/5 tbsps/⅓ cup milk
Pinch salt
15ml/1 tbsp chopped parsley, basil and
    thyme, mixed

FILLING
1 onion, finely slicd
225g/½lb tomatoes, skinned and thickly
    sliced
15ml/1 tbsp olive oil
16 black olives, stoned
1 tbsp capers
8 anchovies
1.25ml/¼ tsp oregano or basil
60g/2oz/½ cup Gruyère cheese, grated

To make pastry: Sift flour with salt and cut in the butter until mixture resembles fine breadcrumbs. Add herbs and milk, and mix to a soft dough. It may not be necessary to add all the milk. Turn out and knead lightly Divide dough into 4 pieces

Terrine of Duck and Cherries with Tarragon Sauce

PREPARATION TIME: 15 minutes

MICROWAVE COOKING TIME: 15 minutes

SERVES: 6-8 people

TERRINE
1 2kg/5lb duck, skinned and boned
6 slices boiled ham
145g/5oz/⅓ cup ground/minced pork
145g/5oz/⅓ cup ground/minced veal
½ clove garlic, crushed
225g/8oz can black/morello cherries,
    drained and pitted
60ml/4 tbsps white wine
Allspice
10ml/2 tsps tarragon, chopped
15ml/1 tbsp kirsch
Salt
Pepper

SAUCE
1 egg
45ml/3 tbsps tarragon vinegar
1.25ml/¼ tsp chopped fresh tarragon
45g/1½ oz/2 tbsps sugar
140ml/¼ pint/½ cup whipping cream

To prepare terrine: Mince duck meat in a food processor and mix with pork and veal. Add garlic, kirsch, wine, tarragon, allspice and seasoning. Fold in the cherries. Line a 450g/

Facing page: Terrine of Duck and Cherries with Tarragon Sauce. This page: Ham and Mushroom Pâté (left) and Stuffed Tomatoes Provençal (right).

and roll each out to line a muffin pan or 8 tart pans.
To make filling and assemble tarts: Bring 570ml/1 pint/2 cups water to the boil for 3 minutes on HIGH. Put in the tomatoes for 5 seconds, remove and plunge them into cold water. Peel, drain and slice them. Put olive oil in a bowl, add onion, and cook for 3 minutes on HIGH or until softened. Season, mix with half the cheese. Put into the bottom of each pastry shell. Layer tomatoes,

seasoning and sprinkling the herbs between each layer. Decorate with anchovies, capers and olives, and sprinkle with remaining cheese. Bake for 4 minutes on HIGH, turning pans once. Brown under a grill/broiler if desired. Do not overbake or pastry will become hard.

Ham and Mushroom Pâté

PREPARATION TIME: 10 minutes
MICROWAVE COOKING TIME: 20 minutes
SERVES: 6-8 people

450g/1lb cooked ham, minced
120g/4oz/1 cup fresh white breadcrumbs
3 eggs
45g/1½ oz/3 tbsps butter
120g/4oz mushrooms, finely chopped
1 shallot, finely chopped
1 clove garlic, crushed
30ml/2 tbsps dry sherry
1.25ml/¼ tsp thyme
1.25ml/¼ tsp parsley
Nutmeg
Salt and pepper

Melt the butter in a small bowl and add the shallot. Cover with pierced plastic wrap and cook for 2 minutes on HIGH. Add the thyme, parsley and mushrooms, and cook for a further 4 minutes, uncovered, on HIGH. Add the seasoning and 30g/1oz/¼ cup of the breadcrumbs. Leave to cool. Add 1 beaten egg only if necessary to bind together. Mix ham, remaining breadcrumbs, garlic, sherry, nutmeg and seasonings. Beat in up to 2 of the eggs, 1 at a time, until mixture holds together. Put half the ham mixture into a 450g/1lb glass loaf dish and pack down firmly. Make a channel down the centre and mound the mushroom mixture into it. Cover with remaining ham mixture, packing it carefully around the mushroom mixture to cover it completely. Cover dish with plastic wrap and put into the microwave oven with a ramekin dish of water. Cook for 10 minutes on MEDIUM, leave to stand for 2 minutes, then cook for another 2 minutes on MEDIUM until firm. Cover with foil and weight the top of the dish. Chill for 4-5 hours and cut into slices to serve with toast or French bread.

Stuffed Tomatoes Provençal

PREPARATION TIME: 10 minutes

MICROWAVE COOKING TIME: 6 minutes

SERVES: 4 people

4 large ripe tomatoes
225g/8oz mushrooms, finely chopped
1 shallot, finely chopped
30g/1oz/2 tbsps butter or margarine
45g/1½ oz/1 cup fresh white
    breadcrumbs
15ml/1 tbsp white wine
1 clove garlic, crushed
1 tsp Dijon mustard
5ml/1 tsp chopped parsley
5ml/1 tsp chopped basil
1.25ml/¼ tsp thyme

GARNISH
Parsley sprigs

Cut the rounded ends of the tomatoes off to form caps, and remove the green cores from the bottoms. Scoop out the pulp and seeds, and strain the juice. Put the butter into a small bowl with the garlic and shallot and cook for 2 minutes on HIGH. Stir in the mushrooms and wine and cook for 2 minutes on HIGH. Add bread-crumbs, herbs, seasoning, mustard

and tomato pulp, and mix well. Stuff the tomatoes and put into a shallow dish. Place the tops on at a slight angle and cook, uncovered, for 2 minutes on HIGH. Garnish with the parsley sprigs.

Langoustine Parisienne

PREPARATION TIME: 10 minutes

MICROWAVE COOKING TIME: 14 minutes

SERVES: 4 people

450g/1lb scampi/langoustines, shelled
    and uncooked (Gulf shrimp may be
    substituted)
225g/8oz mushrooms
75g/2½ oz/⅔ cup butter or margarine
45g/1½ oz/3 tbsps flour/plain flour
1 shallot, finely chopped
430ml/¾ pint/1½ cups milk
15ml/1 tbsp chopped parsley
30ml/2 tbsps dry sherry
60g/2oz/⅓ cup dry breadcrumbs
Lemon juice
Paprika
Salt
Pepper

Cut mushroom stalks level with the caps and cut mushrooms into quarters. Put 45g/1½ oz/3 tbsps of the butter into a large bowl, then add shallot and cook for 1 minute on HIGH. Stir in the mushrooms and cook, uncovered, for 6 minutes on HIGH. Add flour and seasoning, and stir in the milk and sherry. Cook for 3 minutes on HIGH, stirring frequently. Add parsley, and set aside. Put scampi into a small bowl with 2 tbsps water, cover with pierced plastic wrap and cook for 2 minutes on HIGH. Cut each scampi into 2 or 3 pieces if large, then stir them into the mushroom sauce. Heat a brown-ing tray and melt the remaining butter. Stir in the breadcrumbs and cook until golden brown and crisp. Put the shellfish-mushroom mixture into 4 ramekins or shells and scatter over the crumbs. Sprinkle over the paprika and heat for 2 minutes on HIGH. If using a microwave convection oven, melt the butter for 1 minute on HIGH microwave

setting, mix in the crumbs, fill the ramekins with the shellfish-mushroom mixture and scatter the crumbs over. Sprinkle with paprika and cook for 3 minutes on the Combination setting to brown.

Chicken Liver Pâté

PREPARATION TIME: 8 minutes

MICROWAVE COOKING TIME: 9 minutes

SERVES: 4 people

450g/1lb/chicken livers
1 shallot, finely chopped
1 clove garlic, crushed
1 large sprig rosemary
5ml/1 tsp parsley
15ml/1 tbsp Madeira
15ml/1 tbsp cream
45g/1½ oz/⅓ cup butter
Nutmeg
Salt
Pepper

GARNISH
Juniper berries
Small sprigs of rosemary

Pick over the livers, removing any discolored parts. Put livers, shallot, garlic, 1 sprig rosemary, half the butter, seasonings and a pinch of nutmeg into a bowl. Cover with pierced plastic wrap and cook for 6 minutes on HIGH, stirring once. Remove rosemary and put the mixture into a food processor with the Madeira, cream and parsley, and purée until smooth. Divide between 4 ramekin dishes. Put remaining butter in a bowl and cook for 3 minutes on HIGH until boiling. Leave to stand and skim off salt rising to surface. Spoon the butter oil over each pâté to seal. Chill until firm, decorate with small sprigs of rosemary and juniper berries, and serve with hot toast or French bread.

Facing page: Chicken Liver Pâté (top) and Langoustine Parisienne (bottom).

Microwave
SOUPS AND APPETIZERS

MEAT AND SEAFOOD APPETIZERS

Sparkling Shrimp

PREPARATION TIME: 5 minutes

MICROWAVE COOKING TIME:
2½ minutes

SERVES: 4 people

675g/1½lbs peeled shrimp or prawns
15ml/1 tbsp peppercorns packed in brine,
  rinsed
140ml/¼ pint/½ cup dry sparkling white
  wine
140ml/¼ pint/½ cup heavy/double
  cream
Juice and grated rind of half an orange
Salt
Pepper

GARNISH
12 thin orange slices

Put orange rind and juice, peppercorns, seasoning and wine into a
bowl. Heat for 30 seconds on HIGH.
Stir in the prawns and heat for
1 minute on HIGH. Lightly whip the
cream, fold in, and heat for a further
1 minute on HIGH. Adjust seasoning
before putting into serving dishes.
Garnish with the orange slices.

Moûles Marinière à la Moutarde

PREPARATION TIME: 5 minutes

MICROWAVE COOKING TIME:
9 minutes

SERVES: 4 people

1 litre/2 pints mussels
20g/¾ oz/1½ tbsps butter or margarine
2 shallots, finely chopped
1 clove garlic, crushed
4 tbsps Dijon mustard

280ml/½ pint/1 cup white wine
140ml/¼ pint/½ cup heavy/double
  cream
15g/½ oz/1 tbsp flour/plain flour
15ml/1 tbsp parsley, chopped
15ml/1 tbsp dill, chopped
Salt
Pepper

**This page: Moûles Marinière à la
Moutarde.
Facing page: Sparkling Shrimp.**

Scrub mussels well and discard any
that are open or broken. Put butter
into a large bowl and cook for

1 minute on HIGH. Add shallot, garlic, wine and seasoning. Cover with pierced plastic wrap and cook for 2 minutes on HIGH. Add mussels, and cover and cook for 3 minutes or until the shells are open. Stir half-way through the cooking time. Remove mussels from the bowl, put into a serving dish and keep them warm. Strain the liquid from them and set it aside. Put flour into a clean bowl and gradually pour on the mussel liquid, stirring well to mix. Cook, uncovered, for 2 minutes on HIGH or until thick, stirring occasionally. Stir in the mustard, cream and chopped herbs and heat through for 1 minute on HIGH. Pour over the mussels and serve with French bread.

Pork Satay with Peanut Sauce

PREPARATION TIME: 10 minutes and 1 hour to marinate pork

MICROWAVE COOKING TIME: 13 minutes

SERVES: 4 people

675g/1½lbs pork fillet/tenderloin, cut
*   into 2.5cm (1") cubes*
1 large red pepper, cut into 2.5cm (1")
*   slices*
30ml/2 tbsps oil
Lime juice
1 clove garlic, crushed
1 small green chili pepper, finely chopped
60g/2oz/½ cup crunchy peanut butter
140ml/¼ pint/½ cup chicken or vegetable
*   stock*
5ml/1 tsp ground cumin
5ml/1 tsp ground coriander
1 shallot, finely chopped
Salt
Pepper

GARNISH
1 bunch fresh coriander leaves (optional)
Lemon wedges

Mix lime juice, salt and pepper together and mix in the pork. Leave in a cool place for 1 hour. Heat 1 tbsp oil in a small bowl and add shallot. Cook for 2 minutes on HIGH, add chili pepper and cook for 1 minute

more on HIGH. Stir in stock, peanut butter, spices and seasoning. Cook for 1 minute on HIGH. Set aside. Thread meat and red pepper onto 12 small, wooden skewers. Heat a browning tray for 5 minutes on HIGH. Add oil and brown the satay for 3 minutes on HIGH, turning frequently. Transfer onto a roasting rack, and cook for 6 minutes on MEDIUM. Arrange sprigs of coriander leaves on serving plates and put the satay on top. Spoon over some of the peanut sauce and serve the rest separately.

Spicy Chicken Kebabs with Avocado Sauce

PREPARATION TIME: 10 minutes

MICROWAVE COOKING TIME: 6 minutes

SERVES: 4 people

CHICKEN AND MARINADE
3 chicken breasts, skinned and boned
30ml/2 tbsps vegetable oil
1 clove garlic, crushed

This page: Pork Satay with Peanut Sauce (top) and Spicy Chicken Kebabs with Avocado Sauce (bottom).
Facing page: Stuffed Zucchini/ Courgettes.

15ml/1 tbsp curry powder
1.25ml/¼ tsp Cayenne pepper
15ml/1 tbsp chopped coriander leaves
Juice and grated rind of 1 lime
Salt
Pepper

SAUCE
1 large avocado, peeled and stone
*   removed*
140ml/¼ pint/½ cup plain yogurt
15ml/1 tbsp vegetable oil
2.5ml/½ tsp finely chopped onion
5ml/1 tsp mango chutney
Lime juice

Cut chicken into strips 2.5cm (1") wide. Combine ingredients for the marinade and mix in the chicken to coat each piece. Leave to marinate for 1 hour. Thread the meat onto wooden skewers and put onto a roasting rack. Cook for 5 minutes on

HIGH. Turn kebabs while cooking. Leave to stand, covered in plastic wrap, for 1 minute. Put oil and onion for the sauce into a small bowl. Cook for 1 minute on HIGH, and stir in chutney. Put avocado flesh into a food processor with seasoning, yogurt and lime juice. Add onion and chutney, and process until smooth. Serve with the chicken kebabs.

Stuffed Zucchini/ Courgettes

PREPARATION TIME: 10 minutes

MICROWAVE COOKING TIME: 18 minutes

SERVES: 4 people

4 small, even-sized zucchini/courgettes
120g/¼lb crabmeat, fresh or frozen
1 shallot, finely chopped
140ml/¼ pint/½ cup cream cheese
60g/2oz/½ cup mushrooms, chopped
¼ tsp tomato paste
45g/1½oz/¼ cup grated Parmesan cheese
60g/2oz/4 tbsps dry breadcrumbs
30ml/2 tbsps milk
15ml/1 tbsp chopped parsley
60g/2oz/4 tbsps butter, melted
Tabasco
Salt and pepper

Top and tail the zucchini/courgettes and put into a large dish with 1 cup of water. Cover with pierced plastic wrap and cook for 4-5 minutes on HIGH. Rinse in cold water until completely cooled. Cut in half lengthways, and carefully scoop out the flesh with a teaspoon, leaving a thin lining of flesh inside the skin. Leave to drain. Chop flesh roughly and set aside. Melt 30g/1oz/2 tbsps of butter in a bowl for 1 minute on HIGH. Add the shallot and mushrooms, and cook, covered, for 2 minutes on HIGH. Add zucchini/ courgette flesh, cover and cook for 1 minute on HIGH. Beat the cream cheese, tomato paste and milk together. Add crabmeat, parsley, seasoning, and a few drops of tabasco. Stir into the zucchini/ courgette mixture and pile the filling into each zucchini/courgette shell.

Mix breadcrumbs and Parmesan cheese together, and top each filled zucchini/courgette. Melt the remaining butter and sprinkle over the zucchini/courgettes. Heat through, uncovered, for 5 minutes on HIGH and brown under a grill/broiler or on the Combination setting of a microwave convection oven for 10 minutes. Serve immediately.

Potted Smoked Fish

PREPARATION TIME: 15 minutes

MICROWAVE COOKING TIME: 8 minutes

SERVES: 4 people

2 smoked white, or kippered, fish fillets
15g/½ oz/1 tbsp butter or margarine
15g/½ oz/1 tbsp flour/plain flour
90ml/5 tbsps/⅓ cup cream cheese
90ml/5 tbsps/⅓ cup milk
6-8 pimento-stuffed olives, sliced
2 tsps Dijon mustard
Salt and pepper

GARNISH
60g/2oz/½ cup butter for clarifying
Pimento-stuffed olives
Black peppercorns

Skin the fish fillets and break up into small pieces. Melt butter for 1 minute on HIGH. Stir in the flour and cook for 2 minutes on HIGH. Blend in the cheese, milk, half the olives, mustard and seasoning. Add fish and mix until well blended. Put into 4 ramekin dishes and smooth the top. Cover each with plastic wrap and cook for 1 minute on HIGH to set the mixture. Put butter into a medium bowl and heat for 3-4 minutes on HIGH, or until boiling. Leave to stand for 10-15 minutes. Skim the salt off the top and spoon the butter oil carefully over each pot of fish. Fill nearly to the top, and leave until almost set. Then place the remaining olives and peppercorns on top of the butter. Chill and when set, cover the decoration with another thin layer of clarified butter and refrigerate again until set. Serve with hot toast.

Artichokes with Mustard Butter

PREPARATION TIME: 8 minutes

MICROWAVE COOKING TIME: 21 minutes

SERVES: 4 people

4 globe artichokes
15ml/1 tbsp lemon juice
Pinch salt
570ml/1 pint/2 cups water
15ml/1 tbsp oil
1 bay leaf
1 slice onion

SAUCE
60g/2oz/½ cup butter
3 tbsps Dijon mustard
Salt and pepper
Squeeze of lemon juice

Break stems from the base of each artichoke and twist to remove any stringy fibres. Trim the base of each so the artichokes sit level. Trim tips of artichoke leaves using kitchen scissors. Wash artichokes under cold running water. Put lemon juice, salt, water, oil, bay leaf and onion slice into a large bowl and cook 3-4 minutes on HIGH, or until the water boils. Put artichokes upright in the bowl, cover with plastic wrap and pierce several times. Cook for 15 minutes on HIGH, or until lower leaves can be pulled away easily. Leave to stand covered while preparing the sauce. Put butter, seasoning and lemon juice into a glass measuring cup or jug and cook for 2 minutes on HIGH, or until butter has melted. Beat in the mustard until sauce holds together. Put artichokes onto special artichoke serving plates, or onto small serving plates each on top of a larger plate, to give room for the discarded leaves. Serve the sauce separately, or remove the "choke" and serve the sauce in the centre of the artichoke.

Facing page: Potted Smoked Fish (top) and Artichokes with Mustard Butter (bottom).

CHEESE AND EGG APPETIZERS

Eggs Florentine

PREPARATION TIME: 15 minutes

MICROWAVE COOKING TIME: 18 minutes

SERVES: 4 people

1kg/2¼lbs fresh spinach, washed and stems removed
30g/1oz/2 tbsps butter or margarine
4 eggs
2 tomatoes, skinned and seeded
Nutmeg
Salt
Pepper

MORNAY SAUCE
45g/1½ oz/3 tbsps butter or margarine
45g/1½ oz/3 tbsps flour/plain flour
430ml/¾ pint/1½ cups milk
45g/1½ oz/⅓ cup Cheddar cheese, grated
Dry mustard
Cayenne pepper
Salt
Pepper

To prepare spinach and tomatoes: Put spinach into a roasting bag and tie loosely. Stand upright and cook for 5 minutes on HIGH. (Spinach may also be cooked in a bowl covered with pierced plastic wrap.) Drain spinach well, and chop roughly. Boil 570ml/1 pint/2 cups of water in a large bowl on HIGH and put in the tomatoes for 5 seconds. Put the tomatoes immediately into cold water. Peel, squeeze out the seeds and juice, and chop roughly. To poach the eggs: Pour water into each of 4 ramekin dishes/custard cups to a depth of 2.5cm (1″). Put the dishes in a circle and heat on HIGH until the water boils. Break 1 egg into each cup and pierce the yoke with a sharp knife. Cook on DEFROST or LOW for 3 minutes, or until whites have set. Turn the dishes at 1 minute intervals.
To prepare Mornay sauce: Melt butter in a medium bowl for 1 minute on HIGH. Stir in the flour, mustard and a pinch of Cayenne pepper, and add the milk gradually. Cook for 4-5 minutes on HIGH, stirring frequently. Add the cheese, reserving some for the top. Add seasoning and stir until blended. Melt 30g/1oz/2 tbsps of butter for 1 minute on HIGH. Stir in the spinach, seasoning and grated nutmeg to taste. Heat for 1 minute on HIGH, then add tomatoes. Put some of the spinach mixture into each individual serving dish and top with a poached egg. Coat each with Mornay sauce and sprinkle on grated cheese. Brown under a grill/broiler, or on the Combination setting in a microwave convection oven for 2 minutes.

Baked Eggs with Mushrooms and Mustard Cream

PREPARATION TIME: 10 minutes

MICROWAVE COOKING TIME: 9 minutes

SERVES: 4 people

225g/8oz mushrooms, finely chopped
4 eggs
140ml/¼ pint/½ cup cream, whipped
30g/1oz/chopped chives
5ml/1 tsp sherry
10ml/2 tsps Dijon mustard
Paprika
Salt
Pepper

Melt butter in a small bowl for 1 minute on HIGH. Add mushrooms and cook for 4 minutes on HIGH. Add chives, sherry and seasoning and divide into 4 ramekin dishes. Make a slight well in the center of each portion and break an egg into it. Pierce the yoke with a small, sharp knife. Fold the mustard, cream and seasonings together and spoon over the eggs. Sprinkle with paprika and cook for 4 minutes on HIGH. Leave to stand for 1 minute before serving.

Cheese Custards

PREPARATION TIME: 10 minutes

MICROWAVE COOKING TIME: 30 minutes

SERVES: 4 people

30g/1oz/¼ cup butter or margarine
30g/1oz/¼ cup flour/plain flour
2.5ml/½ tsp mustard powder
280ml/½ pint/1 cup light/single cream
140ml/¼ pint/½ cup heavy/double cream
340g/12oz/¾ cup Cheddar cheese, grated
4 eggs, separated
1.25ml/¼ tsp cream of tartar
Cayenne pepper
Salt
Pepper
Paprika

Melt the butter for 1 minute on HIGH. Add the flour, mustard, Cayenne pepper and seasoning to the

Facing page: Eggs Florentine (top) and Cheese Custards (bottom).

bowl and stir in the cream gradually. Cook for 6 minutes on HIGH, stirring frequently until thickened. Add 225g/8oz/½ cup of the cheese and stir to melt. Beat in the egg yolks and whip egg whites with the cream of tartar until stiff but not dry. Fold whites into cheese mixture and pour into 8 ramekin dishes/small custard cups. Arrange in a larger dish filled with hot water. Cook for 3 minutes on HIGH. Turn the cups and cook for 1½ minutes more on HIGH. If the mixture appears set and begins to pull away from the sides of the cups/ dishes, turn the custards out. If not, cook for 30 seconds longer on HIGH. Put the custards into individual baking dishes, allowing 2 per person. Pour over the heavy/double cream and sprinkle on the remaining cheese and paprika. Bake for 2 minutes on HIGH and serve immediately.

Sour Cream and Caviar Cheesecake

PREPARATION TIME: 10 minutes

MICROWAVE COOKING TIME: 15 minutes

SERVES: 4 people

225g/8oz/1 cup Cheddar cheese crackers/biscuits
30g/1oz/¼ cup butter
30g/1oz/2 tbsps Parmesan cheese
225g/8oz package/carton cream cheese
120g/4oz/1 cup Gruyère cheese, grated
60ml/2 fl oz/¼ cup milk
2 eggs
140ml/¼ pint/½ cup sour cream
1 bunch/⅓ cup chives, chopped
1 jar red salmon caviar
1 jar black lumpfish caviar

Crush the crackers/biscuits in a food processor and melt the butter for 1 minute on HIGH. Add half the Parmesan cheese and all the butter to the crumbs in the processor and work until well mixed. Mix cream cheese, Gruyère and remaining Parmesan together. Beat in eggs and sour cream, reserving 30ml/2 tbsps for the top, and stir in the chives. Add seasoning. Line the base of a 15cm (6″) microwave cake pan with

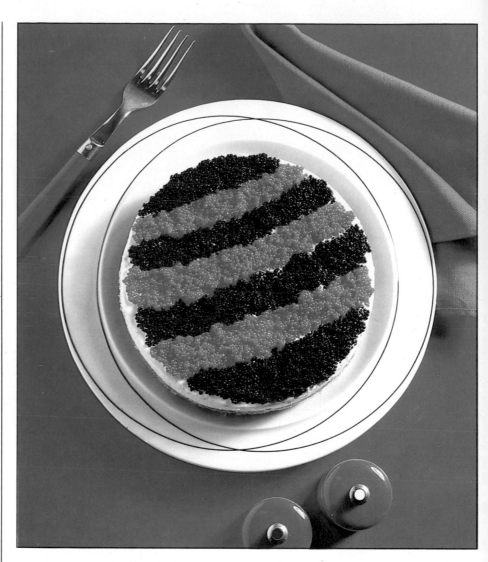

wax/greaseproof paper and pour in the cheesecake mixture. Bake for 5 minutes on HIGH until lightly set. Sprinkle on the crumbs and press down gently. Bake for another 10 minutes on MEDIUM. Leave to cool at room temperature, then chill for 1 hour. Invert onto a serving dish, spread with remaining sour cream and decorate the top with caviar. Cut into wedges to serve.

Eggplant/Aubergine Caviar

PREPARATION TIME: 30 minutes

MICROWAVE COOKING TIME: 13 minutes

SERVES: 4 people

This page: Sour Cream and Caviar Cheesecake.
Facing page: Baked Eggs with Mushrooms and Mustard Cream (top) and Eggplant/Aubergine Caviar (bottom).

1 large or 2 small eggplants/aubergines
1 clove garlic, crushed
60ml/4 tbsps olive oil
Juice of half a lemon
10ml/2 tsps chopped fresh coriander
15ml/1 tbsp chopped parsley
5ml/1 tsp cumin seeds
1 cap pimento, finely chopped
Cayenne pepper
Salt
Pepper
Pitta bread

Dice the aubergine/eggplant, then spread out on paper towels, sprinkle

with salt and leave for 30 minutes to draw out any bitterness. Rinse and dry well. Put into a large bowl with 4 tbsps water, cover with pierced plastic wrap and cook for 10 minutes on HIGH, stirring 2-3 times. Drain and leave to cool. Put cumin seeds on a plate and roast, uncovered, for 3 minutes on HIGH, stirring occasionally. Put the aubergine/eggplant into a food processor with the garlic, and blend until smooth, adding olive oil slowly through the feed tube. Add lemon juice, seasoning, Cayenne pepper and cumin seeds, and process once. Add herbs and pimento and process again once. Adjust seasoning and chill. Wrap pitta bread in paper towels and warm for 30 seconds on HIGH. Cut into triangles and serve·with the aubergine/eggplant caviar.

Pasta Shells Stuffed with Garlic Cheese

PREPARATION TIME: 10 minutes

MICROWAVE COOKING TIME: 20 minutes

SERVES: 4 people

8 large pasta shells (conchiglie) or small shells
2 pkts garlic and herb soft cheese
4 tomatoes, skinned and seeded
45g/1½ oz/3 tbsps butter or margarine
45g/1½ oz/3 tbsps flour/plain flour
570ml/1 pint/2 cups milk
60g/2oz/½ cup Gruyère cheese, grated
15ml/1 tbsp chopped parsley
Nutmeg
Salt and pepper

Heat 1150ml/2 pints/4 cups water on HIGH for 5 minutes, until boiling. Put in the tomatoes for 5 seconds, then remove them and put immediately into cold water. Peel, seed and shred them thinly, then set aside. Put the pasta into the water with 1 tbsp oil and cook for 9 minutes, or until just tender. Leave to stand for 5 minutes. Drain and dry. Beat cheese to soften. Put into a pastry/piping bag fitted with a wide, plain tube. Fill each shell with the garlic cheese and put into 4 baking dishes. Melt butter

in a small bowl for 1 minute on HIGH and stir in the flour. Stir in the milk and seasoning, and blend well. Heat for 2-3 minutes on HIGH, stirring frequently. Add half of the cheese, stirring to melt. Stir in the tomato strips and coat over the pasta shells in the baking dishes. Sprinkle on the remaining cheese. Heat for 2 minutes on HIGH.

This page: Pasta Shells Stuffed with Garlic Cheese.
Facing page: Stuffed Vine Leaves Bordelaise.

VEGETABLE APPETIZERS

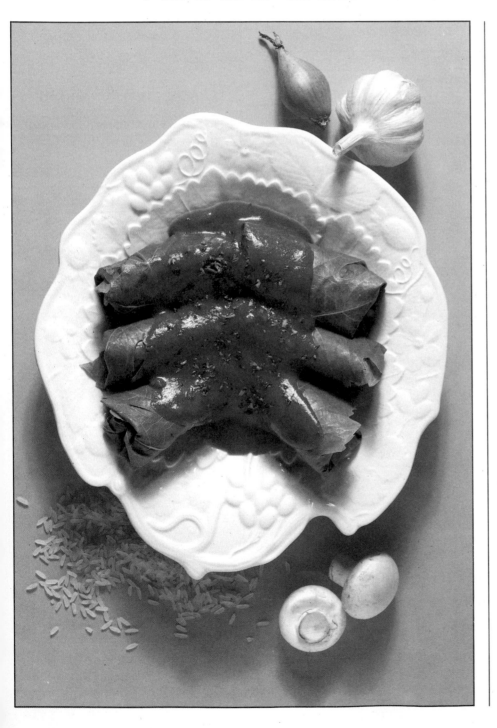

Stuffed Vine Leaves Bordelaise

PREPARATION TIME: 15 minutes

MICROWAVE COOKING TIME:
53 minutes and 5 minutes standing time

SERVES: 4 people

12 packaged vine leaves
30g/1oz/¼ cup butter
1 shallot, finely chopped
175g/6oz/1 cup mushrooms, finely chopped
90g/3oz/½ cup rice
4 strips green streaky bacon (rind and bones removed)
30g/1oz/2 tbsps dried blackcurrants
15ml/1 tbsp parsley
Salt and pepper

SAUCE
1 shallot, finely chopped
15g/½ oz/1½ tbsps flour/plain flour
15g/½ oz/1½ tbsps butter or margarine
180ml/7 fl oz/¾ cup red wine
180ml/7 fl oz/¾ cup beef stock
1 clove garlic, crushed
1 tsp tomato paste

To make stuffed vine leaves: Put 850ml/1½ pints/3 cups water and the rice into a large, deep bowl. Cover with pierced plastic wrap and cook for 14 minutes on HIGH. Add the blackcurrants and leave to stand for 5 minutes. Drain and cool. Put the butter and shallot for the filling into a bowl, cover and cook for 1 minute on HIGH. Add mushrooms and cook for 6 minutes on HIGH, stirring occasionally. Heat a browning dish for 3-4 minutes on HIGH and cook the bacon for 1 minute each side until crisp. Crumble the bacon and add to the mushrooms with the

rice, parsley and seasoning. Mix well and put a mound of filling on each leaf. Roll up, tucking in the sides to enclose the filling completely.
To make the sauce: Heat a browning dish for 3-4 minutes on HIGH. Melt the butter and add shallot and flour. Cook until golden brown, or about 4 minutes on HIGH. Put into a bowl and stir in the stock, wine, garlic, tomato paste and seasoning. Cook, covered with pierced plastic wrap, for 4 minutes on HIGH. Put vine leaves into a casserole, seamed side down, and pour over the sauce. Cover and cook for 5 minutes on HIGH. Serve immediately.

Celeriac Moutarde

PREPARATION TIME: 10 minutes
MICROWAVE COOKING TIME: 15 minutes
SERVES: 4 people

1 large root celeriac, peeled
30ml/2 tbsps white wine

MUSTARD CREAM SAUCE
45g/1½ oz/3 tbsps butter
45g/1½ oz/3 tbsps flour/plain flour
570ml/1 pint/2 cups milk
60ml/4 tbsps Dijon mustard
15ml/1 tbsp celery seed
Salt and pepper
60ml/4 tbsps dry breadcrumbs
30g/1oz/2 tbsps butter or margarine

Cut celeriac into 5mm (¼") slices, then into sticks about 2cm (1") long. Put into a bowl with the wine, and toss to mix. Cover with pierced plastic wrap and cook for 4 minutes on HIGH. Melt butter in a small deep bowl for 1 minute on HIGH. Add flour and cook for 1 minute more on HIGH. Stir in milk, mustard, celery seed and strained cooking liquid from the celeriac. Season and cook for 3 minutes on HIGH, stirring occasionally, until sauce has thickened. Put celeriac into 4 baking/gratin dishes and coat with the sauce. Heat a browning tray for 3-4 minutes on HIGH. Put in 30g/1oz/2 tbsps butter and dry bread-

crumbs, and cook until golden brown. Sprinkle the breadcrumbs on top of the celeriac and heat through for 2 minutes on HIGH. If using a microwave convection oven, melt the butter for 1 minute, then stir in the breadcrumbs. Sprinkle on top of the celeriac and cook on the Combination setting for 5 minutes. Serve immediately.

Vinaigrette de Jardin

PREPARATION TIME: 15 minutes
MICROWAVE COOKING TIME: 7 minutes
SERVES: 4 people

SALAD AND DRESSING
120g/4oz pea pods/mangetout
2 zucchini/courgettes, sliced in rounds
4 spring/green onions, sliced
120g/4oz broccoli flowerets
1 small head cauliflower, cut into flowerets
2 carrots, sliced in rounds
4 tomatoes, seeded and sliced into strips
1 banana pepper, sliced into strips
100ml/6 tbsps olive oil
30ml/2 tbsps white wine vinegar
15ml/1 tbsp Dijon mustard
15ml/1 tbsp herbs (eg chives, chervil, parsley, basil), chopped
Salt and pepper

GARLIC BREAD
1 small loaf French bread
45g/1½ oz/⅓ cup butter
1 clove garlic, crushed
2 tbsps poppy seeds

Cook each of the vegetables on HIGH in 2 tbsps water, in a shallow, covered dish: pea pods/mangetout, 2 minutes; zucchini/courgettes, 3 minutes; broccoli, 3 minutes; cauliflower, 5 minutes; carrots, 5 minutes. When cooked, rinse immediately in cold water to stop the cooking. Drain and leave to dry. Boil 570ml/1 pint/2 cups water for 3-4 minutes on HIGH and put tomatoes in for 5 seconds. Then put them immediately into cold water, peel and quarter them, remove the seeds, and cut them into thin shreds. Cut pepper into thin slices and add,

with the tomato, to the drained vegetables. Mix oil, vinegar, Dijon mustard, herbs and seasoning, and pour over the mixed vegetables. Toss lightly and leave to marinate. Serve with the garlic bread.
To make garlic bread: Cut the loaf into thick slices without cutting through the base. Mix the butter, garlic and poppy seed, and spread between each slice. Wrap loosely in paper towels and heat for 1½ minutes on HIGH or until butter has melted. Serve with the vegetable salad.

Cheese and Herb Soufflés

PREPARATION TIME: 8 minutes
MICROWAVE COOKING TIME: 8-10 minutes
SERVES: 4 people

180g/6oz/1 cup Red Leicester/Colby and Parmesan cheese, grated and mixed
30g/1oz/¼ cup butter or margarine
45g/1½ oz/¼ cup flour/plain flour
430ml/¾ pint/1½ cups milk
6 eggs, separated
5ml/1 tsp cream of tartar
1.25ml/¼ tsp parsley, chopped
1.25ml/¼ tsp chives, chopped
1.25ml/¼ tsp thyme, chopped
1.25ml/¼ tsp sage, chopped
Dry mustard
Paprika
Salt
Pepper

Put the butter in a bowl and heat for 1 minute on HIGH. Stir in the flour, Cayenne pepper and mustard, and blend in the milk. Cook for 4 minutes on HIGH, stirring frequently until thickened. Add cheese, herbs and seasoning. Beat egg yolks into the cheese mixture one at a time. Whisk egg whites until stiff but not dry with the cream of tartar, and fold in carefully. Divide the mixture

Facing page: Cheese and Herb Soufflés (top) and Celeriac Moutarde (bottom).

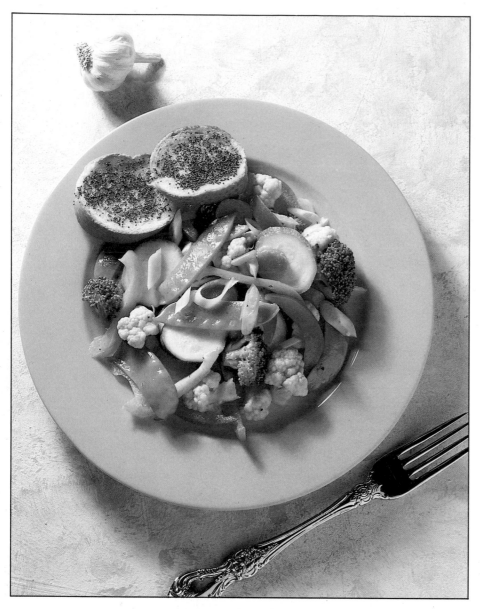

lining inside the shell. Sprinkle the scooped-out flesh and shell with lemon juice. Heat a browning tray for 3 minutes on HIGH, brown bacon for 1 minute each side, crumble it and set aside. Brown shallot, pepper and mushrooms lightly for 1 minute in the bacon fat and combine with avocado flesh. Melt 15g/½ oz/1 tbsp butter for 1 minute on HIGH. Stir in flour and milk. Heat for 2 minutes until thickened, stirring frequently. Add all ingredients save cheese and breadcrumbs. Stir in seasoning and a few drops of tabasco. Pile into the shells. Sprinkle on the cheese and breadcrumbs. Melt remaining butter for 1 minute. Sprinkle over the avocado and cook for 3 minutes in a microwave-convection oven on Combination setting, or brown under a grill/broiler. Serve immediately.

Stuffed Mushrooms

PREPARATION TIME: 8 minutes

MICROWAVE COOKING TIME:
6-8 minutes

SERVES: 4 people

12-16 large mushrooms
120g/4oz ham, finely chopped
60g/2oz/½ cup fresh white breadcrumbs
75g/2½ oz/⅓ cup finely chopped walnuts
1 egg, beaten
1 bunch snipped chives
15ml/1 tbsp chopped parsley
15ml/1 tbsp Dijon mustard
Dry breadcrumbs
45g/1½ oz/3 tbsps butter, melted
Salt
Pepper

Clean the mushrooms, trimming stalks, and chop them finely. Mix with the ham, breadcrumbs, walnuts, herbs, mustard and seasoning. Beat in the egg gradually to bind. Pile on top of the mushrooms, then put on a plate and cook for 5 minutes on

between 4 small soufflé dishes. Cook on MEDIUM for 4-6 minutes. The COMBINATION setting of a microwave convection oven may be used for 6 minutes. Sprinkle with paprika and serve immediately.

Stuffed Avocados

PREPARATION TIME: 10 minutes

MICROWAVE COOKING TIME:
10 minutes

SERVES: 4 people

2 large avocados
4 slices smoked streaky bacon
60g/2oz/1 cup peeled prawns or cooked shrimp, shelled

1 shallot, finely chopped
60g/2oz/½ cup mushrooms, roughly chopped
1 green pepper, roughly chopped
20g/¾ oz/1½ tbsps butter or margarine
30g/1oz/2 tbsps flour/plain flour
140ml/¼ pint/½ cup milk
2 tomatoes, skinned, seeded and chopped
60g/2oz/⅓ cup Parmesan cheese
4 tbsps dry breadcrumbs
15ml/1 tbsp parsley
5ml/1 tsp marjoram
Tabasco
Salt and pepper
Lemon juice

Halve avocados and remove stones. Scoop out flesh, leaving 5mm (¼")

HIGH. Sprinkle over the dry crumbs and melted butter. Cook for a further 1 minute on HIGH. Brown under a grill/broiler, or cook for 2 minutes in a microwave-convection oven on the Combination setting.

Spinach Gnocchi in Ricotta Sauce

PREPARATION TIME: 10 minutes

MICROWAVE COOKING TIME: 8 minutes

SERVES: 4 people

GNOCCHI
450g/1lb fresh spinach, washed and
    stems removed
120g/4oz/1 cup Gruyère cheese, grated
4 slices white bread, crusts removed·
2 tbsps finely chopped walnuts
1 tbsp finely chopped shallot
1 clove garlic, crushed
1 egg, beaten
Nutmeg
Salt
Pepper

RICOTTA SAUCE
225g/8oz Ricotta cheese
45g/1½ oz/3 tbsps grated Parmesan
    cheese
2.5g/½ tsp basil, fresh or dried
1.25g/¼ tsp chopped parsley
190ml/⅓ pint/⅔ cup cream or milk
Salt
Pepper
Paprika

To prepare gnocchi: Put spinach into a roasting bag and tie loosely. Stand upright and cook for 3 minutes on HIGH. (Spinach may also be cooked in a bowl covered with pierced plastic wrap.) Drain the spinach well, and chop finely. Make crumbs from the bread slices using a food processor or liquidiser. Add to the spinach along with the Gruyère, walnuts, nutmeg, seasoning and egg. Beat well and shape into 5cm (2") balls or ovals. Put gnocchi onto a plate, cover loosely with plastic wrap, and cook for 2 minutes on HIGH. Set aside and keep warm.
To make sauce: Mix Ricotta cheese with the other ingredients except the

paprika and heat for 1 minute on HIGH.
Divide the gnocchi between 4 gratin dishes and coat with the sauce. Sprinkle with paprika and heat for 2 minutes on HIGH. Serve at once.

Salade Alsacienne

PREPARATION TIME: 10 minutes

MICROWAVE COOKING TIME: 13-15 minutes

SERVES: 4 people

340g/¾lb new potatoes, scrubbed but not
    peeled (or regular/old potatoes, peeled)
Half head (white) cabbage, shredded
30ml/2 tbsps white wine
225g/8oz smoked sausage or kielbasa
10ml/2 tsps caraway seeds
60g/2oz/½ cup blue cheese, crumbled
140ml/¼ pint/½ cup sour cream
15ml/1 tbsp white wine vinegar
45ml/3 tbsps vegetable oil
1.25ml/¼ tsp French mustard
Salt
Pepper

GARNISH
4 green onions, chopped

Prick potato skins with a fork, if using new potatoes. Put potatoes into a casserole dish with 2 tbsps water, cover, and cook for 10-12 minutes on HIGH until tender. Drain and cut into large pieces. Mix vinegar, oil, mustard and seasoning together and pour over the potatoes. Stir and leave to stand. Prick sausage skin and cook, covered, for 1 minute on

HIGH. Slice thinly and add to the potatoes. Put cabbage into a casserole dish with the wine, caraway seeds and seasoning. Cover and cook for 2 minutes on HIGH. Add to the potatoes and sausages. Add blue cheese and sour cream, and mix carefully, so that the potatoes do not break up. Garnish with chopped green onions.

Fondue Pots

PREPARATION TIME: 10 minutes

MICROWAVE COOKING TIME: 10-13 minutes

SERVES: 4 people

FONDUE
225g/8oz/2 cups Gruyère cheese, grated

Facing page: Spinach Gnocchi in Ricotta Sauce.
This page: Salade Alsacienne (left) and Fondue Pots (right).

225g/8oz/2 cups Swiss cheese, grated
430ml/¾ pint/1½ cups dry white wine
20ml/1½ tbsps cornstarch/cornflour
20ml/1½ tbsps kirsch
1 clove garlic, crushed
Dry mustard
Nutmeg
Salt and Pepper

BREADSTICKS
12 slices white bread, crusts removed
115g/4oz/1 stick butter
60g/4 tbsps herbs (eg thyme, parsley, sage) chopped

To make breadsticks: Roll out each slice of bread to flatten. Mix herbs and half the butter together and spread over the bread. Roll up from each end to the middle and cut in half to form 2 breadsticks. Melt remaining butter for 1 minute on HIGH and brush over breadsticks. Put bread onto a plate and cook for 5 minutes in a microwave convection oven on the Combination setting until pale brown. Keep warm. (Breadsticks may also be baked in a conventional oven for 20 minutes at 200°C, 400°F, Gas Mark 6.)
To make fondue: Put garlic, wine, mustard, nutmeg and seasoning into a bowl and cook for 5 minutes on HIGH. Mix cornflour, kirsch and cheese, and blend well into the wine. Cook for 5-8 minutes on MEDIUM, stirring frequently until thick and

creamy. Heat individual ramekin dishes and pour fondue mixture into each. Serve immediately with the warm breadsticks or raw vegetables.

Garlic Mushrooms

PREPARATION TIME: 5 minutes

MICROWAVE COOKING TIME: 6 minutes

SERVES: 4 people

675g/1½lbs mushrooms, cleaned and quartered
2 cloves garlic, crushed
30g/1oz/¼ cup butter
45ml/3 tbsps white wine
8 slices French bread, 1.5cm (½") thick
1.25ml/¼ tsp fresh thyme, chopped
1.25ml/¼ tsp fresh sage, chopped
1.25ml/¼ tsp parsley, chopped
Salt
Pepper

GARNISH
30ml/2 tbsps chopped chives

Heat butter for 1 minute on HIGH or until melted in a large bowl. Add garlic and cook for 2 minutes on HIGH. Mix in the herbs, wine, seasoning and mushrooms. Pour into a shallow casserole, and cook, uncovered, for 3 minutes on HIGH. Heat the bread for 1 minute on HIGH. Garnish with snipped chives and serve on French bread.

Leek and Ham Tarts Bernaise

PREPARATION TIME: 10 minutes

MICROWAVE COOKING TIME: 19½ minutes

SERVES: 4 people

TART SHELLS AND FILLING
8-12 slices wholewheat bread, crusts removed
1-2 leeks, washed and sliced
30g/1oz/¼ cup butter or margarine
115g/4oz ham, chopped
45g/1½ oz/2½ tbsps flour
45ml/3 tbsps white wine
30ml/2 tbsps milk or chicken stock

BERNAISE SAUCE
60g/2oz/½ cup butter
3 egg yolks
15ml/1 tbsp white wine or tarragon vinegar

This page: Leek and Ham Tarts Bernaise (top) and Garlic Mushrooms (bottom).
Facing page: Pumpkin Creams with Dill Sauce.

1 bay leaf
1 blade mace
5ml/1 tsp chopped tarragon
5ml/1 tsp chopped parsley
Salt
Pepper
Lemon juice

To prepare shells and filling: Roll out the slices of bread to flatten slightly. Cut out large rounds with a pastry cutter. Melt half the butter for 1 minute on HIGH and brush over both sides of the bread rounds. Mould into custard cups/ramekin dishes or a muffin pan and cook for 3 minutes on HIGH until crisp. Melt the remaining butter in a bowl for 1 minute on HIGH and add the leek slices. Cover with pierced plastic wrap and cook for 8 minutes on HIGH, stirring occasionally. Add ham and flour, and cook for 1 minute on HIGH. Stir in the wine, milk or stock, and seasoning. Cook, uncovered, for 2 minutes or until sauce thickens. Set aside.

To make Bernaise sauce: Have a bowl of ice water ready. Melt the butter in a deep bowl on HIGH for 1 minute. Put vinegar, bay leaf and mace in a small dish and heat through for 30 seconds on HIGH. Beat egg yolks and seasoning together and strain on the vinegar. Pour into the bowl with the butter and stir well. Cook for 15 seconds on HIGH, remove bowl and stir sauce. Repeat until sauce has thickened – which takes about 2 minutes. Put jug/bowl immediately into ice water to stop the cooking. Remove the prepared shells from the custard cups/ramekin dishes and put onto a plate. Fill with the ham and leek mixture and coat each with a spoonful of the Bernaise sauce. Broil/grill until lightly browned. Serve immediately.

Pumpkin Creams with Dill Sauce

PREPARATION TIME: 15 minutes

MICROWAVE COOKING TIME: 27 minutes

SERVES: 4 people

450g/1lb/2½ cups mashed pumpkin
1 shallot, finely chopped
60g/2oz/½ cup Ricotta cheese
90g/3oz/½ cup Parmesan cheese, grated
2 eggs
60ml/2 fl oz/¼ cup sour cream
140ml/¼ pint/½ cup heavy/double cream
15ml/1 tbsp parsley
2 bunches dill
Crushed garlic (optional)
Nutmeg
Salt
Pepper

GARNISH
Whole sprigs of dill

Put the mashed pumpkin into a food processor and add eggs, shallot, cheeses, parsley, nutmeg and seasoning. Process until well blended. Divide between 4 ramekin dishes and cook for 6 minutes on HIGH until set. Leave to stand for 5 minutes before turning out. Heat the cream for 2 minutes on HIGH in a small bowl with the crushed garlic, if desired. Chop the dill finely, reserving 4 whole sprigs. Stir the chopped dill into the hot cream with the sour cream. Turn out the pumpkin creams and serve immediately with the dill sauce. Garnish with whole sprigs of dill.

Microwave
FISH AND SEAFOOD

Microwave
FISH AND SEAFOOD

A microwave oven is a fish kettle par excellence. In fact, many people prefer microwaved fish and shellfish to that cooked by conventional methods. Microwave cooking retains the natural moisture of food, something that is important in well-prepared fish. Fish and shellfish both require quick cooking, so the microwave oven really comes into its own.

Poaching is the fish cooking method that the microwave oven performs best. Use a shallow dish or a cooking bag and add white wine or water and lemon juice with peppercorns, onion slices and aromatic herbs, spices and vegetables. In a microwave oven all the flavor cooks into the fish, and low evaporation means plenty of liquid to make a good sauce.

A whole fish, such as a salmon or sea bass, can easily be poached providing the fish is not too large to allow it to turn freely. It is best to choose a fish no heavier than 1kg/2.2lbs in weight. Use a large cooking bag, securely tied, or a large, shallow dish covered with plastic wrap/cling film. Wrap the head and tail with foil to keep them from over-cooking and falling off. Cook 7-10 minutes on HIGH, or slightly longer on MEDIUM. The fish will continue to cook as it stands, so

keep it covered while preparing sauces to accompany the fish. If you are not sure whether the fish is cooked, check close to the bone in an inconspicuous place. The flesh should be firm and opaque.

Even frying is possible, after a fashion, in a microwave oven. Dredge fish fillets or small whole fish with seasoned flour and preheat a browning dish. Fry in butter briefly on both sides to get a light brown, slightly crisp coating; a surprising result from a microwave oven.

Shellfish need careful cooking in a microwave oven or they toughen. Cook them no longer than 3 minutes on the highest setting or add them to a hot sauce at the last minute.

In the classification of fish there are four main categories: Flat fish, such as sole; Round fish, such as trout; Shellfish and Smoked fish, more popular in England and Europe than in the United States. Flat fish and round fish can be subdivided into oily fish, such as trout or salmon, and whitefish, such as sole or cod. But whatever fish you choose, your microwave oven will help you cook it to perfection.

Microwave
FISH AND SEAFOOD

FISH SOUPS

Spicy Clam Chowder

PREPARATION TIME: 15 minutes

MICROWAVE COOKING TIME: 12 minutes

SERVES: 4 people

30g/1oz/2 tbsps butter or margarine
1 green pepper, diced
1 onion, finely sliced
340g/12oz/1½ cups potatoes, diced
450g/1lb can plum tomatoes
450g/1lb can clams, liquid reserved
1 small chili pepper, finely chopped
Pinch cinnamon
Pinch nutmeg
Salt and pepper

Melt the butter in a large bowl for 30 seconds on HIGH. Add the green pepper, onion, potatoes and the liquid from the clams. Cover the bowl loosely and cook for 10 minutes on HIGH or until the potatoes are tender. Add the plum tomatoes, clams, chili pepper, cinnamon, nutmeg, and salt and pepper. Cook, uncovered, for 2 minutes more on HIGH. Serve immediately.

Mariners' Chowder

PREPARATION TIME: 15 minutes

MICROWAVE COOKING TIME: 12 minutes

SERVES: 4 people

225g/8oz whitefish
225g/8oz/½ pint clams
225g/8oz/½ pint mussels
225g/8oz raw shrimp/prawns, peeled
45g/1½ oz/3 tbsps butter
45g/1½ oz/3 tbsps flour/plain flour
1 onion, finely chopped

850ml/1½ pints/4 cups milk
60ml/2 fl oz/¼ cup white wine
140ml/¼ pint/½ cup cream
1 bay leaf
30g/1oz/2 tbsps chopped parsley
Salt and pepper

This page: **Mariners' Chowder** (top) and **Spicy Clam Chowder** (bottom). Facing page: **Cheese and Clam Chowder** (top) and **Curried Prawn Soup** (bottom).

Scrub the clams and mussels well. Discard any with broken or open shells. Put into a bowl with 30ml/ 2 tbsps water and cover loosely. Cook for 4 minutes on HIGH until the shells open. Discard any shellfish that do not open, remove the others from their opened shells, and set them aside. Combine the fish, shrimp and wine in a casserole and cook for 4 minutes, covered, on HIGH. Melt the butter for 30 seconds on HIGH in a large bowl. Add the onion and cook for 2 minutes on HIGH. Add the flour, milk, wine from the fish, salt and pepper. Cook for 5 minutes on HIGH, stirring frequently. Add the fish, shellfish, cream and parsley. Heat through for 1 minute on HIGH. Remove the bay leaf and serve.

Cheese and Clam Chowder

PREPARATION TIME: 15 minutes

MICROWAVE COOKING TIME: 13 minutes

SERVES: 4 people

2 450g/1lb cans clams, liquid reserved
340g/12oz/2 cups diced potatoes
1 onion, finely chopped
2 sticks celery, chopped
1 green pepper, chopped
1 litre/1¾ pints/3¼ cups milk
30g/1oz/2 tbsps butter or margarine
30g/1oz/2 tbsps flour/plain flour
2.5ml/½ tsp dry mustard
Light/single cream as necessary
1 bay leaf
1.25ml/¼ tsp thyme
Dash Worcestershire sauce
30ml/2 tbsps chopped parsley
120g/4oz/1 cup grated Colby/Red
   Leicester cheese
Salt and pepper

Put the butter, onion, celery and pepper into a large bowl. Cover loosely and cook on HIGH for 2 minutes. Stir in the flour, mustard, milk and clam liquid. Blend well and add potatoes, thyme, salt and pepper. Put in the bay leaf, and cook on HIGH for 10 minutes, stirring occasionally. Remove the bay leaf and add the clams, cheese and

Worcestershire sauce. Heat for 2 minutes on MEDIUM to melt the cheese. Add light cream to thin the soup if it is too thick. Add the parsley to the soup and serve immediately.

Curried Prawn Soup

PREPARATION TIME: 10 minutes

MICROWAVE COOKING TIME: 8 minutes

SERVES: 4 people

45g/1½ oz/3 tbsps butter or margarine
45g/1½ oz/3 tbsps flour/plain flour
30g/1oz/2 tbsps curry powder
1 shallot, finely chopped
5ml/1 tsp mango chutney
15ml/1 tbsp lime juice
850ml/1½ pints/3 cups milk
280ml/½ pint/1 cup fish or chicken stock
225g/8oz cooked shrimp/prawns
Salt and pepper

GARNISH
Fresh coriander leaves or parsley
Plain yogurt

Melt the butter for 30 seconds on HIGH in a large bowl. Add the curry powder and the shallot and cook for 1 minute on HIGH. Stir in the flour, milk, stock, chutney, lime juice, salt and pepper. Cook for 5-6 minutes on HIGH until thickened. Add the shrimp and cook for 30 seconds on HIGH. Serve garnished with coriander and yogurt.

Lobster Bisque

PREPARATION TIME: 15 minutes

MICROWAVE COOKING TIME: 9 minutes

SERVES: 4 people

1 large lobster tail, uncooked
60g/2oz/4 tbsps butter or margarine
60g/2oz/4 tbsps flour/plain flour
1 shallot, finely chopped
570ml/1 pint/2 cups milk
280ml/½ pint/1 cup cream
280ml/½ pint/1 cup fish or chicken stock
1 bay leaf
Celery salt

Pepper
Cayenne pepper
60ml/2 fl oz/4 tbsps dry sherry

Remove the lobster tail meat from the shell. Break the shell into small pieces. Melt the butter in a small bowl for 30 seconds on HIGH. Put in the shell pieces and the shallot and cook for 1 minute on HIGH or until the shell turns red. Strain the butter into a large, clean bowl. Cut the lobster meat into small pieces and add to the butter. Cook for 1-2 minutes on HIGH. Remove the meat and set it aside. Stir the flour, celery salt and Cayenne pepper into the butter. Add the bay leaf, milk and stock. Cook for 5-6 minutes on HIGH to thicken. Add the sherry and the lobster meat and heat through for 1 minute on HIGH. Remove the bay leaf and swirl the cream through the soup. Serve immediately.

Smoked Salmon Cream Soup

PREPARATION TIME: 15 minutes

MICROWAVE COOKING TIME: 7-8 minutes

SERVES: 4 people

225g/8oz whitefish, cut into 2.5cm (1")
   chunks
225g/8oz smoked salmon, cut into 2.5cm
   (1") pieces
45g/1½ oz/3 tbsps butter or margarine
30g/1oz/2 tbsps flour/plain flour
140ml/¼ pint/½ cup white wine
850ml/1½ pints/3 cups milk
140ml/¼ pint/½ cup light/single cream
Pepper

GARNISH
Sour cream
Chopped chives

Cook the whitefish and wine for 2 minutes on HIGH. Melt the butter for 30 seconds on HIGH. Stir in the

Facing page: Smoked Salmon Cream Soup (top) and Lobster Bisque (bottom).

flour and milk, the whitefish and its cooking liquid. Cook for 5-6 minutes, stirring frequently, until thick. Add pepper, smoked salmon and cream. Work in a food processor until smooth. Re-heat for 1 minute on HIGH and add salt to taste. Garnish each serving with a spoonful of sour cream and a sprinkling of chopped chives.

Creamy Crab Soup

PREPARATION TIME: 15 minutes

MICROWAVE COOKING TIME: 9 minutes

SERVES: 4 people

450g/1lb crabmeat, fresh or frozen
60g/2oz/4 tbsps butter or margarine
60g/2oz/4 tbsps flour/plain flour
1 shallot, finely chopped
850ml/1½ pints/3 cups milk
140ml/¼ pint/½ cup cream
140ml/¼ pint/½ cup stock
30ml/2 tbsps white wine
Cayenne pepper
Salt and pepper

GARNISH
Chopped chives

Put the butter and shallot into a casserole. Cover and cook for 3 minutes on HIGH, stirring occasionally. Stir in the flour, milk, stock, Cayenne pepper, salt and pepper. Cook for 5 minutes on HIGH, stirring frequently until thickened. Add the crabmeat, cream and wine, and cook for a further 1 minute on HIGH. Serve garnished with chopped chives.

Shrimp and Chinese Mushroom Soup

PREPARATION TIME: 15 minutes

MICROWAVE COOKING TIME: 9 minutes

SERVES: 4 people

120g/4oz fine Chinese egg noodles
8 dried Chinese mushrooms
120g/4oz/¾ cup shrimp/prawns, cooked and peeled
1 small can water chestnuts, sliced

1 small can bamboo shoots, sliced
Bunch green/spring onions, sliced diagonally
120g/¼ lb peapods, mangetout, trimmed
15ml/1 tbsp light soy sauce
30ml/2 tbsps dry sherry
5ml/1 tsp sesame seed oil
15g/1 tbsp cornstarch/cornflour
1150ml/2 pints/4 cups chicken or fish stock
Salt and pepper

Put the mushrooms into a small bowl with enough water to cover. Cook on HIGH for 2 minutes and leave to stand. Mix the cornflour with 30ml/ 2 tbsps stock, and set aside. Combine the remaining stock, peapods and noodles. Cook for 2 minutes on HIGH. Add the cornstarch mixture and all the remaining ingredients, and cook for a further 5 minutes on HIGH. Serve immediately.

Oyster and Watercress Soup

PREPARATION TIME: 15 minutes

MICROWAVE COOKING TIME: 13 minutes

SERVES: 4 people

450g/1lb can oysters
Bunch watercress
675g/1½ lbs/3 cups diced potatoes

430ml/¾ pint/1½ cups liquid reserved from oysters
430ml/¾ pint/1½ cups light/single cream
280ml/½ pint/1 cup milk
1 shallot, finely chopped
45g/1½ oz/3 tbsps butter or margarine
Nutmeg
Lemon juice
Salt and pepper

Drain the oysters and add water to the liquid, if necessary, to measure 430ml/¾ pint/1½ cups. Melt the butter in a large bowl for 30 seconds on HIGH. Add the potatoes, shallot, stock, nutmeg, salt and pepper. Cover loosely and cook on HIGH for 10 minutes, or until the potatoes are tender. Add the milk and half the oysters. Chop the watercress, reserving 4 sprigs for garnish, and add to the bowl. Cook, uncovered, for 2 minutes on HIGH. Put into a food processor and purée until smooth. Return to the bowl and add the remaining oysters, cream and lemon juice. Heat through for 1 minute on HIGH. Serve garnished with the reserved watercress.

This page: Shrimp and Chinese Mushroom Soup. Facing page: Creamy Crab Soup (top) and Oyster and Watercress Soup (bottom).

Microwave
FISH AND SEAFOOD

APPETIZERS AND FIRST COURSES

Florentine Shrimp Tarts

PREPARATION TIME: 20 minutes

MICROWAVE COOKING TIME: 9-10 minutes

SERVES: 4 people

4 slices wholewheat bread
60g/2oz/¼ cup butter, melted
675g/1½ lbs fresh spinach, washed (or 340g/¾ lb frozen spinach, thawed)
30ml/2 tbsps heavy/double cream
Nutmeg, grated
8 large, unpeeled shrimp/prawns, cooked

SAUCE
120g/4oz/½ cup butter
3 egg yolks
15ml/1 tbsp white wine vinegar
Cayenne pepper
Salt and pepper

GARNISH
Fresh chives or chervil

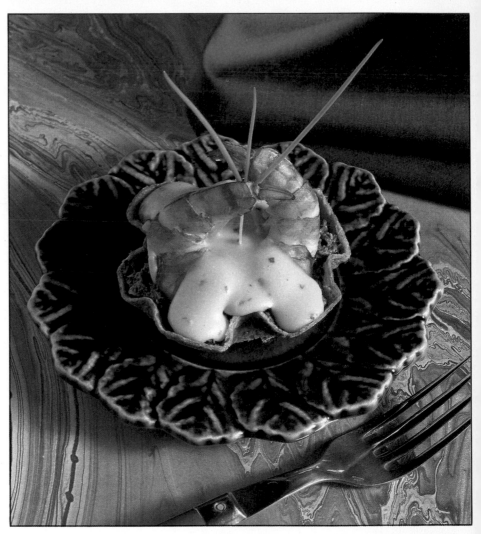

Cut the crusts off the bread and roll out each slice very thinly. Cut out a 10cm (4″) round from each slice and brush both sides with melted butter. Mould into 4 individual pie or flan pans, preferably false-bottomed. Cook on HIGH for 2-3 minutes until crisp. Cook the fresh spinach in a large bowl, loosely covered, for 2 minutes on HIGH with 30ml/ 2 tbsps water. Drain the spinach well, squeezing out all the moisture whether using fresh or frozen spinach. Heat 15g/½ oz/1 tbsp of the remaining butter in a large bowl for 1 minute on HIGH. Toss in the spinach, salt, pepper and nutmeg. Stir in the cream and set aside. Peel the shrimp carefully and set aside. Prepare the sauce by melting the butter in a small, deep bowl for 1 minute on HIGH. Mix the egg yolks, salt, pepper, Cayenne pepper and vinegar together, and pour into the hot butter, beating constantly. Have a bowl of ice water ready. Cook the sauce for 30 seconds on HIGH, then beat well. Repeat until the sauce thickens, which takes about 2 minutes. Put the sauce bowl immediately into ice water to stop the cooking. Remove and set aside.

Put the spinach into the bread shells and top with the shrimp. Heat through for 30 seconds on HIGH. Pour over the sauce and heat for 20 seconds on MEDIUM. Serve garnished with chives or chervil.

This page: Florentine Shrimp Tarts. Facing page: Shrimp Kebabs Vera Cruz.

Shrimp Kebabs Vera Cruz

PREPARATION TIME: 15 minutes
MICROWAVE COOKING TIME: 4 minutes
SERVES: 4 people

2 dozen large shrimp, peeled and
  uncooked
120g/4oz chorizo or pepperoni, cut into
  5mm (¼") slices.
1 large green pepper
30ml/2 tbsps olive oil
1 ripe avocado
2 tomatoes, peeled, seeded and finely
  chopped
1 clove garlic, crushed
Cayenne pepper
Lemon juice
Salt and pepper

Alternate the shrimp, sausage and green pepper on wooden skewers. Brush with oil. Peel and mash the avocado with the garlic, lemon juice, Cayenne pepper, and salt and pepper. Stir in the tomatoes. Cook the kebabs on a roasting rack for 3 minutes on HIGH, and heat the sauce for 30 seconds on HIGH. Serve immediately.

Layered Seafood Terrine

PREPARATION TIME: 20 minutes
MICROWAVE COOKING TIME: 12 minutes, plus 5 minutes standing time
SERVES: 4 people

340g/12oz whitefish, skinned and cut
  into chunks
90g/3oz crabmeat
90g/3oz lobster
60g/2oz/¼ cup cream cheese
2 eggs
60g/2oz/1 cup fresh white breadcrumbs
30ml/1oz/2 tbsps heavy/double cream
30ml/1oz/2 tbsps white wine
Chopped parsley
Cayenne pepper
Salt and pepper

BERNAISE SAUCE
3 egg yolks
120g/4oz/½ cup butter
15ml/1 tbsp chopped mixed herbs

15ml/1 tbsp white wine vinegar
Salt and pepper

Combine the eggs, whitefish, cheese, cream, crumbs, wine, salt and pepper in a food processor and work until smooth. Divide the mixture into thirds. Mix the crab and parsley into one third, the lobster and Cayenne pepper into another third, and leave the remaining third plain. Line a 450g/1lb glass loaf pan/dish with wax/greaseproof paper, and layer in the crabmeat, whitefish and lobster mixtures. Cover well with plastic wrap and cook for 10 minutes on MEDIUM. Put a small dish of water into the oven with the terrine to keep it moist. Allow to stand for 5 minutes while preparing the sauce. Beat the egg yolks, vinegar, herbs and salt and pepper together. Melt the butter for 1 minute on HIGH in a small, deep bowl. Beat the egg yolks into the butter. Have a bowl of ice water ready. Cook the sauce ingredients for 15 seconds on HIGH and then stir well. Repeat the process until the sauce thickens, which takes about 2 minutes. Put the sauce immediately into the bowl of ice water to stop the cooking. Slice the terrine and serve with the Bernaise Sauce.

Crab-Stuffed Pea Pods

PREPARATION TIME: 20 minutes
MICROWAVE COOKING TIME: 2 minutes
SERVES: 4 people

450g/1lb pea pods/mangetout

FILLING
120g/4 oz/½ cup crabmeat
1 package/carton garlic-and-herb soft
  cheese
30ml/2 tbsps white wine
15ml/1 tbsp milk or light/single cream

Mix the filling ingredients together, breaking up the crabmeat well. Wash the pea pods/mangetout and carefully split down one side of each to form pockets. Blanch for 1 minute on HIGH with 60ml/4 tbsps water in a loosely-covered bowl. Rinse under

cold water and dry well. Carefully open each pocket. Put the filling into a pastry bag fitted with a 15mm (½") plain tube and pipe the filling into the pea pods/mangetout. Arrange on individual dishes and heat for 30 seconds on HIGH. Serve with lemon slices or wedges.

Herbed Fish Pâté with Lemon-Orange Hollandaise Sauce

PREPARATION TIME: 20 minutes
MICROWAVE COOKING TIME: 12 minutes, plus 5 minutes standing time
SERVES: 4 people

450g/1lb whitefish (sole, flounder or cod)
120g/4oz Parma ham, thinly sliced
60ml/4 tbsps chopped mixed herbs
60g/2oz/1 cup fresh white breadcrumbs
2 eggs
60g/2oz/¼ cup low-fat soft cheese, or
  Ricotta cheese
30ml/2 tbsps heavy/double cream
Salt and pepper

HOLLANDAISE SAUCE
3 egg yolks
120g/4oz/½ cup butter
15ml/1 tbsp lemon juice
15ml/1 tbsp orange juice and rind
Salt and pepper

Line a 450g/1lb glass loaf pan/dish with the slices of Parma ham. Skin and cut the fish into chunks. Combine all the remaining pâté ingredients in a food processor and work until smooth. Spoon onto the ham and smooth out. Fold the ends of the ham over the pâté mixture. Cover well with plastic wrap and cook on MEDIUM for 10 minutes, or until just firm. Put a small dish of water into the microwave oven with the pâté to keep it moist. Leave to stand for 5 minutes before turning out and slicing for serving. To

Facing page: Layered Seafood Terrine (top) and Herbed Fish Pâté with Lemon-Orange Hollandaise Sauce.

prepare the sauce, melt the butter in a small glass bowl for 1 minute on HIGH. Beat the egg yolks with the salt, pepper, lemon juice, orange juice and rind. Mix the egg yolks with the butter, stirring constantly. Have a bowl of ice water ready. Cook the sauce for 15 seconds on HIGH. Stir well, and repeat the process until the sauce thickens, which takes about 2 minutes. Put the sauce immediately into the bowl of ice water to stop the cooking. Serve with the pâté.

Crab-Stuffed New Potatoes

PREPARATION TIME: 15 minutes	
MICROWAVE COOKING TIME: 5 minutes	
SERVES: 4 people with 3 potatoes each	

12 small new potatoes, uniform in size
90g/3oz/½ cup cream or low-fat soft cheese

90g/3oz/½ cup crabmeat
2.5ml/½ tsp grated horseradish
15ml/1 tbsp snipped chives or chopped green/spring onion
15ml/1 tbsp sesame seeds
15ml/1 tbsp poppy seeds
30ml/2 tbsps butter, melted
Salt and pepper

Scrub, but do not peel, the potatoes, Pierce them several times with a fork. Mix the cheese, crab, horseradish, chives and salt and pepper together. Cook the potatoes with enough water to barely cover for 4 minutes on HIGH. When cooked, slice 1.5cm (½") off the top of each potato and reserve. Spoon 5ml/1 tsp of the crab filling into the bottom portion of the potatoes. Top with the lids and put the filled potatoes onto a plate. Pour some of the melted butter over each potato and sprinkle on a mixture of the sesame and poppy seeds. Heat for 30 seconds on HIGH.

Scallops with Red and Gold Sauces

PREPARATION TIME: 15 minutes	
MICROWAVE COOKING TIME: 12 minutes	
SERVES: 4 people	

900g/2lb fresh scallops
225g/½ lb fresh bean sprouts
1 large, ripe avocado
60ml/2oz/4 tbsps lime juice
2 sweet red peppers
2 yellow peppers
15ml/1 tbsp grated ginger
280ml/½ pint/1 cup water
30ml/2 tbsps desiccated coconut
15ml/1 tbsp ground almonds
Pinch Cayenne pepper
Salt and pepper

Put scallops in a casserole with 60ml/4 tbsps water and 8ml/1½ tsps lime juice. Cover loosely and cook

This page: Scallops with Red and Gold Sauces. Facing page: Crab-Stuffed Pea Pods (top) and Crab-Stuffed New Potatoes (bottom).

on HIGH for 1 minute. Turn the scallops over after 30 seconds. Slice the scallops in half through the middle if they are large. Slice the red and yellow peppers, and put them into separate bowls with half the remaining lime juice and water in each. Cover with pierced plastic wrap and cook each for 5 minutes on HIGH, or until the peppers are very soft. Put the yellow peppers and liquid into a food processor with the ginger and salt and pepper, and work to a smooth purée. Strain if necessary. Work the red peppers in the same way but with the almonds, coconut, Cayenne pepper, and salt and pepper. Peel and slice the avocado thinly. Divide the red sauce evenly on 4 salad plates, covering one side, and put the equivalent gold sauce on the other side of each plate. Arrange the scallops, bean sprouts and avocado slices on top of the sauce to serve.

Oysters Florentine

PREPARATION TIME: 15 minutes

MICROWAVE COOKING TIME: 5 minutes

SERVES: 4 people

2 dozen oysters on the half shell
450g/1lb spinach, washed, or 225g/½ lb
*   frozen spinach, thawed*
60ml/2 fl oz/¼ cup heavy/double cream
Nutmeg
Salt and pepper

SAUCE
3 egg yolks
120g/4oz/½ cup butter
1 shallot, finely chopped
30ml/2 tbsps lemon juice mixed with
*   Tabasco*

GARNISH
Lemon slices

Cook the spinach with 15ml/1 tbsp water for 1 minute on HIGH in a large bowl loosely covered. Drain well and season with salt and pepper. Add the nutmeg and cream. Put a spoonful of spinach on top of each oyster. Melt the butter on HIGH for 1 minute with the shallot. Mix the

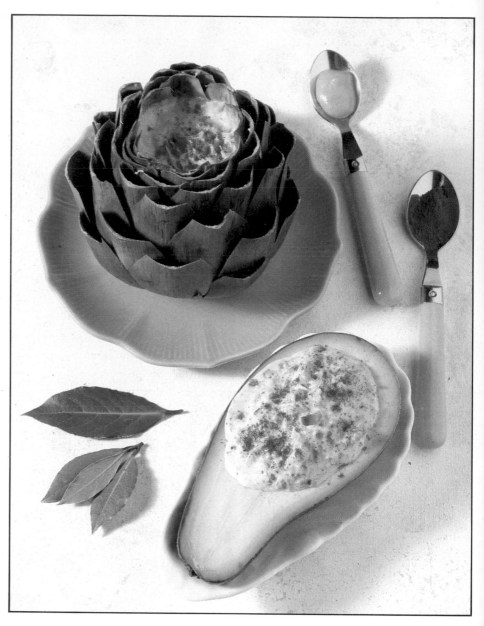

egg yolks with lemon juice and Tabasco, and pour into the hot butter, beating constantly. Have a bowl of ice water ready. Cook for 30 seconds on HIGH and stir. Repeat the process until the sauce thickens (about 2 minutes). Put the sauce bowl immediately into ice water to stop the cooking. Remove and set aside. Top each oyster with a spoon-ful of the sauce and heat through for 30 seconds on MEDIUM. Garnish with lemon slices.

NOTE: Oysters can be opened easily in microwave ovens. Clean the shells well, and leave to soak in clean water

for 2 hours. Cook for 45 seconds on HIGH, insert a knife near the hinge and pry open.

Crab-Stuffed Avocados

PREPARATION TIME: 15 minutes

MICROWAVE COOKING TIME: 3 minutes

SERVES: 4 people

This page: Crab-Stuffed Artichoke (top) and Crab-Stuffed Avocados (bottom). Facing page: Oysters Florentine.

*2 ripe avocados, cut in half and stones
    removed*
225g/½ lb crabmeat
1 green pepper, diced
2 sticks celery, diced
2 green/spring onions, chopped
*280ml/½ pint/1 cup prepared
    mayonnaise*
30ml/2 tbsps heavy/double cream
15ml/1 tbsp chili sauce
Lemon juice
Salt and pepper
Paprika

Scoop out some of the avocado and chop the flesh roughly. Sprinkle the shell and the chopped flesh with lemon juice. Put the pepper, celery and onion into a small bowl with 30ml/2 tbsps water. Cover loosely and cook for 2 minutes on HIGH to soften. Drain away the water and mix in the crab, mayonnaise, cream, chili sauce and salt and pepper. Carefully fold in the reserved avocado flesh. Pile into the avocado shells and sprinkle with paprika. Cook for 1 minute on HIGH, with the narrow end of the avocados pointing to the middle of the dish. Serve immediately.

Stuffed Artichokes

PREPARATION TIME: 20 minutes

MICROWAVE COOKING TIME:
17-19 minutes

SERVES: 4 people

4 globe artichokes
1 bay leaf
1 slice lemon

FILLING
225g/8oz/1 cup crabmeat, flaked
45g/1½ oz/3 tbsps butter
45g/1½ oz/3 tbsps flour/plain flour
30ml/1oz/2 tbsps Dijon mustard
30ml/2 tbsps snipped chives
280ml/½ pint/1 cup milk
140ml/¼ pint/½ cup white wine
Salt and pepper

Trim the points of the artichoke leaves and cut the stems so that the artichokes will sit upright. Put them into a large, deep bowl with enough water to barely cover. Add the bay

leaf and lemon slice. Cook for 15 minutes on HIGH. Drain upside-down. Melt the butter in a small, deep bowl for 30 seconds on HIGH. Stir in the flour, milk, wine, salt and pepper. Cook for 2-3 minutes on HIGH. Stir every 30 seconds. Add the mustard and chives. Add the crabmeat and keep warm. Remove the center leaves of the artichoke and carefully lift away the thistle-like choke with a teaspoon. Pour in the crabmeat filling and serve hot.

Lobster Julienne

PREPARATION TIME: 20 minutes

MICROWAVE COOKING TIME:
9-10 minutes

SERVES: 4 people

1 large lobster tail, uncooked
30g/1oz/2 tbsps butter or margarine
2 carrots, cut in thin, 5cm (2") strips
1 leek, cut in thin, 5cm (2") strips
*2 zucchini/courgettes, cut into 5cm (2")
    strips*
2 sticks celery, cut in 5cm (2") strips
8 mushrooms, thinly sliced
140ml/¼ pint/½ cup white wine
10ml/2 tsps cornstarch/cornflour
15ml/1 tbsp lemon juice
140ml/¼ pint/½ cup whole milk yogurt
10ml/2 tsps crushed tarragon
Salt and pepper

GARNISH
Chopped parsley

Melt half the butter for 30 seconds on HIGH in a small casserole. Add the carrot and celery and 15ml/1 tbsp white wine. Cover and cook for 1 minute on HIGH. Add the zucchini/courgette, leek and mushrooms. Cover the casserole and cook for 2 minutes on HIGH and set aside. Heat a browning dish for 3 minutes on HIGH. Remove the lobster tail meat from the shell and cut into 1.5cm (½") slices. Drop the remaining butter into the browning dish and add the lobster meat. Cook for 1 minute on HIGH. Remove the lobster and mix with the vegetables. Mix the cornstarch with the lemon juice, remaining wine, tarragon, salt

and pepper. Cook for 1-2 minutes on HIGH until thickened. Stir in the yogurt and heat through for 30 seconds on HIGH. Toss the lobster and vegetables with the sauce and serve immediately, garnished with chopped parsley.

Chinese Shrimp/Prawn Parcels

PREPARATION TIME: 20 minutes

MICROWAVE COOKING TIME:
6-7 minutes

SERVES: 4 people

1 head Chinese cabbage/Chinese leaves

FILLING
90g/3oz/½ cup cashew nuts
4 green/spring onions, chopped
225g/8oz cooked shrimp/prawns
*120g/4 oz/½ cup chopped water
    chestnuts*
450g/1lb/2 cups bean sprouts
8 dried Chinese mushrooms, soaked
1 red pepper, chopped
15g/½ oz/1 tbsp cornstarch/cornflour
30ml/1oz/2 tbsps white wine

**SWEET AND SOUR MUSTARD
SAUCE**
30ml/2 tbsps honey
30ml/2 tbsps white wine vinegar
60ml/4 tbsps Dijon mustard
15g/½ oz/1 tbsp cornstarch/cornflour
140ml/¼ pint/½ cup white wine
140ml/¼ pint/½ cup water
30ml/2 tbsps soy sauce

Separate 8 of the largest and best-looking leaves of the Chinese cabbage. Trim down their spines to make them easier to roll up. Put them into a large bowl with 30ml/ 2 tbsps water. Cover the bowl loosely and cook the leaves for 30 seconds on HIGH to soften slightly. Slice the mushrooms and roughly chop the cashews, then mix with the remaining

**Facing page: Lobster Julienne
(top) and South Seas Tidbits
(bottom).**

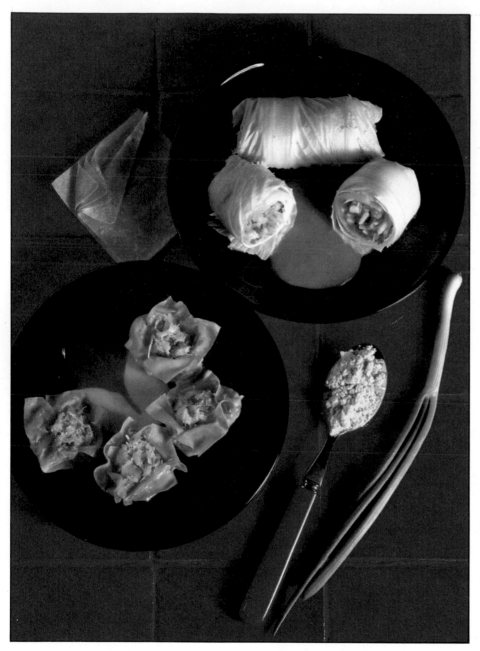

1 papaya, peeled and cut into 2.5cm (1")
  chunks
225g/8oz raw shrimp, peeled
225g/8oz scallops

SAUCE
30g/1oz/2 tbsps brown sugar
15g/½ oz/1 tbsp cornstarch/cornflour
15ml/½ oz/1 tbsp soy sauce
15ml/½ oz/1 tbsp cider vinegar
Large pinch ground ginger
30g/1oz/2 tbsps desiccated coconut
2 green/spring onions, chopped

Mix all the sauce ingredients, except the coconut, together with 180ml/ 6 fl oz/¾ cup reserved pineapple juice. Cook for 2-3 minutes on HIGH, stirring until thickened. Add the shrimp and scallops and cook for a further 2 minutes on HIGH. Add the pineapple, papaya and coconut and cook for a further 30 seconds on HIGH. Serve as an appetizer.

Steamed Crabmeat Wontons

PREPARATION TIME: 20 minutes

MICROWAVE COOKING TIME:
5 minutes for wontons; 2-3 minutes per sauce

SERVES: 4 people

30 fresh wonton skins

FILLING
340g/12oz cooked crabmeat, fresh or
  frozen
2 green/spring onions, chopped
6 water chestnuts, chopped
15ml/1 tbsp grated fresh ginger root
15ml/1 tbsp sherry or white wine
15ml/1 tbsp sesame seed oil
1 egg
Salt and pepper

SWEET AND SOUR SAUCE
180ml/6 fl oz/¾ cup orange juice
30ml/2 tbsps soy sauce
25ml/1½ tbsps brown sugar
25ml/1½ tbsps cider vinegar
10ml/2 tsps cornstarch/cornflour
25ml/1½ tbsps ketchup

HOT MUSTARD SAUCE
60ml/4 tbsps dry mustard
8ml/1½ tsps cornstarch/cornflour

filling ingredients. Put 2 leaves together, slightly overlapping, and divide the filling equally among all the leaves. Tuck the sides of the leaves around the filling and roll up. Repeat with the remaining leaves and filling. Put folded edge down in a large casserole with 30ml/2 tbsps water. Cover loosely and cook for 3 minutes on HIGH. Set aside while preparing the sauce. Mix all the sauce ingredients together and cook for 2-3 minutes on HIGH. Stir every 30 seconds until the sauce thickens. Set aside

Above: Chinese Shrimp/Prawn Parcels (top) and Steamed Crabmeat Wontons (bottom).

South Seas Tidbits

PREPARATION TIME: 15 minutes

MICROWAVE COOKING TIME:
5-6 minutes

SERVES: 4 people

450g/1lb can pineapple chunks, juice
  reserved

60ml/4 tbsps white wine vinegar
140ml/¼ pint/½ cup water
60ml/2 fl oz/¼ cup honey
Salt

Mix all the filling ingredients together. Just before filling each skin, brush both sides with water. Put a rounded tsp of the filling in the center of each skin and pinch the edges together, leaving some of the filling showing. Lightly grease a plate or microwave baking sheet and place the wontons on it. Pour 30ml/1oz/ 2 tbsps water over the wontons. Cover them loosely with plastic wrap and cook for 1 minute on HIGH. Lower the setting to LOW and cook for 4 further minutes. Cook in two batches. Brush the wontons several times with water while cooking. Serve with one or both of the sauces. For the sweet and sour sauce, mix the sauce ingredients and cook in a small, deep bowl, uncovered, for 2-3 minutes on HIGH. Stir every 30 seconds until the sauce has thickened. For the hot mustard sauce, mix the mustard and cornstarch/cornflour together. Beat in the water, vinegar and honey gradually until the sauce is smooth. Add salt and cook, uncovered, in a small, deep bowl for 2-3 minutes on HIGH. Stir every 30 seconds until thickened.

Coriander Mussels

PREPARATION TIME: 15 minutes

MICROWAVE COOKING TIME: 4-6 minutes

SERVES: 4 people

900g/2lbs/1 quart mussels
2 shallots, finely chopped
280ml/½ pint/1 cup white wine
15ml/½ oz/1 tbsp coriander seeds, crushed
15g/½ oz/1 tbsp butter
15g/½ oz/1 tbsp flour/plain flour
140ml/¼ pint/½ cup cream
15ml/½ oz/1 tbsp chopped coriander
15ml/½ oz/1 tbsp chopped parsley
Salt and pepper

Scrub the mussels well and discard any with broken or open shells. Put the mussels into a large bowl with the shallots, wine and coriander seeds. Cook for 1-2 minutes on HIGH, stirring every 30 seconds, until shells open. Discard any mussels that do not open. Strain the cooking liquid. Melt the butter in a small, deep bowl for 30 seconds on HIGH. Stir in the flour, cream, strained liquid, and salt and pepper. Cook for 2-3 minutes on HIGH until thickened, stirring every 30 seconds. Add the chopped coriander and parsley. Divide the mussels into individual bowls and pour over the sauce to serve.

Above: Coriander Mussels.

Brandied Shrimp

PREPARATION TIME: 10 minutes

MICROWAVE COOKING TIME: 4 minutes

SERVES: 4 people

1kg/2¼ lbs uncooked shrimp, peeled
175g/6oz/1½ cups dry breadcrumbs
60ml/2 fl oz/4 tbsps brandy

120g/4oz/½ cup butter
2 shallots, chopped
60ml/4 tbsps chopped parsley
Paprika
Salt and pepper

GARNISH
4 lemon wedges

Mix the shallot, salt, pepper, parsley and shrimp together and divide between 4 small baking dishes. Pour brandy over each dish and cook for 30 seconds on HIGH. Heat a browning dish for 5 minutes on HIGH. Drop in the butter and cook for a further 30 seconds on HIGH. Stir in the breadcrumbs and cook for 1-2 minutes to brown. Spoon the breadcrumbs over the shrimp and sprinkle on the paprika. Cook for 1 minute on HIGH or until the shrimp are cooked. Serve with lemon wedges.

Marinated Herring with Tomatoes

PREPARATION TIME: 20 minutes	
MICROWAVE COOKING TIME: 5-7 minutes	
SERVES: 4 people	

8 herring fillets

MARINADE
2 onions, finely chopped
200ml/6 fl oz/¾ cup red wine vinegar
60ml/2 fl oz/¼ cup water
60g/2oz/¼ cup sugar
6 black peppercorns
2 whole allspice berries

SAUCE
4 tomatoes, peeled, seeded and cut into
  thin strips
30ml/2 tbsps tomato purée/paste
30ml/2 tbsps snipped chives
90ml/3 fl oz/⅓ cup vegetable oil
60ml/2 fl oz/¼ cup reserved marinade
Salt and pepper

Combine the marinade ingredients and cook, uncovered, for 5-7 minutes on HIGH until rapidly boiling. Allow to cool slightly, and pour over the fish fillets. Leave the fish to cool

completely in the marinade. Mix the oil and strained reserved marinade together with the tomato purée, chives, salt and pepper. Pour over the herring and top with the tomato strips to serve.

Smoky Cheese and Shrimp Dip

PREPARATION TIME: 15 minutes	
MICROWAVE COOKING TIME: 5 minutes	
SERVES: 4 people	

180g/6oz/1½ cups shredded Cheddar cheese

This page: Smoky Cheese and Shrimp Dip. Facing page: Brandied Shrimp (top) and Marinated Herring with Tomatoes (bottom).

120g/4oz/1 cup shredded smoked or
  smoky cheese
15g/½ oz/1 tbsp butter
1 shallot, finely chopped
120g/4oz/½ cup shrimp, chopped
180ml/6 fl oz/¾ cup light/single cream
15g/½ oz flour/plain flour
Salt and pepper
Raw vegetables

Melt the butter in a small, deep bowl for 30 seconds on HIGH. Add the shallot and cook for 1 minute on

HIGH to soften. Toss the cheese and flour together and add to the bowl with the shallot. Stir in the cream, salt and pepper. Cook for 4 minutes on MEDIUM or until the cheese has melted. Stir the mixture twice while cooking. Serve hot with vegetable crudités for dipping.

Herring in Mustard Dill Sauce

PREPARATION TIME: 20 minutes

MICROWAVE COOKING TIME: 7-9 minutes

SERVES: 4 people

4 herring fillets, cut in chunks

MARINADE
2 onions, finely chopped
200ml/6 fl oz/¾ cup white wine vinegar
60ml/2 fl oz/¼ cup water
60g/2oz/¼ cup sugar
4 sprigs fresh dill
15ml/1 tbsp dried dill
6 black peppercorns
2 whole allspice berries

SAUCE
15g/½ oz/1 tbsp flour/plain flour
30ml/1oz/2 tbsps mustard
15ml/1 tbsp chopped dill
60ml/2 fl oz/¼ cup sour cream

Combine the marinade ingredients and cook, uncovered, for 5-7 minutes until rapidly boiling. Allow to cool slightly, and pour over the fish. Leave the fish to cool in the marinade. Strain the marinade and beat gradually into the flour. Add the mustard and cook for 2 minutes on HIGH, stirring every 30 seconds until thickened. Mix with the chopped dill, and chill. Mix in the sour cream and herring. Serve as an appetizer/starter, or on a bed of lettuce as a first course.

Oysters Romanoff

PREPARATION TIME: 10 minutes

MICROWAVE COOKING TIME: 1 minute

SERVES: 4 people

2 dozen oysters on the half shell
20ml/1½ tbsps snipped chives
280ml/½ pint/1 cup sour cream
1 jar red lumpfish or salmon caviar
Lemon juice
Salt and pepper

Put a drop of lemon juice on each oyster. Mix the chives and cream together with salt and pepper. Put a spoonful of the mixture on top of each oyster. Heat through for 1 minute on HIGH on a large plate. Heat in 2 batches if necessary. Put a spoonful of the caviar on each oyster before serving. Serve with lemon wedges and watercress.

This page: Pickled Mussels (top) and Herring in Mustard Dill Sauce (bottom). Facing page: Oysters Romanoff.

Pickled Mussels

PREPARATION TIME: 15 minutes

MICROWAVE COOKING TIME: 6 minutes

SERVES: 4 people

900g/2lbs/1 quart mussels
140ml/¼ pint/½ cup white wine
140ml/¼ pint/½ cup white wine vinegar

30g/1oz/2 tbsps sugar
15ml/½ oz/1 tbsp mustard seed
1 cinnamon stick
4 whole allspice berries
4 black peppercorns
4 whole cloves
2 shallots, finely chopped
Salt and pepper

Scrub the mussels well and discard any with broken or open shells. Put the mussels into a large bowl with 30ml/2 tbsps water. Cook on HIGH for 45-50 seconds, until the shells open, stirring twice. Discard any mussels that do not open. Combine the remaining ingredients, and cook for 5 minutes on HIGH or until boiling. Allow to cool slightly. Remove the mussels from their shells and combine with the pickling mixture. Leave to cool and then refrigerate. Keep no longer than 2 days.

Salmon Terrine

PREPARATION TIME: 15 minutes

MICROWAVE COOKING TIME: 10 minutes

SERVES: 4 people

450g/1lb salmon
2 eggs
60g/2oz/1 cup fresh white breadcrumbs
60g/2oz/¼ cup cream cheese
30ml/2 tbsps heavy/double cream
Salt and pepper

DRESSING
1 cucumber, grated
280ml/½ pint/1 cup sour cream
140ml/¼ pint/½ cup prepared
  mayonnaise
30ml/2 tbsps chopped dill
Salt and pepper

GARNISH
Red lumpfish caviar

Skin the salmon and cut into chunks. Combine with the remaining terrine ingredients in a food processor and work until smooth. Line the bottom of a 450g/1lb glass loaf pan/dish with waxed/greaseproof paper. Fill with the salmon mixture and smooth out.

Cover well with plastic wrap and cook for 10 minutes on MEDIUM, with a small dish of water to keep it moist. Allow to cool and then chill well. Turn out and cut into slices. Mix all the dressing ingredients together and serve with the terrine. Garnish with the lumpfish caviar.

Smoked Oyster Pâté

PREPARATION TIME: 15 minutes

MICROWAVE COOKING TIME:
10 minutes, plus 5 minutes standing time

SERVES: 4 people

1 can smoked oysters
450g/1lb whitefish
60g/2oz/1 cup fresh white breadcrumbs
Butter
2 eggs
60g/2oz/¼ cup cream cheese
30ml/2 tbsps cream
15ml/½ oz/1 tbsp chopped parsley
10ml/2 tsps Worcestershire sauce
15ml/1 tbsp lemon juice
Salt and pepper

Roughly chop the smoked oysters. Combine the remaining ingredients in a food processor and work until smooth. Fold in the oysters. Line the bottom of a 450g/1lb glass loaf pan/dish with waxed/greaseproof paper. Spoon in the pâté mixture and smooth out. Cover well with plastic wrap and cook for 10 minutes on MEDIUM. Put a small dish of water into the oven with the pâté to keep it moist. Leave to stand for 5 minutes, then chill before serving. Serve with buttered toast.

Paprika Shrimp

PREPARATION TIME: 15 minutes

MICROWAVE COOKING TIME:
10 minutes

SERVES: 4 people

900g/2lbs raw shrimp/prawns, peeled
60g/2oz/¼ cup butter or margarine
15ml/1 tbsp paprika
2 chopped shallots
1 red pepper, thinly sliced

30ml/2 tbsps chopped parsley
430ml/¾ pint/1½ cups sour cream
15ml/1 tbsp lemon juice
Salt and pepper

TOPPING
60g/2oz/¼ cup butter or margarine
120g/4oz/½ cup breadcrumbs

Heat a browning dish for 5 minutes on HIGH. Melt the butter for the topping and stir in the breadcrumbs. Cook on HIGH for 2 minutes, stirring every 30 seconds. Set aside. Melt the remaining butter in a large casserole for 30 seconds on HIGH. Add the paprika, shallot and sliced pepper. Cook for 2 minutes on HIGH, stirring frequently. Add the shrimp, lemon juice, salt and pepper, and continue cooking for 2 minutes more on HIGH. Stir in the sour cream. Put into individual serving dishes and sprinkle over the browned crumbs. Cook for 30 seconds on MEDIUM to heat through, and serve with hot rolls or French bread.

Calamares España

PREPARATION TIME: 20 minutes

MICROWAVE COOKING TIME:
8 minutes

SERVES: 4 people

2 medium-sized squid
30ml/2 tbsps olive oil
30g/1oz/2 tbsps flour/plain flour
1 clove garlic, finely chopped
450g/1lb/2 cups canned plum tomatoes
1 chili pepper, finely chopped
Grated rind and juice of 1 orange
140ml/¼ pint/½ cup white wine
15ml/1 tbsp tomato purée/paste
5ml/1 tsp oregano
5ml/1 tsp basil
1 bay leaf
Salt and pepper

GARNISH
Fresh coriander leaves

Facing page: Smoked Oyster Pâté (top) and Salmon Terrine (bottom).

This page: Garlic Shrimp/Prawns and Mushrooms. Facing page: Paprika Shrimp (top) and Calamares España (bottom).

Separate heads of the squid from the tails. Remove the ink-sac and reserve for the sauce if desired. Remove the quill and discard. Cut the tentacles above the eyes, and reserve. Discard the eyes and head. Peel the purplish membrane off the tail portion of the squid. Split the tail in half, length-wise, and wash it well. Cut the tail into pieces about 5cm (2″) wide. Score each section in a lattice pattern at 5mm (¼″) intervals. Separate the tentacles. Put the squid, bay leaf and onion into a casserole with hot water. Cover loosely and cook for 1 minute on HIGH. Heat the olive oil for 30 seconds on HIGH in a medium-sized bowl. Add the garlic and onion, and cook for a further 1 minute on HIGH. Stir in the flour. Mix the cooking liquid from the squid with the tomatoes and the other sauce ingredients. If using the ink, break the ink-sac into the sauce ingredients. Cook the sauce, uncovered, for 5 minutes on HIGH. Mix with the squid and serve garnished with fresh coriander leaves.

Garlic Shrimp/Prawns and Mushrooms

PREPARATION TIME: 10 minutes	
MICROWAVE COOKING TIME: 3-4 minutes	
SERVES: 4 people	

4-8 (depending on size) oyster or wild mushrooms
120g/4oz/½ cup butter
675g/1½ lbs raw shrimp/prawns, peeled
1 large clove garlic, chopped
30ml/2 tbsps chopped parsley
Salt and pepper
Lemon juice

Leave the mushrooms whole, but remove the stalks. Melt the butter in a shallow casserole for 30 seconds on HIGH. Add the mushrooms, garlic, salt, pepper and lemon juice. Cook for 2 minutes on HIGH. Remove and set aside. Add the shrimp to the casserole and cook on HIGH for 1 minute, stirring several times. Cook for 30 seconds more on HIGH, if required, to cook the shrimp thoroughly. Mix in the parsley and add more seasoning if necessary. Arrange the mushrooms in individual dishes and spoon over the shrimp and any remaining butter in the dish. Serve with French bread.

Microwave

FISH AND SEAFOOD

LIGHT DISHES

Codfish Pie

PREPARATION TIME: 15 minutes

MICROWAVE COOKING TIME:
11-12 minutes

SERVES: 4 people

4 cod fillets
30ml/2 tbsps lemon juice
30ml/2 tbsps water
1 bay leaf

SAUCE
45g/1½ oz/3 tbsps butter
1 shallot, finely chopped
45g/1½ oz/3 tbsps flour/plain flour
430ml/¾ pint/1½ cups milk
30ml/2 tbsps chopped parsley
Salt and pepper

TOPPING
2 large potatoes, peeled and very thinly
  sliced
60g/2oz/¼ cup grated Colby/Red
  Leicester cheese
Paprika

Put the fillets in a casserole with the water, lemon juice and bay leaf. Cover loosely and cook for 2 minutes on HIGH. Melt the butter in a deep bowl for 30 seconds on HIGH. Add the shallot and cook for a further 1 minute on HIGH. Stir in the flour, milk, liquid from the fish, salt, pepper and parsley. Cook for 2-3 minutes on HIGH or until thick, stirring frequently. Pour over the cod. Slice the potatoes on a mandolin or with the fine blade of a food

This page: Codfish Pie (top) and Tuna, Pea and Fennel Casserole (bottom). Facing page: Sea Lion.

processor. Layer on top of the cod and season with salt and pepper. Cover the dish tightly and cook for 3 minutes on HIGH. Sprinkle on the cheese and paprika and cook, uncovered, for a further 2 minutes on MEDIUM to melt the cheese. Serve immediately.

Crab Lasagne

PREPARATION TIME: 15 minutes

MICROWAVE COOKING TIME: 10 minutes

SERVES: 4 people

8 quick-cooking green lasagne noodles
4 tomatoes, peeled and sliced
225g crabmeat, flaked
340g/12oz Ricotta cheese
60g/2oz/¼ cup grated Parmesan cheese
140ml/¼ pint/½ cup milk
1 small clove garlic, minced
Pinch marjoram
Pinch nutmeg
Pinch dry mustard
Salt and pepper

TOPPING
60g/2oz/¼ cup seasoned dry
   breadcrumbs
15g/½ oz/1 tbsp butter
Paprika

Boil 1 litre/1¾ pints/3½ cups water on HIGH with a pinch of salt. Put in the lasagne and leave for 1 minute. Remove the noodles and rinse under hot water. Dry on paper towels. Mix the remaining ingredients, except the tomatoes, together. If the mixture is very thick, add more milk. Layer up the noodles, tomatoes and crabmeat filling, ending with filling. Melt the butter on HIGH for 30 seconds and stir in the breadcrumbs. Scatter over the top of the lasagne and sprinkle on some paprika. Cook for 3 minutes on HIGH and serve immediately.

Sea Lion

PREPARATION TIME: 20 minutes

MICROWAVE COOKING TIME: 5 minutes

SERVES: 4 people

CRABMEAT BALLS
450g/1lb crabmeat, flaked
45ml/1½ fl oz/3 tbsps sherry
15ml/½ fl oz/1 tbsp soy sauce
4 water chestnuts, finely chopped
2 green/spring onions, finely chopped
30ml/2 tbsps cornstarch/cornflour
1 egg white, lightly beaten
Pinch ginger
Salt and pepper

ACCOMPANIMENT
1 head Chinese cabbage/leaves, shredded
15ml/1 tbsp cornstarch/cornflour
30ml/2 tbsps soy sauce
5ml/1 tsp sugar
140ml/¼ pint/½ cup chicken stock

GARNISH
Sesame seeds

Mix all the ingredients for the crabmeat balls together and shape into 5cm (2″) balls. Place them in a large casserole with 30ml/1 fl oz/ 2 tbsps water. Cover loosely and cook for 2 minutes on MEDIUM. Remove from the casserole and keep warm. Combine the ingredients for the accompaniment and cook in the casserole for 2 minutes on HIGH, or until the cornstarch/cornflour thickens. Put the crabmeat balls on top of the cabbage and heat through for 1 minute on HIGH. Sprinkle over the sesame seeds to serve.

Monkfish Provençale

PREPARATION TIME: 20 minutes

MICROWAVE COOKING TIME: 19 minutes

SERVES: 4 people

675g/1½ lbs monkfish tails
1 aubergine/eggplant, cut in 1.5cm (½″)
   chunks
2 zucchini/courgettes, cut in 1.5cm (½″)
   chunks
1 large red pepper, cut in thin strips
90g/3oz/¾ cup sliced mushrooms
1 large onion, thinly sliced
30ml/1oz/2 tbsps olive oil
1 clove garlic, crushed
140ml/4oz/½ cup white wine
200g/7oz can plum tomatoes
30ml/1oz/2 tbsps tomato purée/paste

Pinch dried thyme
1 bay leaf
Salt and pepper
120g/4oz/½ cup grated cheese

Cut the eggplant/aubergine in half lengthways and lightly score the surface. Sprinkle with salt and leave to stand for 30 minutes. Wash and pat dry before cutting in cubes. Heat the olive oil in a browning dish for 3 minutes on HIGH. Add the vegetables and garlic. Cook for 2 minutes on HIGH. Add the canned tomatoes, tomato paste, thyme, bay leaf, half the wine, salt and pepper. Pour the contents into a casserole dish, cover, and cook for 10 minutes on HIGH. Stir 3 or 4 times during cooking. Cook the fish separately in the remaining wine for 2 minutes on HIGH. Transfer the fish to a baking dish and cover with the Provençale vegetables. Sprinkle on the cheese and cook for 2 minutes on MEDIUM to melt.

Tuna, Pea and Fennel Casserole

PREPARATION TIME: 15 minutes

MICROWAVE COOKING TIME: 10 minutes, plus 10 minutes standing time

SERVES: 4 people

225g/8oz green and whole-wheat
   noodles
120g/4oz/1 cup frozen peas
1 small bulb Florentine fennel chopped
225g/8oz can tuna, drained
45g/1½ oz/3 tbsps butter or margarine
45g/1½ oz/3 tbsps flour/plain flour
60ml/2oz/¼ cup white wine
360ml/⅔ pint/1¼ cups milk
Pinch oregano
1 small clove garlic, minced
Salt and pepper

TOPPING
Paprika
Parmesan cheese

Facing page: Monkfish Provençale (top) and Crab Lasagne (bottom).

Put the noodles in a large bowl with 1 litre/1¾ pints/3½ cups water. Cook for 6 minutes on HIGH and then leave to stand for 10 minutes. Drain, rinse under hot water, then leave to dry. Put the fennel into a casserole with 30ml/1 fl oz/2 tbsps water. Cover and cook for 1 minute on HIGH. Drain and combine with the noodles, tuna and peas. Melt the butter for 30 seconds on HIGH with the garlic. Stir in the flour, wine, milk, oregano, salt and pepper. Pour over the noodles and mix well. Sprinkle on grated Parmesan cheese and paprika. Heat for 2 minutes on HIGH before serving.

Shrimp/Prawn Curry

PREPARATION TIME: 10 minutes

MICROWAVE COOKING TIME: 5-7 minutes

SERVES: 4 people

45g/1½ oz/3 tbsps butter or margarine
45g/1½ oz/3 tbsps flour/plain flour
1 small onion, finely chopped
15g/½ oz/1 tbsp curry powder
430ml/¾ pint/1½ cups milk
60ml/2oz/¼ cup plain yogurt
1 cap pimento, chopped
225g/8oz shrimp/prawns, cooked and peeled

This page: Seafood Stir-fry. Facing page: Shrimp/Prawn Curry (top) and Pasta alla Vongole (bottom).

Desiccated coconut or chopped green/ spring onion

Melt the butter for 30 seconds on HIGH. Add the onion and cook for 30 seconds on HIGH to soften. Stir in the curry powder and cook for 1 minute on HIGH. Add the flour, salt, pepper and milk. Cook for 3-4 minutes, stirring often until thickened. Add the yogurt, pimento and shrimp. Heat for 30 seconds on

HIGH and serve on a bed of rice. Sprinkle on the coconut or onion.

Seafood Stir-fry

PREPARATION TIME: 20 minutes

MICROWAVE COOKING TIME: 16 minutes

SERVES: 4 people

120g/4oz thin Chinese egg noodles
30ml/1 fl oz/2 tbsps vegetable oil
2 large or 4 small scallops
90g/3oz/½ cup crabmeat, flaked
90g/3oz/½ cup shrimp/prawns, cooked and peeled
4 water chestnuts, sliced
4 ears baby corn
60g/2oz peapods/mangetout
1 small red pepper, sliced
225g/8oz bean sprouts
140ml/¼ pint/½ cup chicken or fish stock
30ml/1 fl oz/2 tbsps soy sauce
15ml/1 tbsp cornstarch/cornflour
15ml/1 tbsp sherry
Dash sesame seed oil
Salt and pepper

Boil 1 litre/1¾ pints/3½ cups water with a pinch of salt for 5 minutes on HIGH. Put in the noodles and leave them to stand for 6 minutes. Drain and rinse under hot water and leave to dry. Heat the oil for 5 minutes on HIGH in a browning dish. Cook the scallops for 3 minutes on HIGH, turning several times. Add the pepper, peapods/mangetout and baby corn. Cook for 1 minute on HIGH. Add the bean sprouts and noodles. Mix the remaining ingredients together and add to the dish with the shrimp and crab. Toss the ingredients together and heat for 2 minutes on HIGH or until the sauce thickens. Serve immediately.

Pasta alla Vongole

PREPARATION TIME: 15 minutes

MICROWAVE COOKING TIME: 9 minutes, plus 10 minutes standing time

SERVES: 4 people

180g/6oz/2 cups red, green and plain pasta shells (or other shapes)

3 tomatoes, peeled, seeded and sliced in strips
45g/1½ oz/3 tbsps butter or margarine
½ clove garlic, crushed
2 shallots, finely chopped
45g/1½ oz/3 tbsps flour/plain flour
140ml/¼ pint/½ cup white wine
280ml/½ pint/1 cup milk, or light/single cream
30ml/1 tbsp chopped parsley
Pinch oregano or basil
340g/12oz/1½ cups small clams, shelled
Salt and pepper
Grated Parmesan cheese

Put the pasta into 1 litre/1¾ pints/ 3½ cups hot water with a pinch of salt. Cook for 6 minutes on HIGH. Leave to stand for 10 minutes, then drain and rinse in hot water. Melt the butter in a small, deep bowl for 30 seconds on HIGH. Add the garlic and shallot and cook for 30 seconds on HIGH to soften. Stir in the flour, wine and milk or cream, and add the herbs, salt and pepper. Cook for 2-3 minutes on HIGH, stirring every 30 seconds. Cut the tomatoes into thin strips and add to the hot sauce with the clams. Heat through for a further 30 seconds on HIGH. Toss the sauce and pasta together and serve with grated Parmesan cheese if desired.

Microwave

FISH AND SEAFOOD

MAIN DISHES

Turbot with Almonds and Emerald Sauce

PREPARATION TIME: 20 minutes

MICROWAVE COOKING TIME: 11 minutes

SERVES: 4 people

4 turbot fillets
1 slice onion
1 bay leaf
2 black peppercorns
140ml/¼ pint/½ cup water

SAUCE
450g/1lb fresh spinach, well washed
15ml/1 tbsp fresh chives, chopped
15ml/1 tbsp white wine vinegar
Nutmeg
Cayenne pepper
15g/1 tbsp butter
140ml/¼ pint/½ cup cream

GARNISH
90g/3oz/½ cup sliced/flaked almonds

Heat a browning dish for 5 minutes on HIGH and toast the almonds for 1-2 minutes on HIGH, stirring frequently until browned. Put the fish into a casserole with the slice of onion, bay leaf, peppercorn, lemon juice and water. Cover loosely and cook on HIGH for 2 minutes. Set aside. Put the spinach, nutmeg, Cayenne pepper and butter into a large bowl with 15ml/1 tbsp water. Cover loosely and cook on HIGH for 2 minutes. Purée in a food

This page: Salmon and Broccoli Fricassee. Facing page: Turbot with Almonds and Emerald Sauce.

processor. Add the cream, chives and some of the fish cooking liquid if the sauce is too thick. Sprinkle the toasted almonds on the fish and serve with the emerald sauce.

Garlic-Braised Tuna Steaks

PREPARATION TIME: 20 minutes

MICROWAVE COOKING TIME: 11-12 minutes

SERVES: 4 people

4 tuna steaks, cut 2.5cm (1") thick
1 clove garlic, peeled and cut in thin slivers
225g/8oz button or pickling onions, peeled
15g/½ oz/1 tbsp butter
140ml/¼ pint/½ cup red wine
140ml/¼ pint/½ cup water
1 bay leaf

SAUCE
Cooking liquid from the fish
15g/½ oz/1 tbsp butter or margarine
15g/½ oz/1 tbsp flour/plain flour
15ml/1 tbsp tomato paste or purée
2.5ml/½ tsp thyme
15ml/1 tbsp chopped parsley
Squeeze lemon juice
Salt and pepper

GARNISH
450g/1lb fresh spinach, washed and thinly shredded
15g/½ oz/1 tbsp butter

Make small slits in the tuna steaks with a knife and insert a sliver of garlic into each slit. Heat a browning dish for 3 minutes on HIGH. Drop in 15g/½ oz/1 tbsp butter and the peeled onions. Heat for 1-2 minutes on HIGH, stirring occasionally, until the onions begin to brown. Pour in the water and wine. Transfer the contents of the browning dish to a large casserole. Add the bay leaf and fish to the casserole, cover loosely and cook for 5 minutes on HIGH. Remove the fish and onions from the casserole and keep them warm. Melt 15g/½ oz/1 tbsp butter in a small, deep bowl for 30 seconds on HIGH. Stir in the flour and cook for 1-2 minutes on HIGH or until the flour

is lightly browned. Pour in the cooking liquid from the fish, and add the tomato purée and thyme. Cook for 2-3 minutes on HIGH, stirring occasionally until thickened. Add the parsley, lemon juice, salt and pepper, and set aside with the fish. Melt the remaining butter in a small casserole on HIGH for 30 seconds. Put in the spinach, cover loosely and cook for 1-2 minutes on HIGH. Spread the spinach onto a serving plate and combine the fish and sauce to re-heat for 30 seconds on HIGH. Arrange the fish and onions on top of the bed of spinach and pour over the sauce to serve.

Salmon and Broccoli Fricassee

PREPARATION TIME: 20 minutes

MICROWAVE COOKING TIME: 10-12 minutes

SERVES: 4 people

900g/2lbs salmon fillets or tail pieces
60g/2oz/½ cup sliced/flaked almonds, toasted
450g/1lb broccoli
140ml/¼ pint/½ cup white wine
180g/6oz/1 cup sliced mushrooms
15g/½ oz/1 tbsp butter
15g/½ oz/1 tbsp flour/plain flour
120g/4oz/1 cup chow mein noodles
5ml/1 tsp chopped dill
5ml/1 tsp chopped parsley
200ml/6 fl oz/¾ cup cream
Salt and pepper

Put the fillets into a casserole with enough water to barely cover. Cover the dish loosely and cook for 2 minutes on HIGH. Reserve the cooking liquid, flake the fish and set aside. Put the broccoli into a bowl with 30ml/2 tbsps water. Cover loosely and cook for 4 minutes on HIGH. Drain and arrange the broccoli in a casserole with the flaked salmon. Melt the butter in a small bowl for 30 seconds on HIGH. Stir in the flour, cream, fish liquid and sliced mushrooms. Cook for 2-3 minutes on HIGH. Season with salt and pepper. Add dill and parsley and pour over the fish and broccoli.

Sprinkle over the almonds and noodles. Heat through for 2 minutes on HIGH before serving.

Halibut à la Normande

PREPARATION TIME: 15 minutes

MICROWAVE COOKING TIME: 5-7 minutes

SERVES: 4 people

4 halibut fillets or steaks
140ml/¼ pint/½ cup white wine, dry cider or unsweetened apple juice
60ml/4 tbsps/¼ cup water
15g/½ oz/1 tbsp flour/plain flour
30g/1oz/2 tbsps butter or margarine
1 shallot, finely chopped
2 medium-sized apples/dessert apples
60ml/2oz/¼ cup light/single cream
1 bay leaf
Salt and pepper
Lemon juice

GARNISH
Chopped parsley

Put the halibut into a casserole with the wine, cider or juice, water and bay leaf. Cover loosely and cook for 2 minutes on HIGH. Set aside and keep warm. In a small bowl melt half the butter. Add the shallot and cook, uncovered, for 1 minute on HIGH, stirring once. Peel and chop one of the apples. Add the shallot, cover the bowl loosely and cook for 2 minutes on HIGH, or until the apple is soft. Stir in the flour, add the cooking liquid from the fish and heat for 2 minutes on HIGH. Stir the sauce twice until thickened. Add the cream and heat for 30 seconds on HIGH. Season with salt, pepper and lemon juice to taste. Heat a browning dish for 5 minutes on HIGH and drop in the remaining butter. Core and slice the second apple, but do not peel it. Brown the slices for 1-2 minutes on HIGH in the butter. Coat the fish with the sauce and garnish with the parsley. Serve surrounded with the apple slices.

Facing page: Garlic-Braised Tuna Steaks.

Monkfish Medallions Piperade

PREPARATION TIME: 15 minutes

MICROWAVE COOKING TIME: 7 minutes, plus 1 minute standing time

SERVES: 4 people

900g/2lbs monkfish tails
140ml/¼ pint/½ cup white wine
430ml/¾ pint/1½ cups tomato sauce
1 shallot, finely chopped
1 red pepper, sliced
1 green pepper, sliced
1 yellow pepper, sliced
1 clove garlic, finely minced
2.5ml/½ tsp thyme
1 bay leaf
Salt and pepper

GARNISH
Chopped parsley

Cut the monkfish tails into round slices 15mm (½″) thick. Put into a casserole with the wine and bay leaf. Cover loosely and cook for 2 minutes on HIGH. Set aside. Combine the shallot, garlic and thyme in a small, deep bowl. Pour on the fish cooking liquid and cook, uncovered, for 3 minutes on HIGH to reduce by half. Add the tomato sauce, peppers, salt and pepper. Cover loosely and cook for 2 minutes on HIGH. Leave to stand for 1 minute and pour over the fish to serve.

Salmon in Chive Sauce

PREPARATION TIME: 15 minutes

MICROWAVE COOKING TIME: 5 minutes

SERVES: 4 people

1 side of salmon (about 675-900g/ 1½-2lbs)
30g/1oz/2 tbsps butter or margarine
280ml/½ pint/1 cup sour cream
120ml/¼ pint/½ cup light/single cream
5ml/1 tsp cornstarch/cornflour
45g/1½ oz/3 tbsps snipped chives
5ml/1 tsp coarsely ground black pepper
Salt

Slice the salmon horizontally into very thin slices. Heat a browning dish for 3 minutes on HIGH. Drop in the butter and heat for 30 seconds on HIGH. Lay in the salmon slices and cook for 30 seconds each side. Cook the fish in several batches. Remove the fish from the dish. Cover and keep warm. Mix the cream, sour cream, and cornstarch together. Pour into the dish and cook for 30 seconds on HIGH. Stir well and repeat the process until the cornstarch has cooked and thickened

This page: Monkfish Medallions Piperade. Facing page: Halibut à la Normande (top) and Salmon in Chive Sauce (bottom).

the sauce. The sauce should not bubble too rapidly, but the cornstarch will help prevent the sour cream from curdling. Stir in the chives, pepper and salt, and pour over the salmon slices. Serve with fine green noodles.

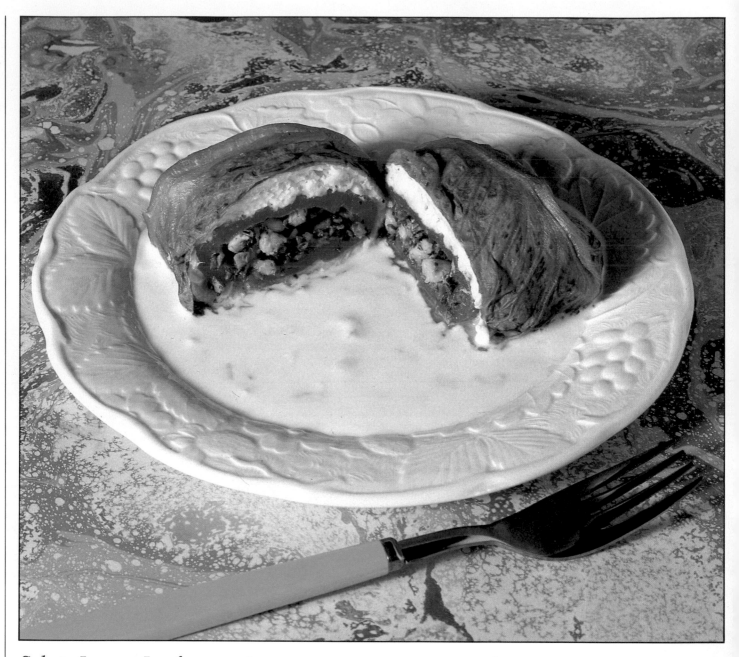

Sole in Lettuce Leaf Parcels

PREPARATION TIME: 20 minutes

MICROWAVE COOKING TIME: 5 minutes

SERVES: 4 people

4 double fillets of sole or flounder
8 large leaves of romaine/cos lettuce
225g/8oz small shrimp/prawns
1 finely chopped shallot
90g/3oz/½ cup chopped mushrooms
60ml/2 tbsps chopped parsley

4 large caps canned pimento
1 cap pimento, chopped
140ml/¼ pint/½ cup white wine
140ml/¼ pint/½ cup heavy/double cream
120g/4oz/1 cup low-fat soft cheese
Salt and pepper

Combine the shrimp/prawns, mushrooms, half the parsley, salt and pepper, and stuff the pimento caps with the mixture. Roll the fish fillets around the pimento and set aside. Put the lettuce leaves into a large casserole with 30ml/2 tbsps water.

This page: **Sole in Lettuce Leaf Parcels.** Facing page: **Mackerel and Mustard (top) and Trout with Hazelnuts (bottom).**

Cover tightly and cook for 30 seconds on HIGH to soften. Roll the leaves carefully around the stuffed fillets. Put seam-side down into a casserole with the wine and shallot. Cover loosely and cook for 3 minutes on HIGH. Remove the parcels and keep them warm. Cook

the wine for a further 2-3 minutes on HIGH to reduce. Stir in the cream and bring to the boil for 2 minutes on HIGH. Add the cheese, salt, pepper, the remaining parsley and chopped pimento. Serve the sauce with the sole parcels.

Trout with Hazelnuts

PREPARATION TIME: 15 minutes

MICROWAVE COOKING TIME: 12-13 minutes

SERVES: 4 people

4 small rainbow trout, cleaned
60g/2oz/4 tbsps butter
120g/4oz/¾ cup crushed hazelnuts
4 green/spring onions, shredded
Juice of 1 lemon
Salt and pepper

Heat a browning dish for 5 minutes on HIGH. Put in the hazelnuts and cook for 2-3 minutes on HIGH, stirring often until browned. Set aside. Melt half the butter in the browning dish. Add the trout and cook for 5 minutes per side. If the butter has browned too much, wipe out the dish. Melt the remaining butter and allow to brown lightly. Add the nuts, lemon juice and green onion, and season with salt and pepper. Pour over the fish to serve.

Hangchow Fish

PREPARATION TIME: 15 minutes

MICROWAVE COOKING TIME: 19 minutes

SERVES: 4 people

1 sea or freshwater bass, 900-1kg/
    2-2¼ lbs in weight, cleaned
140ml/¼ pint/½ cup white wine
140ml/¼ pint/½ cup water
1 small ginger root, sliced
60g/2oz/¼ cup sugar
90ml/3 fl oz/⅓ cup rice vinegar
30ml/1 fl oz/2 tbsps soy sauce
15g/½ oz/1 tbsp cornstarch/cornflour
1 clove garlic, minced
1 carrot, thinly sliced in rounds
4 water chestnuts, thinly sliced

4 green/spring onions, diagonally sliced
Salt and pepper

Combine the wine, water and a few slices of ginger in a large casserole. Cut 2 or 3 slashes on each side of the fish to help it cook faster, and put it into the casserole. Cover and cook for 25 minutes on MEDIUM. Set the fish aside and keep it warm. Combine the cornstarch, sugar, vinegar, soy sauce, salt, pepper and 140ml/¼ pint/½ cup of the fish cooking liquid. Add the garlic and cook on HIGH for 2 minutes, stirring frequently. Add the water chestnuts, carrots and remaining slices of ginger. Cook the sauce for a further 1-2 minutes on HIGH. Add the green/spring onions and pour over the fish to serve.

Mackerel and Mustard

PREPARATION TIME: 15 minutes

MICROWAVE COOKING TIME: 14-16 minutes

SERVES: 4 people

4 small mackerel, cleaned
280ml/½ pint/1 cup white wine
5ml/1 tsp whole mustard seed
3 whole peppercorns
1 bay leaf
1 slice onion

SAUCE
25g/¾ oz/1½ tbsps flour/plain flour
25g/¾ oz/1½ tbsps butter
30ml/1oz/2 tbsps Dijon or spicy brown
    mustard
30ml/1oz/2 tbsps chopped herbs
    (eg chives, parsley, thyme, dill)
140ml/¼ pint/½ cup milk
Salt and pepper

Put the mackerel into one or two casseroles (do not crowd the fish) and cook in two batches if necessary. Pour over the white wine and add the mustard seed, peppercorns, bay leaf and onion. Cover loosely and cook for 12 minutes on HIGH. Set aside and keep warm. Melt the butter in a small, deep bowl for 30 seconds on HIGH. Stir in the flour, milk and strained liquid from the fish. Cook, uncovered, for 2-3 minutes on

HIGH, stirring often until thickened. Add salt, pepper, mustard and herbs. Peel the skin from one side of the mackerel and coat each one with some of the sauce to serve. Serve the remaining sauce separately.

Crab-Stuffed Trout

PREPARATION TIME: 15 minutes

MICROWAVE COOKING TIME: 14 minutes

SERVES: 4 people

4 rainbow trout
60g/2oz/4 tbsps butter
Juice of 1 lemon

STUFFING
225g/8oz flaked crabmeat
3 green/spring onions, chopped
2 sticks celery, finely chopped
1 small green pepper, finely chopped
60g/2oz/¼ cup black olives, sliced
Fresh breadcrumbs from 4 slices of white
    bread, crusts removed
30ml/2 tbsps chopped parsley
30ml/2 tbsps sherry
Salt and pepper

GARNISH
Lemon slices
Chopped chives

Buy the trout fresh or frozen with the bones removed. Mix the stuffing ingredients together and fill the trout. Put the trout into a large casserole and cook, covered, in two batches if necessary. Cook 4 trout together for 12 minutes on HIGH, or 2 trout for 6 minutes on HIGH. Melt the butter for 2 minutes on HIGH and add the lemon juice and pour over the trout before serving. Garnish with lemon slices and chives.

Facing page: Hangchow Fish.

Sole and Asparagus Rolls

PREPARATION TIME: 15 minutes

MICROWAVE COOKING TIME:
7 minutes

SERVES: 4 people

8 fillets of sole
16 asparagus spears
140ml/¼ pint/½ cup water
15ml/1 tbsp lemon juice

SAUCE
3 egg yolks
30ml/2 tbsps lemon juice
120g/4oz/½ cup butter
Cayenne pepper
Salt

This page: Sole and Asparagus Rolls. Facing page: Crab-Stuffed Trout.

Cook the asparagus with 30ml/
2 tbsps water for 2 minutes on
HIGH in a covered casserole. Rinse
under cold water and drain dry.
Divide the asparagus evenly between
all the sole fillets and roll the fish
around them. Tuck the ends of the
fillets under the asparagus evenly
between all the sole fillets and roll
the fish around them. Tuck the ends
of the fillets under the asparagus and

place in a casserole. Pour over the water and 15ml/1 tbsp lemon juice. Cover the dish loosely and cook for 2-3 minutes on HIGH. Set aside and keep warm. Melt the butter in a small, deep bowl for 1 minute on HIGH. Beat the egg yolks, lemon juice, salt and Cayenne pepper together. Have a bowl of iced water ready. Pour the yolk mixture into the butter and beat well. Cook for 30 seconds on HIGH and beat well. Repeat the process until the sauce thickens – about 2 minutes. Put the sauce bowl into the iced water to stop the cooking. Pour over the hot fish and asparagus rolls to serve. Sprinkle on paprika if desired.

Sole with Limes and Chili Peppers

PREPARATION TIME: 15 minutes

MICROWAVE COOKING TIME: 6 minutes

SERVES: 4 people

900g/2lbs sole fillets
2 limes
1 green chili pepper, very thinly sliced
1 small bunch chives
30g/1oz/2 tbsps butter
Salt and pepper

Melt the butter in a large casserole for 1 minute on HIGH. Put in the fish and cook for 30 seconds each side on HIGH. Remove from the casserole and keep warm. Grate the peel off one of the limes, pare off the white pith and cut the lime into very thin rounds. Squeeze the remaining lime for its juice. Pour the lime juice into the casserole with the butter. Add the chili pepper slices and cook for 30 seconds on HIGH. Add the lime slices, rind and snipped chives. Season and pour over the fish fillets to serve.

Salmon with Tomato Chive Hollandaise

PREPARATION TIME: 15 minutes

MICROWAVE COOKING TIME: 4 minutes

SERVES: 4 people

4 salmon fillets or tail portions
2 tomatoes, peeled, seeded and chopped
30ml/2 tbsps snipped chives
3 egg yolks
120g/4oz/½ cup butter
5ml/1 tsp red wine vinegar
Salt and pepper

Poach the fish fillets in enough water to come half way up the side of the fillets. Cover loosely and cook for 2 minutes on HIGH. Keep warm. Beat the yolks with salt, pepper and chives. Add the vinegar and set aside. Melt the butter for 1 minute on HIGH in a small, deep bowl. Beat the yolks into the butter. Have a bowl of iced water ready. Put the sauce ingredients into the oven and cook for 20 seconds on HIGH. Stir and cook for 20 seconds more. Repeat until the sauce thickens – about 2 minutes. Put the bowl into the iced water to stop the cooking process. Add the tomatoes to the sauce and serve with the salmon fillets.

Sole Bonne Femme

PREPARATION TIME: 20 minutes

MICROWAVE COOKING TIME: 8-11 minutes

SERVES: 4 people

900g/2lbs sole fillets
225g/8oz whole mushrooms, stalks removed
120g/4oz button or pickling onions, peeled
140ml/¼ pint/½ cup white wine
1 bay leaf

WHITE SAUCE
30g/1oz/2 tbsps butter or margarine
30g/1oz/2 tbsps flour/plain flour
140ml/¼ pint/½ cup milk
Salt and pepper

BUTTER SAUCE
2 egg yolks
60g/2oz/¼ cup butter
7ml/½ tbsp white wine vinegar
Salt and pepper

For the butter sauce, melt 60g/2oz/¼ cup butter in a small, deep bowl for 30 seconds on HIGH. Mix the egg yolks, vinegar, salt and pepper together and beat into the butter. Have a bowl of iced water ready. Cook the sauce for 15 seconds on HIGH and beat well. Repeat until the sauce has thickened – about 1 minute. Put immediately into a bowl of iced water to stop the cooking. Set the sauce aside. Tuck the ends of each sole fillet under and place the fish into a large casserole. Add the mushrooms, onions, wine and bay leaf. Cover loosely and cook for 5-6 minutes on HIGH. Arrange the fish, mushrooms and onions in a clean casserole or serving dish and keep warm. In a small bowl melt the remaining butter on HIGH for 30 seconds. Stir in the flour, milk, cooking liquid from the fish, salt and pepper. Cook for 2-3 minutes on HIGH, stirring frequently until thickened. Beat in the butter sauce and pour over the fish to serve.

Cod with Bacon

PREPARATION TIME: 15 minutes

MICROWAVE COOKING TIME: 12 minutes

SERVES: 4 people

4 fillets of cod
60ml/2oz/¼ cup white wine
8 strips bacon/streaky bacon, rind and bones removed
1 green pepper, diced
2 green/spring onions, chopped
15g/½ oz/1 tbsp flour/plain flour
140ml/¼ pint/½ cup milk
1 bay leaf
Salt and pepper

Put the cod, wine and bay leaf into a large casserole. Cover loosely and cook on HIGH for 3 minutes. Set aside. Heat a browning dish for 3 minutes on HIGH. Chop the bacon

Facing page: Sole Bonne Femme (top) and Salmon with Tomato Chive Hollandaise (bottom).

roughly, put it into the browning dish and cook for 2-3 minutes on HIGH. Stir frequently until the bacon has browned. Add the pepper and onion and cook for 30 seconds on HIGH. Stir in the flour, milk, salt, pepper and liquid from the fish. Cook for 2-3 minutes on HIGH, stirring frequently until the sauce has thickened. Pour over the fish and re-heat for 30 seconds on HIGH. Serve with parsley new potatoes.

Sole with Oranges

PREPARATION TIME: 15 minutes

MICROWAVE COOKING TIME: 5 minutes

SERVES: 4 people

900g/2lbs sole fillets
200ml/6 fl oz/¾ cup orange juice
15ml/1 tbsp lemon juice
10g/2 tsps butter
10g/2 tsps flour
200ml/6 fl oz/¾ cup heavy/double
    cream
15ml/1 tbsp chopped basil
Salt and pepper

GARNISH
2 oranges, peeled and cut in segments
Fresh basil leaves, if available

Tuck in the ends of the sole fillets. Put into a casserole with the orange and lemon juice. Cover loosely and cook on HIGH for 2 minutes. Set aside. Melt the butter in a small, deep bowl for 30 seconds on HIGH. Add the flour and fish cooking liquid. Stir in the cream, basil, salt and pepper, and cook, uncovered, for 2 minutes on HIGH. Stir frequently until the sauce thickens. Pour over the fish and serve with the orange segments and basil leaves.

Cod with Crumb Topping

PREPARATION TIME: 10 minutes

MICROWAVE COOKING TIME: 5-7 minutes

SERVES: 4 people

4 cod fillets
Lemon juice
140ml/¼ pint/½ cup water

TOPPING
60g/2oz/4 tbsps butter or margarine
180g/6oz/1½ cups seasoned breadcrumbs
30ml/2 tbsp paprika
60g/2oz/¼ cup grated Parmesan cheese
30ml/1oz/2 tbsps sesame seeds
Salt and pepper

GARNISH
Lemon wedges

Heat a browning dish for 3 minutes on HIGH. Melt the butter in the dish and add the breadcrumbs. Stir well and heat for 1 minute on HIGH to lightly brown. Add the remaining

This page: Cod with Crumb Topping (top) and Cod with Bacon (bottom). Facing page: Sole with Limes and Chili Peppers (top) and Sole with Oranges (bottom).

ingredients and heat for 1 minute more on HIGH. Set aside. Put the cod, a squeeze of lemon juice, and water into a casserole. Cover loosely and cook for 3-4 minutes on HIGH. Drain the fillets and top each one with the breadcrumb mixture. Heat through for 30 seconds on HIGH. Serve with lemon wedges.

Lychee Sole

PREPARATION TIME: 20 minutes

MICROWAVE COOKING TIME:
4-5 minutes

SERVES: 4 people

900g/2lbs sole fillets
225g/8oz lychees (canned or fresh),
   peeled
225g/8oz can pineapple chunks, 140ml/
   ¼ pint/½ cup juice reserved
Juice and rind of 2 limes
15-30g/½-1oz/1-2 tbsps sugar
15ml/½ fl oz/1 tbsp light soy sauce

10ml/2 tsps cornstarch/cornflour
2 green/spring onions, shredded
Salt and pepper

With a swivel peeler, peel strips off
the limes, and cut into thin slivers.
Cover well and set aside. Squeeze the
lime juice, and mix with the
pineapple juice, sugar, soy sauce and
constarch in a small, deep bowl. Fold
the fish fillets in half and place in a
large casserole, thinner ends of the
fillets towards the middle of the dish.
Pour over enough water to cover
1.5cm (½″) of the sides of the fillets.
Cover the dish loosely and cook for

**This page: Lychee Sole. Facing
page: Sole Italienne (top) and
Halibut and Green Grapes
(bottom).**

2 minutes on HIGH. Set aside and
keep warm. Cook the sauce
ingredients for 2-3 minutes on
HIGH, stirring often until thickened.
Add the cooking liquid from the fish,
strained. Stir in the pineapple
chunks, lychees, green/spring onions
and lime rind. Add a pinch of salt
and pepper and pour the sauce over
the fish. Serve with fried rice or chow
mein noodles.

Halibut and Green Grapes

PREPARATION TIME: 10 minutes

MICROWAVE COOKING TIME: 10-13 minutes

SERVES: 4 people

900g/2lbs halibut steaks
1 small bunch green seedless grapes
140ml/¼ pint/½ cup white wine
Lemon juice
200ml/6 fl oz/¾ cup heavy/double cream
5ml/1 tsp tarragon
Salt and pepper

Put the fish into a casserole and pour on the wine and lemon juice. Cook for 4-5 minutes on HIGH. Remove the fish from the casserole, cover and keep warm. Heat the wine for 2-3 minutes on HIGH to reduce by half. Cut the grapes in half if large, and add to the wine. Add the tarragon, salt and pepper, and cream. Heat through for 1 minute on HIGH. Pour over the fish to serve.

Halibut in Sesame Ginger Sauce

PREPARATION TIME: 20 minutes

MICROWAVE COOKING TIME: 6 minutes

SERVES: 4 people

4 halibut steaks
2 carrots, cut in Julienne strips
280ml/½ pint/1 cup water
45ml/1½ fl oz/3 tbsps ginger wine
60g/2oz/¼ cup light brown sugar
60g/2oz/¼ cup sesame seeds
30ml/2 tbsps chopped fresh ginger root
30ml/2 tbsps rice vinegar
10ml/2 tsps cornstarch/cornflour
Dash of sesame seed oil
Salt and pepper

Put the fish into a casserole with the ginger wine and water. Cover and cook for 2 minutes on HIGH. Put the carrots into a small bowl with 15ml/1 tbsp water. Cover loosely and cook for 1 minute on HIGH. Leave to stand while preparing the sauce. Combine the sugar, cornstarch,

ginger, sesame seed oil, rice vinegar, sesame seeds and cooking liquid from the fish. Cook for 4 minutes on HIGH, stirring often until thickened. Add the carrot, salt and pepper and pour over the fish to serve.

Sole Italienne

PREPARATION TIME: 15 minutes

MICROWAVE COOKING TIME: 6-8 minutes

SERVES: 4 people

8 sole fillets
120g/4oz Parma ham
140ml/¼ pint/½ cup white wine
15g/½ oz/1 tbsp butter or margarine
15g/½ oz/1 tbsp flour/plain flour
200ml/6 fl oz/¾ cup heavy/double cream
Pinch sage
Pinch thyme
Pinch chopped parsley
1 bay leaf
Salt and pepper

GARNISH
Fresh sage or bay leaves

Cut the ham into 1.5cm (½") strips. Wrap the ham strips lattice fashion around the fish and tuck the ends underneath. Put into a casserole with the bay leaf and wine. Cook for 3-4 minutes on HIGH. Remove the fish from the dish, cover and keep it warm. Discard the bay leaf. Melt the butter for 30 seconds on HIGH in a small casserole. Stir in the flour and fish cooking liquid, and add the thyme, parsley, sage, salt and pepper. Cook for 2 minutes on HIGH and stir in the cream. Cook for a further 1 minute on HIGH and spoon over the fish. Garnish with sage or bay leaves.

Fillets of Salmon with Peppercorn Sauce

PREPARATION TIME: 15 minutes

MICROWAVE COOKING TIME: 8-12 minutes

SERVES: 4 people

1 side of salmon, about 675-900g/ 1½-2lbs
30g/1oz/2 tbsps butter or margarine
280ml/½ pint/1 cup heavy/double cream
90ml/3 fl oz/⅓ cup dry vermouth
30ml/1 tbsp canned green peppercorns, rinsed and drained
Salt and pepper

Slice the salmon horizontally into very thin slices. Heat a browning dish for 3 minutes on HIGH. Drop in the butter and heat for 30 seconds on HIGH. Lay in the salmon slices and cook for 30 seconds each side. Cook the fish in several batches. Remove the cooked fish from the dish, cover it, and keep it warm. Pour the vermouth into the dish and add the peppercorns. Cook on HIGH for 2 minutes or until reduced by half. Add the cream, stir well, and cook for 2-3 minutes on HIGH until bubbling. Season with salt and pepper. Pour over the salmon scallops to serve. Serve with lightly cooked green/French beans or pea-pods/mangetout.

Fruits of the Sea

PREPARATION TIME: 15 minutes

MICROWAVE COOKING TIME: 5-9 minutes

SERVES: 4 people

900g/2lbs mixture of:
    raw scallops, cut in half
    raw shrimp/prawns, peeled
    1 lobster tail, shelled and cut into 2.5cm (1") chunks
    sole fillets, cut into 5cm (2") chunks
    oysters, shelled
    mussels, shelled
280ml/½ pint/1 cup white wine
10ml/2 tsps cornstarch/cornflour
15ml/1 tbsp lemon juice
140ml/¼ pint/½ cup whole milk yogurt
30ml/1oz/2 tbsps chopped chives
225g/8oz edible seaweed, soaked or cooked in 30ml/2 tbsps water
Salt and pepper

Facing page: Fruits of the Sea (top) and Fillets of Salmon with Peppercorn Sauce (bottom).

Cook all the seafood in the wine for 2-3 minutes on HIGH. Cook the seaweed with 30ml/1 fl oz/2 tbsps water for 1-2 minutes on HIGH. Mix the cornstarch and lemon juice. Remove the fish from the casserole and arrange on a serving dish with the seaweed. Combine the cornstarch and lemon juice with the cooking liquid from the seafood. Cook for 2-3 minutes on HIGH, stirring frequently until thickened. Add the yogurt and chives and heat through for 30 seconds on HIGH. Season with salt and pepper and pour over the seafood.

Salmon in Madeira

PREPARATION TIME: 15 minutes

MICROWAVE COOKING TIME: 8 minutes

SERVES: 4 people

4 salmon steaks, about 2.5cm (1") thick
225g/8oz mushrooms, stalks trimmed
5 sprigs fresh rosemary
280ml/½ pint/1 cup Rainwater Madeira
140ml/¼ pint/½ cup water
15g/½ oz/1 tbsp butter or margarine
15g/½ oz/1 tbsp flour/plain flour
Small pinch ground cloves
60ml/2 fl oz/¼ cup heavy/double cream
Salt and pepper

Put the salmon steaks in a casserole with the Madeira. Strip the leaves off one sprig of rosemary and add to the salmon. Cover the dish loosely and cook for 5 minutes on HIGH. Add the mushrooms half way through the cooking time. Melt the butter in a small casserole for 2 minutes on HIGH until browning slightly. Add the flour and cook for 1 minute on HIGH. Stir in the cooking liquid from the fish and a pinch of cloves. Season with salt and pepper. Arrange the salmon and mushrooms on plates and pour over the Madeira sauce. Drizzle 15ml/1 tbsp cream over each salmon steak and garnish each with a sprig of fresh rosemary.

Curried Cod Nuggets

PREPARATION TIME: 15 minutes

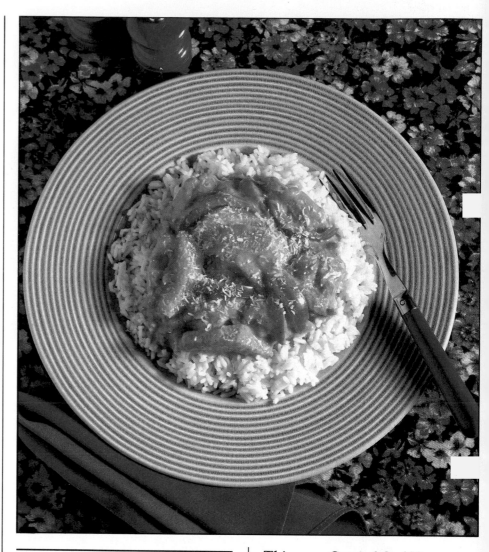

MICROWAVE COOKING TIME: 7 minutes

SERVES: 4 people

900g/2 lbs cod, cut in 5cm (2") chunks
60ml/2 oz/¼ cup lime juice
200ml/6 fl oz/¾ cup water
30g/1oz/2 tbsps butter or margarine
30g/1oz/2 tbsps flour/plain flour
1 large onion, chopped
15g/1 tbsp curry powder
140ml/¼ pint/½ cup orange juice
2 oranges, peeled and segmented
2 tomatoes, peeled and seeded
Desiccated coconut

Combine the cod, lime juice and water in a large casserole. Cover loosely and cook on HIGH for 2 minutes. Set aside and keep warm. Melt the butter for 30 seconds on HIGH in a small, deep bowl. Add the

This page: **Curried Cod Nuggets.** Facing page: **Halibut in Sesame Ginger Sauce** (top) and **Salmon in Madeira** (bottom).

onion, cover loosely and cook for 1 minute on HIGH. Stir in the curry powder and cook for 1 minute on HIGH. Add the flour, orange juice and cooking liquid from the fish. Stir well and cook, uncovered, for 2-3 minutes. Stir often until the sauce is thick. Slice the tomatoes into thin strips and add to the sauce with the orange segments. Cook the sauce for 10 seconds on HIGH to heat the orange and tomato through. Pour the sauce over the cod nuggets and sprinkle with desiccated coconut.

Monkfish and Ribbons

PREPARATION TIME: 20 minutes

MICROWAVE COOKING TIME:
5-6 minutes

SERVES: 4 people

900g/2lbs monkfish tails
140ml/¼ pint/½ cup white wine
2 carrots, peeled
2 zucchini/courgettes, ends trimmed
1 large or 2 small leeks, washed and
   trimmed, retaining some green
140ml/¼ pint/½ cup heavy/double
   cream
30ml/2 tbsps chopped parsley
2.5ml/½ tsp ground oregano
1 bay leaf
Salt and pepper

Cut the monkfish tails into 1.5cm
(½″) rounds. Put the pieces into a
casserole with the wine and bay leaf.
Cover loosely and cook for 2
minutes on HIGH. Set aside and
keep warm. With a swivel vegetable
peeler, pare thin ribbons of carrot and
zucchini/courgettes. Cut the leeks in
half lengthwise and then into 1.5cm
(½″) strips. Put the vegetables into a
small casserole with 15ml/1 tbsp
water. Cover loosely and cook for 1
minute on HIGH. Set aside. Remove
the fish from the casserole and heat
the wine for 2-3 minutes on HIGH
to reduce. Pour in the cream, and add
the oregano, salt and pepper. Heat
through for 30 seconds on HIGH.
Pour the sauce over the fish and
sprinkle on the chopped parsley.
Surround with the vegetable ribbons
to serve.

Cod Steaks with Mushrooms

PREPARATION TIME: 15 minutes

MICROWAVE COOKING TIME:
5-7 minutes

SERVES: 4 people

4-8 cod steaks, depending on size
140ml/¼ pint/½ cup white wine
1 bay leaf
2 shallots, finely chopped
30g/1oz/2 tbsps butter
180g/6oz/1½ cups sliced mushrooms
15g/1 tbsp flour/plain flour
140ml/¼ pint/½ cup milk
5ml/1 tsp Worcestershire sauce
5ml/1 tsp chopped parsley
Salt and pepper

Put the cod and wine into a casserole
with the bay leaf and shallot. Cover
loosely and cook for 2 minutes on
HIGH. Leave covered and set aside.
Melt the butter in a small bowl for
30 seconds on HIGH. Add the
mushrooms. Cover loosely and cook
for 1 minute on HIGH to soften
slightly. Stir in the flour, milk and
Worcestershire sauce. Remove the
bay leaf from the fish and add the
fish cooking liquid to the sauce
ingredients. Cook, uncovered, for 2-3
minutes on HIGH, stirring often
until thickened. Add salt, pepper and
parsley. Pour over the cod to serve.

Sole Aurora

PREPARATION TIME: 15 minutes

MICROWAVE COOKING TIME:
6-7 minutes

SERVES: 4 people

900g/2lbs sole fillets
140ml/¼ pint/½ cup white wine
1 bay leaf

SAUCE
30g/1oz/2 tbsps butter or margarine
30g/1oz/2 tbsps flour/plain flour
280ml/½ pint/1 cup milk
Rind and juice of 1 orange
15ml/1 tbsp tomato purée/paste
Salt and pepper

GARNISH
4 tomatoes, peeled, seeded and cut into
   thin strips

Cook the fish with the wine and the
bay leaf for 3 minutes on HIGH in a
loosely covered casserole. Melt the
butter in a small, deep bowl for
30 seconds on HIGH. Add the flour,
milk, tomato paste, fish cooking

**Facing page: Monkfish and
Ribbons.**

liquid, salt and pepper. Cook for 2-3 minutes on HIGH, stirring frequently until thickened. Add the rind and juice of the orange and cook for 30 seconds more on HIGH. Pour the sauce over the fish and top with the tomato strips.

Sea Bass and Fennel

PREPARATION TIME: 15 minutes

MICROWAVE COOKING TIME: 23 minutes

SERVES: 4 people

1 sea bass, weighing 900g-1kg/2-2¼ lbs, cleaned and trimmed

2 bulbs Florentine fennel
4 oranges
Juice of 1 lemon
1 tbsp anise liqueur
430ml/¾ pint/1½ cups whole-milk yogurt
Salt
Coarsely ground pepper

GARNISH
Samphire
Orange slices

Squeeze the juice from one of the oranges and slice the others. Sprinkle the inside of the bass with salt and put it into a large, shallow casserole. Pour over the orange juice and lemon

This page: Sole Aurora (left) and Cod Steaks with Mushrooms (right). Facing page: Sea Bass and Fennel.

juice, cover and cook for 20 minutes on HIGH. Carefully lift out the fish and keep it warm. Cook the fennel in 30ml/2 tbsps water for 2 minutes on HIGH and set aside. Stir the liqueur, pepper and yogurt into the fish cooking liquid and heat through for 30 seconds on HIGH. Do not let the sauce boil. Peel the skin from the fish if desired and pour over the sauce. Garnish with the samphire and orange slices to serve. Prepare with other varieties of large whole fish if desired.

Microwave
MEAT & POULTRY

Microwave
MEAT & POULTRY

When you cook in a microwave oven you get far more for your meat money. Microwave roasting means less shrinkage and, contrary to popular belief, meat *will* brown. Leave a thin layer of fat on the roast/joint, or rub butter into a chicken or turkey and the high heat of the microwave oven will turn the fat golden brown. Alternatively, there are many marinades, pastes and coatings to give appetizing color to meat, poultry and game.

Because liquids evaporate much more slowly in a microwave oven, there will be more meat juices left to make good sauces and gravies. If you want, use a browning dish to brown the flour for gravies. Red wine, soy sauce, gravy browning and spices also give good color to brown sauces.

In general, stews and braises should be cooked on MEDIUM, regardless of what variety of meat is used. The highest setting in a microwave oven will toughen the cuts of meat used in stews and braises. When cooking small cuts of meat such as chops or steaks in a sauce, a medium setting is also recommended for a tender result. Stir-frying and pan-frying are both possible with a browning dish and the highest setting. Offal/variety meats cook very quickly, so a high setting suits them as well.

When roasting poultry and game birds, cover the legs and wings with foil to prevent them from drying out. Uncover for a portion of the cooking time and the whole bird will be evenly cooked. Depending on your oven, you may find that all roast meats need to be covered with foil on both ends for part of their cooking time. This is especially important for roasts/joints that are uneven in thickness.

Microwave roasts must be left to stand after cooking just like any roast meat. The standing time helps to finish off the cooking, so microwaved roast meat, poultry and game are usually covered for 5-15 minutes before carving.

Special microwave meat thermometers take the guesswork out of roasting, but times will vary from oven to oven. The following chart will serve as a quick reference, but is meant only as a guideline.

Time and Setting per 450g/1lb		
	HIGH	**MEDIUM**
Beef		
Rare	6-7 minutes	11-13 minutes
Medium	7-8 minutes	13-15 minutes
Well done	8-9 minutes	15-17 minutes
Chicken (whole)	6-8 minutes	9-11 minutes
Duck (whole)	6-8 minutes	9-11 minutes
Leg of Lamb	8-10 minutes	11-13 minutes
Pork	9-11 minutes	13-15 minutes
Veal	8-9 minutes	11-12 minutes
Steaks (7.5cm/1½" thick)		
Rare	9 minutes	
Medium rare	10 minutes	
Medium	12 minutes	
Well done	14 minutes	

There is also a method of roasting, Hazelnut Lamb is an example, which cuts down on the cooking time and depends on a longer standing time to finish cooking to the desired doneness. Also, meats and poultry can be roasted for part of their cooking time on HIGH and part on MEDIUM.

All the recipes were tested in both a conventional 700 watt microwave oven and a Combination microwave-convection oven with a maximum setting of 600 watts. The Combination oven does a superb job of roasting. It is nearly as fast as the conventional microwave oven, yet browns and crisps like a regular convection oven. These new ovens have a variety of settings, so it is best carefully to follow the instruction booklet that each manufacturer provides. Either way, the time saving is impressive, and the result delicious when a microwave oven is used on meat, poultry and game.

LAMB DISHES

Lamb Shanks with Leeks and Rosemary

PREPARATION TIME: 15 minutes

MICROWAVE COOKING TIME: 45 minutes

SERVES: 4 people

30ml/2 tbsps vegetable oil
900g-1kg/2-2¼ lbs lamb shanks
1 clove garlic, roughly chopped
2 sprigs fresh rosemary
280ml/½ pint/1 cup red wine
280ml/½ pint/1 cup beef stock
15g/1 tbsp butter
15g/1 tbsp flour
2-4 leeks, washed and thinly sliced
Salt and pepper

Heat the oil in a browning dish for 5 minutes on HIGH. Put in the lamb shanks and cook for 5 minutes on HIGH. Turn the lamb over and cook for further 5 minutes on HIGH. Add the garlic, rosemary, salt and pepper, wine and stock. Cover and cook on MEDIUM for 25 minutes. Melt the butter in a small bowl for 30 seconds on HIGH. Stir in the flour. Pour on the cooking juices from the lamb and stir well. Pour the sauce over the lamb and scatter over the sliced leeks. Cook a further 5 minutes on HIGH, until the leeks soften and the sauce has thickened. Remove the rosemary before serving.

Spiced Lamb Chops with Peaches

PREPARATION TIME: 15 minutes

MICROWAVE COOKING TIME: 20 minutes

SERVES: 4 people

4 lamb chops, fat slightly trimmed
30g/1oz/2 tbsps butter or margarine
15ml/1 tbsp ground allspice
15ml/1 tbsp ground ginger
15ml/1 tbsp brown sugar
Salt and pepper
225g/8oz sliced peaches, juice reserved
45ml/3 tbsps soy sauce
45ml/3 tbsps brown sugar
30ml/2 tbsps cider vinegar
5ml/1 tsp cornstarch/cornflour
10ml/2 tsps water

This page: Spiced Lamb Chops with Peaches (top) and Lamb Shanks with Leeks and Rosemary (bottom). Facing page: Orange Glazed Lamb with Haricot Beans.

Heat a browning dish for 5 minutes on HIGH. Drop in the butter and heat 30 seconds on HIGH. Mix 15ml/1 tbsp brown sugar with the spices, salt and pepper and rub into both sides of the chops. Fry the chops in the butter on HIGH for

2 minutes each side. Mix the peach juice with the soy sauce, remaining brown sugar, vinegar and additional salt and pepper. Pour over the chops and cover loosely. Lower the setting to MEDIUM and cook 10 minutes, turning the chops once and stirring the liquid frequently. Remove the chops and set aside to keep warm. Mix the cornstarch/cornflour with the water and stir into the hot liquid. Cook on HIGH for 1 minute, stirring frequently until the sauce is clear. Add the peaches to heat through for 30 seconds on HIGH and serve with the chops.

Lamb in Sour Cream Dill Sauce

PREPARATION TIME: 15 minutes

MICROWAVE COOKING TIME:
31 minutes

SERVES: 4 people

900g/2lbs leg of lamb, cut into 2.5cm/
  1 inch cubes
1 onion, sliced
1 bay leaf
15ml/1 tbsp dried dill or dill seed
430ml/¾ pint/1½ cups light stock
140ml/4 fl oz/½ cup white wine
45g/1½ oz/3 tbsps butter or margarine
45g/1½ oz/3 tbsps flour
30g/2 tbsps chopped fresh dill or 15g/
  1 tbsp dried dill
140ml/¼ pint/½ cup sour cream
Salt and pepper

Make sure all the fat is trimmed from the lamb. Put the lamb cubes, onion, bay leaf, dried dill or dill seed, salt, pepper, stock and wine into a casserole. Cover and cook on MEDIUM for 25 minutes. Set aside to keep warm. Melt the butter 30 seconds on HIGH. Stir in the flour and strain on the stock from the lamb. Stir well and cook for 5 minutes on HIGH, stirring frequently, until thickened. Add the dill, adjust the seasoning and stir in the sour cream. Pour over the lamb and heat through 1 minute on HIGH, without boiling. Serve with rice or pasta.

Orange Glazed Lamb with Haricot Beans

PREPARATION TIME: 15 minutes

MICROWAVE COOKING TIME:
24 minutes

SERVES: 4 people

2 racks/best-end necks of lamb

GLAZE
60g/2oz/¼ cup dark brown sugar
60ml/2 fl oz/¼ cup red wine
15ml/1 tbsp red wine vinegar
Juice and rind of 1 orange

ACCOMPANIMENT
450g/1lb canned haricot/navy beans or
  flageolets, drained
4 green/spring onions, chopped
60ml/2 fl oz/¼ cup dry white wine
Pinch thyme
Salt and pepper

Trim some of the fat from the lamb and score the remaining fat. Mix the glaze ingredients together and brush over the lamb. Put the lamb on a roasting rack. The bone ends may be covered with foil to protect them during the cooking. Cook on MEDIUM for 10 minutes. Raise the setting to HIGH and cook for 5 minutes, basting often during the whole of the cooking time. Leave to stand 5 minutes before carving. Cook for 20 minutes on the Combination setting of a microwave convection oven until the fat has browned. Mix the beans, wine, onions, thyme, salt and pepper together and cook 4 minutes on HIGH. Reheat any remaining glaze and pour over the lamb. Serve with the beans.

Peppercorn Lamb

PREPARATION TIME: 13 minutes

MICROWAVE COOKING TIME:
21-22 minutes

SERVES: 4 people

675g/1½ lbs lamb fillet or meat from the
  leg cut into 5mm/¼ inch slices
60g/2oz/4 tbsps butter or margarine

2 shallots, finely chopped
1 clove garlic, finely minced
45g/1½ oz/3 tbsps flour
5ml/1 tsp ground allspice
280ml/½ pint/1 cup beef stock
15ml/1 tbsp canned green peppercorns,
  rinsed and drained
2 caps pimento cut into thin strips
5ml/1 tsp tomato paste/purée
60ml/2 fl oz/¼ cup heavy/double cream
Salt and pepper

Heat a browning dish for 5 minutes on HIGH. Melt the butter for 1 minute on HIGH and add the slices of lamb. Cook for 2 minutes on HIGH, in 2 or 3 batches. Remove the meat and set aside. Cook the shallots and flour to brown slightly. Add the garlic, allspice, stock and tomato paste/purée. Season with salt and pepper and cook 2-3 minutes on HIGH, until starting to thicken. Add the lamb, cover and cook 10 minutes on MEDIUM, or until the lamb is tender. Add the peppercorns, pimento and cream and cook for 2 minutes on HIGH. Serve with rice.

Leg of Lamb with Aromatic Spices

PREPARATION TIME: 15 minutes

MICROWAVE COOKING TIME:
31 minutes, plus
5-15 minutes standing time

SERVES: 6-8 people

1.5kg/3lbs leg of lamb, fat completely
  trimmed off
140ml/¼ pint/½ cup stock

MARINADE
280ml/½ pint/1 cup plain yogurt
1 small piece fresh ginger root, grated
5ml/1 tsp crushed coriander seeds
1.25ml/¼ tsp cloves
5ml/1 tsp curry powder
5ml/1 tsp cumin
1.25ml/¼ tsp cardamom seeds, removed
  from the pods
1 clove garlic, minced
Salt and pepper

Facing page: Lamb in Sour Cream Dill Sauce (top) and Peppercorn Lamb (bottom).

SAUCE
Remaining marinade and stock
15ml/1 tbsp chopped fresh coriander
140ml/¼ pint/½ cup plain yogurt

Blend all the marinade ingredients together. In the lamb, make incisions with a sharp knife about 5cm/ 2 inches apart. Place the lamb in a shallow casserole. Push some of the marinade into each cut and spread the remaining marinade over the surface of the lamb. Cover and leave overnight in the refrigerator. Pour the stock into the casserole around the lamb. Cover the casserole loosely and cook on HIGH for 12 minutes, basting frequently. Turn the lamb over and cook a further 15 minutes, basting frequently. Leave the lamb to stand for 5 minutes in a covered dish if serving rare. For well-done or medium lamb leave it to stand for 15-20 minutes. Meanwhile heat the remaining marinade and stock for 3 minutes on MEDIUM. Stir in the yogurt and coriander leaves. Add more salt and pepper if necessary and heat through 1 minute on HIGH. Do not allow the sauce to boil. Serve with the carved lamb.

Hazelnut Lamb

PREPARATION TIME: 15 minutes
MICROWAVE COOKING TIME: 25-30 minutes, plus 5-15 minutes standing time
SERVES: 6-8 people

2kg/4½ lbs leg of lamb
1 clove garlic, finely minced
120g/4oz/1 cup dry breadcrumbs
120g/4oz/1 cup ground, roasted hazelnuts
30ml/2 tbsps chopped parsley
60g/2oz/¼ cup butter
Salt and pepper

Trim the fat off the lamb. Mix together the remaining ingredients except the breadcrumbs. Spread the hazelnut paste over the surface of the lamb and press over the crumbs. Cook 25-30 minutes on MEDIUM. Increase the setting to HIGH for 2 minutes. Cook 40 minutes on a Combination setting of a microwave

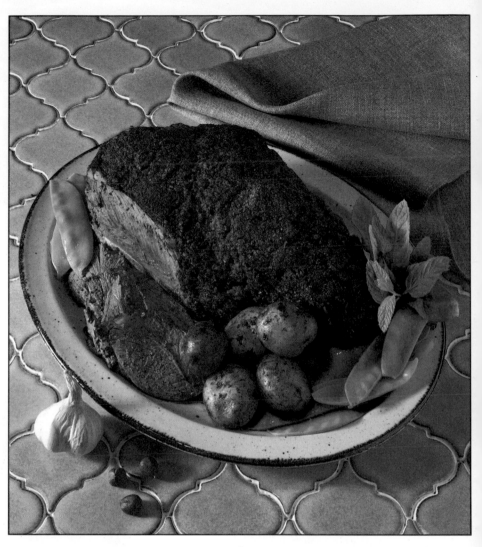

convection oven. Leave the lamb to stand, loosely covered, 5 minutes before carving for rare. Leave 10-15 minutes if medium to well-done lamb is desired. Serve with minted new potatoes and peapods/mangetout.

Moroccan Lamb

PREPARATION TIME: 20 minutes
MICROWAVE COOKING TIME: 35 minutes
SERVES: 4 people

790g/1¾ lbs lamb fillet or meat from the leg cut in 2.5cm/1 inch cubes
1 clove garlic, minced
10ml/2 tsps ground cinnamon
1.25ml/¼ tsp ground cloves
1.25ml/¼ tsp ground cumin
10ml/2 tsps paprika

This page: Hazelnut Lamb. Facing page: Leg of Lamb with Aromatic Spices.

1 large red pepper
570ml/1 pint/2 cups light beef stock
340g/¾ lb okra, trimmed
120g/¼ lb/1 cup whole blanched almonds
60g/2oz/¼ cup currants
15ml/1 tbsp honey
15ml/1 tbsp lemon juice
Salt and pepper

Combine the lamb, garlic, spices, red pepper, salt and pepper in a large casserole. Add the stock, cover the dish and cook on MEDIUM for 25 minutes. Add the okra, currants and almonds. Cook a further 5 minutes on MEDIUM. Remove the

meat and vegetables and almonds to a serving dish. Add the honey and lemon juice to the sauce and cook on HIGH for 5 minutes to reduce it slightly. Pour over the lamb and serve with rice.

Lamb Hot-Pot

PREPARATION TIME: 15 minutes

MICROWAVE COOKING TIME:
30 minutes

SERVES: 4 people

2 large onions, peeled and thinly sliced
30ml/2 tbsps oil
450g/1lb ground/minced lamb
30ml/2 tbsps chopped parsley
Pinch thyme
225g/8oz whole mushrooms
225g/8oz/1 cup canned tomatoes
30ml/2 tbsps Worcestershire sauce
3 potatoes, peeled and thinly sliced
1 red pepper, cut in rings
1 green pepper, cut in rings
Salt and pepper

**This page: Navarin of Lamb.
Facing page: Moroccan Lamb
(top) and Lamb Hot-Pot (bottom).**

GARNISH
Fresh bay leaves

In a large casserole, heat the oil for 30 seconds on HIGH. Put in the onions and cover the casserole loosely. Cook 5 minutes on HIGH to soften the onions. Add the lamb and thyme and cook 10 minutes on MEDIUM, mashing the lamb with a fork to break it up while it cooks. Add the mushrooms, tomatoes, parsley, salt and pepper and Worcestershire sauce. Arrange the slices of potato neatly on top of the lamb mixture and sprinkle with more salt and pepper. Cover the casserole and cook on MEDIUM for 15 minutes or until the potatoes are tender. Cook on a Combination

setting of a microwave convection oven for 15 minutes or until potatoes are cooked and slightly browned. Three minutes before the end of cooking time, arrange the pepper rings overlapping on top of the potatoes. Garnish with fresh bay leaves to serve.

Navarin of Lamb

PREPARATION TIME: 20 minutes

MICROWAVE COOKING TIME:
40 minutes

SERVES: 4 people

4 lamb chops
30ml/2 tbsps oil
30g/2 tbsps flour/plain flour
2 cloves garlic, finely minced
15ml/1 tbsp tomato paste/purée
280ml/½ pint/1 cup white wine
570ml/1 pint/2 cups stock
2 sprigs fresh rosemary or 15ml/1 tbsp
  dried
1 sprig fresh thyme or 5ml/1 tsp dried
Salt and pepper

GARNISH
2 carrots, cut lengthwise in quarters
120g/4oz green/French beans, trimmed
  and cut in 5cm/2 inch pieces
8 small new potatoes, scrubbed but not
  peeled
2 sticks celery, cut in 5cm/2 inch strips
12 small mushrooms, left whole
4 small turnips, peeled

Heat a browning dish 5 minutes on HIGH. Pour in the oil and put in the lamb chops. Cook 1 minute on HIGH. Turn the chops over and cook 2 minutes on HIGH on the other side. Remove the chops and stir in the flour, tomato purée/paste, wine, stock and garlic. Cook for 2 minutes on HIGH, stirring twice. Season with salt and pepper and return the chops to the dish or transfer the whole to a casserole. Cover and cook on MEDIUM for 15 minutes. Add the vegetables, except the beans and mushrooms, and cook 15 minutes further on MEDIUM. Add remaining vegetables 5 minutes before the end of cooking. Remove the herbs, if using fresh, and the bay leaf before serving.

PORK AND HAM

Glazed Ham and Spiced Peaches

PREPARATION TIME: 20 minutes

MICROWAVE COOKING TIME:
57 minutes, plus
5 minutes standing time

SERVES: 6-8 people

1.5kg/3lb ham/gammon, boneless and
　pre-cooked

GLAZE
30ml/2 tbsps Dijon mustard
120g/4oz/½ cup dark brown sugar
120g/4oz/1 cup dry breadcrumbs
Pinch powdered cloves
Pinch ginger

PEACHES
6 fresh peaches or 12 canned peach halves
120g/4oz/½ cup light brown sugar
5ml/1 tsp each ground cinnamon, cloves
　and allspice
140ml/¼ pint/½ cup water or canned
　peach juice
30ml/2 tbsps cider vinegar
12 walnut halves

If using fresh peaches, put them into
a large bowl and cover with boiling
water. Heat on HIGH for 3 minutes
or until the water boils. Peel the
peaches, cut in half and remove the
stones. Mix the remaining ingredients
for the peaches together and heat
2 minutes on HIGH, stirring
frequently until the sugar dissolves.
Add the peaches and cook 2 minutes
on MEDIUM. Remove the peaches
and cook the syrup a further
5 minutes on HIGH. Pour the syrup
over the peaches and set them aside.
Cover the ham with plastic wrap/
cling film, or put into a roasting bag.

This page: Pork à l'Orange. Facing
page: Glazed Ham and Spiced
Peaches.

Cook on MEDIUM for 15 minutes
per lb or ½ kg. Pour the glaze over
during the last 10 minutes of cooking.
Put a walnut half in the hollow of
each peach. Let the ham stand
5 minutes before slicing. Serve either
hot or cold with the peaches.

Pork à l'Orange

PREPARATION TIME: 15 minutes

MICROWAVE COOKING TIME:
24-25 minutes

SERVES: 4 people

30g/2 tbsps butter or margarine
675g/1½ lbs pork tenderloin/fillet cut in
　1.25cm/½ inch slices
3 carrots, cut in 1.25cm/½ inch diagonal
　slices
3 small or 2 large leeks, washed and
　trimmed and cut in 1.25cm/½ inch
　diagonal slices
60g/2oz/¼ cup dried currants

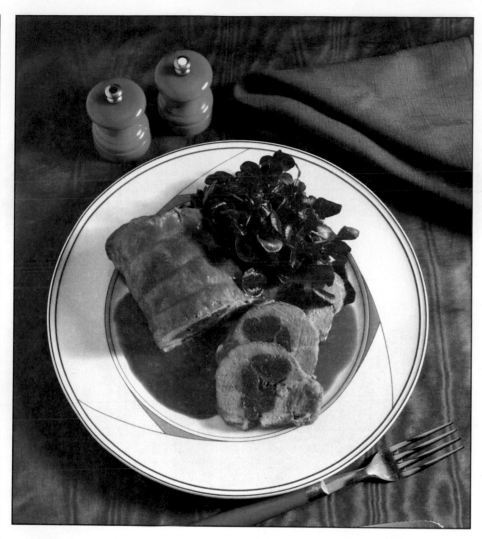

1.25ml/¼ tsp ground ginger
1 bay leaf
280ml/1½ pints/1 cup orange juice
60ml/2 fl oz/¼ cup orange liqueur
10ml/2 tsps cornstarch/cornflour
Salt and pepper

Heat a browning dish 5 minutes on HIGH. Drop in the butter and add the pork slices. Cook 2 minutes each side on HIGH. Cook the meat in 2 or 3 batches. Add the leeks, carrots, bay leaf, ginger, salt and pepper. Pour over the orange juice and cover the dish loosely. Cook 15 minutes on MEDIUM or until the pork and vegetables are tender. Add the currants during the last 3 minutes of cooking. Remove the pork and vegetables and keep them warm. Mix the liqueur and cornstarch/cornflour together and stir into the sauce. Cook, uncovered, 2 to 3

This page: Ginger Apricot Stuffed Pork. Facing page: Pork Creole (top) and Sausages, Apples and Cheese (bottom).

minutes on HIGH, stirring frequently until the sauce thickens and looks clear. Return the meat and vegetables to the sauce and stir carefully. Serve with rice.

Pork Creole

PREPARATION TIME: 15 minutes

MICROWAVE COOKING TIME:
13 minutes

SERVES: 4 people

15ml/1 tbsp butter
750g/1½ lbs lean pork shoulder or
   tenderloin/fillet cut into strips

1 clove garlic, finely minced
1 large onion, sliced
1 large green pepper, sliced
120g/4oz mushrooms, sliced
15ml/1 tbsp tomato paste/purée
30ml/2 tbsps molasses/treacle
225g/8oz canned tomatoes
1 bay leaf
Pinch Cayenne pepper
Salt and pepper

Melt the butter in a casserole for 30 seconds on HIGH and put in the pork pieces, garlic, onions and mushrooms. Cook 5 minutes on MEDIUM. Add the remaining ingredients and cook a further 5 minutes on MEDIUM, loosely covered. If the pork is not tender after 10 minutes, cook an additional 3 minutes on MEDIUM. Remove the bay leaf before serving.

Ginger Apricot Stuffed Pork

PREPARATION TIME: 15 minutes

MICROWAVE COOKING TIME:
33-34 minutes, plus
5 minutes standing time

SERVES: 6-8 people

1.5kg/3lbs loin of pork, boned
570ml/1 pint/2 cups light stock
1 bay leaf
1 carrot, sliced

STUFFING
120g/4oz/¾lb dried apricots
30ml/2 tbsps green ginger wine
30ml/2 tbsps lemon juice
60ml/2 fl oz/¼ cup water
1 spring/green onion, finely chopped
Salt and pepper

SAUCE
280ml/½ pint/1 cup strained reserved
   stock from the pork
Apricot soaking liquid
30g/1oz/2 tbsps butter or margarine
30g/1oz/2 tbsps flour
Dash soy sauce

Mix the stuffing ingredients, except the onion, together in a bowl. Cover well and cook 1 minute on HIGH, then leave to stand to soften the

apricots. Trim most of the fat from the pork. Turn the meat over and sprinkle the surface with pepper. Drain the apricots and reserve the juice. Spread the apricots evenly over the pork and sprinkle on the onion. Roll up the pork starting on the thickest side. Tie at even intervals with string. Place in a deep casserole with the bay leaf, stock and carrot. Cover well and cook 30 minutes on MEDIUM or until the pork is tender and no longer pink. Strain the stock and reserve it. Cover the pork and leave to stand 5 minutes before slicing. Melt the butter in a deep bowl for 30 seconds on HIGH. Stir in the flour and 280ml/½ pint/1 cup stock and the reserved apricot juice. Cook 2 to 3 minutes on HIGH to thicken. Add salt and pepper to taste and serve with the pork.

Speedy Ham Casserole

PREPARATION TIME: 10 minutes
MICROWAVE COOKING TIME: 6 minutes
SERVES: 4 people

225g/8oz cooked ham, cut in 1.25cm/ ½ inch strips
1 can concentrated cream of mushroom soup
1 can water chestnuts, drained and sliced
2 sticks celery, finely chopped
225g/8oz frozen, sliced green/French beans
30ml/1 fl oz/2 tbsps dry sherry
280ml/½ pint/1 cup light/single cream
Pinch thyme
Salt and pepper

TOPPING
1 can French-fried onions
or
60g/2oz/¼ cup seasoned breadcrumbs mixed with 5ml/1 tsp paprika

Mix all the ingredients, except the topping ingredients, together in a serving casserole. Cook 5 minutes on HIGH, stirring occasionally, or until the beans have cooked. Sprinkle on the topping and cook a further 1 minute on HIGH.

Sweet and Sour Ham

PREPARATION TIME: 20 minutes
MICROWAVE COOKING TIME: 2-3 minutes
SERVES: 4 people

450g/1lb cooked ham, cut into 1.25cm/ ½ inch cubes

SAUCE
60g/2oz/¼ cup brown sugar
60ml/2 fl oz/¼ cup rice vinegar
30ml/2 tbsps tomato ketchup
30ml/2 tbsps soy sauce
225g/8oz/1 can pineapple chunks/ pieces, drained and juice reserved
30g/1oz/2 tbsps cornstarch/cornflour
1 green pepper, sliced
2 green/spring onions, sliced diagonally
60g/2oz/½ cup blanched, whole almonds
3 tomatoes, quartered
Salt and pepper

Combine the sugar, vinegar, ketchup, soy sauce, cornstarch/cornflour and reserved pineapple juice and chunks. Add pepper, almonds, salt, pepper and ham. Cook 2-3 minutes on HIGH until the sauce clears and thickens. Add the tomatoes and green/spring onions and heat 30 seconds on HIGH. Serve with rice or crisp noodles.

Sausages, Apples and Cheese

PREPARATION TIME: 15 minutes
MICROWAVE COOKING TIME: 10-12 minutes
SERVES: 4 people

1 ring smoked sausage
4 medium cooking apples, cored and thinly sliced
30ml/2 tbsp brown sugar
30ml/2 tbsp flour
1 shallot, finely chopped
15ml/1 tbsp chopped sage
120g/4oz/1 cup shredded Cheddar cheese
Pinch salt and pepper

Toss the apples, brown sugar, flour,

sage and onion together. Slice the sausage in 1.25cm/½ inch diagonal slices and arrange on top of the apples. Cover loosely and cook on HIGH 5 to 7 minutes or until the apples are tender. Sprinkle over the cheese and cook 5 minutes on Medium to melt. Serve immediately.

Ham Loaf with Mustard Chive Sauce

PREPARATION TIME: 15 minutes
MICROWAVE COOKING TIME: 27-28 minutes, plus 5 minutes standing time
SERVES: 4 people

340g/12oz/¾ lb ground/minced, cooked ham
340g/12oz/¾ lb ground/minced pork
60g/2oz/½ cup dry breadcrumbs
140ml/¼ pint/½ cup milk
2 shallots, finely chopped
1 clove garlic, crushed
Salt and pepper

SAUCE
45g/1½ oz/3 tbsps butter or margarine
45g/1½ oz/3 tbsps flour/plain flour
30ml/2 tbsps Dijon mustard
280ml/½ pint/1 cup milk
140ml/¼ pint/½ cup light stock
30ml/2 tbsps chopped chives
Salt and pepper

Combine all the ingredients for the ham loaf and press into a glass loaf dish. Cook on HIGH for 5 minutes. Reduce setting to MEDIUM, cover with plastic wrap/cling film and cook 20-25 minutes, or until firm. Turn the dish after 10 minutes. Leave in the dish for 5 minutes before turning out to slice. Melt the butter for the sauce 30 seconds on HIGH. Stir in the flour and remaining ingredients, except for the chives. Cook 2-3 minutes on HIGH, stirring often until thick. Add the chives and serve with the ham loaf.

Facing page: Speedy Ham Casserole (top) and Sweet and Sour Ham (bottom).

Cranberry-Orange Ham Slices

PREPARATION TIME: 10 minutes

MICROWAVE COOKING TIME:
7-9 minutes

SERVES: 4 people

4 ham steaks
15g/1 tbsp butter or margarine

SAUCE
Juice and rind of 1 orange
225g/8oz whole cranberry sauce
60ml/2 fl oz/¼ cup red wine
5ml/1 tsp cornstarch/cornflour
1 bay leaf
Pinch salt and pepper

GARNISH
1 orange, sliced

Heat a browning dish 5 minutes on HIGH. Put in the butter and brown the ham 2 minutes on the first side and 1 minute on the other. Combine sauce ingredients in a small, deep bowl. Cook 1-2 minutes on HIGH, until the cornstarch/cornflour clears. Remove the bay leaf and pour over the ham to serve. Garnish with the orange slices.

Polynesian Ham Steaks

PREPARATION TIME: 20 minutes

MICROWAVE COOKING TIME:
9-10 minutes

SERVES: 4 people

4 ham steaks
15ml/1 tbsp oil
1 small fresh pineapple, sliced
1 papaya, sliced
2 bananas, peeled and sliced
1 fresh coconut, grated
280ml/½ pint/1 cup orange juice
Juice and grated rind of 1 lime
10ml/2 tsps cornstarch/cornflour
30ml/2 tbsps brown sugar

Heat a browning dish 5 minutes on HIGH. Add the oil to the dish and lay in the ham steaks. Cook 2 minutes on the first side and 1 minute on the other. Set the ham

aside. Combine the orange juice, lime juice and rind, cornstarch/cornflour and sugar in a large bowl. Cook 1-2 minutes on HIGH, stirring frequently until thickened. Add the fruit and coconut and heat through 1 minute on HIGH. Pour over the ham steaks to serve.

Swedish Meatballs

PREPARATION TIME: 15 minutes

MICROWAVE COOKING TIME:
13-15 minutes

SERVES: 4 people

This page: Cranberry-Orange Ham Slices (top) and Polynesian Ham Steaks (bottom). Facing page: Ham Loaf with Mustard Chive Sauce.

MEATBALLS
225g/8oz ground/minced pork
225g/8oz ground/minced beef
225g/8oz ground/minced veal
2 shallots, finely chopped
60g/2oz/¼ cup dry breadcrumbs
Pinch ground cloves, nutmeg and allspice
60ml/2 fl oz/¼ cup milk
1 egg, beaten
Salt and pepper

SAUCE
30g/1oz/2 tbsps flour/plain flour
280ml/½ pint/1 cup milk
140ml/¼ pint/½ cup light/single cream
10ml/2 tsps fresh dill or 5ml/1 tsp dried dill
15ml/1 tsp lemon juice
5ml/1 tsp grated lemon rind
Salt and pepper

Combine all the meatball ingredients in a large bowl and mix very well. Shape into 2.5cm/1 inch balls and arrange in a large baking dish. Cook, uncovered, for 10 to 12 minutes on HIGH, or until firm and no longer pink. Rearrange the meatballs twice during cooking, bringing the ones from the edges of the dish to the middle. When the meatballs are cooked remove them to a serving dish to keep warm. Stir in the flour and add the milk, cream, dill and salt and pepper. Cook, stirring frequently, 3 to 5 minutes on HIGH. Add the lemon juice and rind and pour over the meatballs to serve.

Pork with Prunes and Apples

PREPARATION TIME: 15 minutes and 1 hour soaking time for prunes

MICROWAVE COOKING TIME: 26 minutes

SERVES: 4 people

4 pork chops
120g/4oz/½ cup prunes, stones removed
580ml/1 pint/2 cups tea
2 apples, peeled and sliced
5ml/1 tsp lemon juice
Pinch mace
Pinch thyme
30g/1oz/2 tbsps butter
30g/1oz/2 tbsps flour/plain flour
140ml/¼ pint/½ cup heavy/double cream

GARNISH
Parsley sprigs

Boil 580ml/1 pint/2 cups water in a covered bowl for 8 minutes on HIGH. Put in 2 tea bags and the prunes. Leave to soak 1 hour. Heat a browning dish 5 minutes on HIGH.

Melt the butter and brown the pork for 2 minutes on each side. Remove the chops and set aside. Add the flour to the dish and stir in well. Strain 280ml/½ pint/1 cup of the prune soaking liquid into the dish and add the lemon juice, mace, thyme, salt and pepper. Add the pork and cover the dish loosely. Cook 10 minutes on MEDIUM. Add the apples and prunes during the last 4 minutes of cooking. Stir in the cream and heat 1 minute on HIGH. Serve garnished with parsley sprigs.

Italian Pork Rolls

PREPARATION TIME: 20 minutes

MICROWAVE COOKING TIME: 24 minutes

SERVES: 4 people

4 pork escalopes or pork steaks
30g/1oz/2 tbsps vegetable oil

FILLING
60g/2oz/¼ cup ricotta cheese
60g/2oz salami, roughly chopped
120g/4oz/1 cup fresh breadcrumbs
120g/4oz/1 cup pimento stuffed olives, roughly chopped
60g/2oz/½ cup pistachio nuts
2 shallots, finely chopped
15ml/1 tbsp chopped basil
15ml/1 tbsp chopped parsley
Pinch oregano
Salt and pepper
1 egg, beaten

SALPICON
225g/8oz tomatoes, peeled, seeded and quartered
225g/8oz mushrooms, sliced
1 green pepper, cut in thin strips
1 onion, thinly sliced
60ml/2 fl oz/¼ cup dry white wine or vermouth
15ml/1 tbsp tomato paste/purée
Salt and pepper

Flatten the pork pieces with a meat mallet or rolling pin until very thin. Mix the filling ingredients together and spread evenly over the meat. Roll up, tucking in the sides, and fasten with a wooden pick/cocktail stick. Heat a browning dish for 5 minutes on HIGH. Add the oil and

place in the pork rolls in a circle. Cover loosely and cook on MEDIUM for 10 minutes. Rearrange the rolls twice to cook evenly. Cook a further 3 minutes on MEDIUM if the pork is still pink. Remove to a serving dish to keep warm. Cook the onion and the mushrooms in the meat juices for 3 minutes on HIGH. Add the wine, purée/paste, peppers, allspice, salt and pepper. Cook further 2 minutes on HIGH. Add the tomatoes and cook 1 minute on MEDIUM to heat through. Remove the wooden picks from the pork and serve it with the salpicon.

Pork with Plums and Port

PREPARATION TIME: 15 minutes

MICROWAVE COOKING TIME: 24-25 minutes

SERVES: 4 people

675g/1½ lbs pork tenderloin/fillet cut in 1.5cm/½ inch slices
30g/1oz/2 tbsps butter or margarine
30g/1oz/2 tbsps flour
1 bay leaf
2 whole cloves
280ml/½ pint/1 cup stock
140ml/¼ pint/½ cup port
450g/1lb purple or red plums
Pinch sugar
5ml/1 tsp lemon juice

GARNISH
Chopped parsley

Heat a browning dish 5 minutes on HIGH. Melt the butter and put in the pork slices. Cook 2 minutes each side. Cook in 2 to 3 batches. Remove the pork and stir in the flour. Cook 2 minutes on HIGH, stirring frequently to brown the flour lightly and evenly. Stir in the stock and port and add the cloves, bay leaf, salt and pepper. Replace the meat and cover the dish loosely. Cook 10 minutes on MEDIUM. Cut the plums in half and

Facing page: Swedish Meatballs (top) and Pork with Prunes and Apples (bottom).

remove the stones. Cut in quarters if the plums are large. Add to the meat and cook 5 minutes further on MEDIUM. Taste the sauce and add sugar and/or lemon juice to taste. Remove the bay leaf and cloves. Sprinkle on the chopped parsley before serving.

Smoked Pork with Melon

PREPARATION TIME: 15 minutes

MICROWAVE COOKING TIME: 16 minutes

SERVES: 4 people

1 small, ripe melon
90g/3oz peapods/mangetout
4 smoked pork chops, fat trimmed
15ml/1 tbsp butter or margarine
Grated rind and juice or 1 orange
Salt and pepper
Chopped parsley or coriander

Scoop out the flesh of the melon in balls and set it aside. Spoon out any remaining flesh and blend with the orange juice, salt and pepper in a food processor. Add the orange rind. Trim the peapods/mangetout and cook 1 minute with 15ml/1 tbsp water in a covered bowl. Heat a

This page: Italian Pork Rolls. Facing page: Pork with Plums and Port (top) and Smoked Pork with Melon (bottom).

browning dish for 5 minutes on HIGH. Melt the butter and cook the chops 2 minutes each side on HIGH. Pour over the sauce and cook 5 minutes on MEDIUM. Add the reserved melon balls, peapods/mangetout and parsley or coriander. Heat 1 minute on HIGH before serving.

BEEF, VEAL AND OFFAL

Spinach and Ricotta Stuffed Veal

PREPARATION TIME: 25 minutes

MICROWAVE COOKING TIME:
34-35 minutes

SERVES: 6 people

900g-1.5kg/2-3lbs loin of veal, boned
    and trimmed
1 bay leaf
1 slice onion
280ml/½ pint/1 cup stock or water

STUFFING
450g/1lb fresh spinach, washed well
120g/4oz/½ cup ricotta cheese
1 egg, beaten
30g/2 tbsps pine nuts, roughly chopped
½ clove garlic, minced
5ml/1 tsp chopped basil
Grated nutmeg
Salt and pepper

SAUCE
Pan juices made up to 430ml/¾ pint/
    1½ cups with stock
30g/1oz/2 tbsps flour/plain flour
30g/1oz/2 tbsps butter or margarine
30ml/2 tbsps dry white wine
Salt and pepper

Cook the spinach with 15ml/1 tsp
water for 2 minutes on HIGH, in a
covered bowl. Drain well and chop
roughly. Mix the remaining stuffing
ingredients with the spinach and
spread on one side of the veal. Roll
up from the thicker end of the meat
to the thin end. Tie at even intervals
with string. Place in a casserole with
1 cup water or stock. Cover loosely
and cook for 30 minutes on
MEDIUM. Leave to stand 5 minutes
before carving. Heat the butter

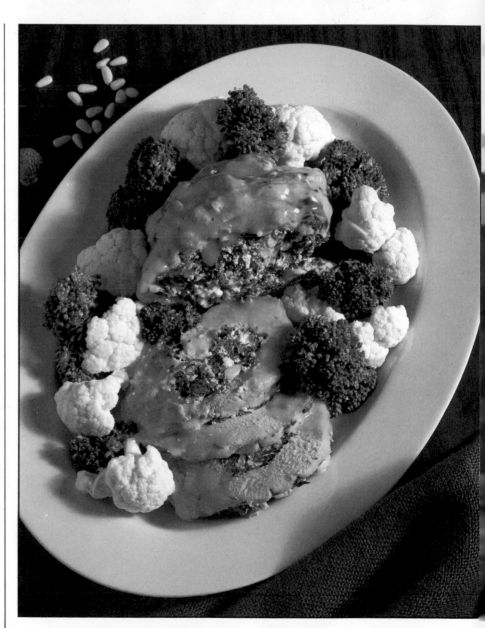

1 minute on HIGH and add the flour,
stock, wine, salt and pepper. Stir to
blend well and cook 2-3 minutes on
HIGH, until thickened. Serve with
the veal and a selection of vegetables.

**This page: Spinach and Ricotta
Stuffed Veal. Facing page: Veal
Involtini (top) and Veal Ragout
(bottom).**

Liver Lyonnaise with Orange

PREPARATION TIME: 20 minutes

MICROWAVE COOKING TIME: 13-18 minutes

SERVES: 4 people

450g/1lb liver, sliced
45g/1½ oz/3 tbsps flour
30g/1oz/2 tbsps butter or margarine
1 onion, sliced
Rind and juice of 1 orange
140ml/¼ pint/½ cup stock
Pinch thyme
Salt and pepper

GARNISH
Orange slices
Chopped parsley

Heat a browning dish 5 minutes on HIGH. Melt the butter in the dish for 1 minute on HIGH. Dredge the liver in the flour and add to the butter in the dish. Cook the liver for 1 minute on HIGH. Turn over and cook 1 minute further on HIGH. Remove from the dish. Cook the onions 1 minute on HIGH. Peel 1 orange and cut the peel into very thin strips. Squeeze the juice and add to the liver along with the remaining ingredients. Cook 10-15 minutes on MEDIUM, until the liver is tender. Turn the slices over frequently during cooking. Serve garnished with the orange slices and chopped parsley.

Veal Involtini

PREPARATION TIME: 20 minutes

MICROWAVE COOKING TIME: 21-22 minutes

SERVES: 4 people

8 veal escalopes/cutlets
8 slices Parma ham
8 slices cheese
10ml/2 tbsps chopped sage
Salt and pepper
30ml/2 tbsps oil

SAUCE
1 400g/14oz can plum tomatoes
1 clove garlic, crushed
1 small onion, finely chopped
30ml/2 tbsps tomato purée
Pinch oregano
Pinch basil
Pinch sugar
1 bay leaf
Salt and pepper

Flatten the veal escalopes. Place on the ham and cheese and sprinkle on the sage, salt and pepper. Roll up, folding in the ends, and secure with wooden picks/cocktail sticks. Heat a browning dish 5 minutes on HIGH. Pour in the oil and heat 1 minute on HIGH. Add the veal rolls and cook 2 minutes, turning several times. Combine all the sauce ingredients in a deep bowl. Cook 3-4 minutes on HIGH. Remove bay leaf and blend in a food processor until smooth. Pour over the veal and cook, covered, on MEDIUM for 10 minutes. Serve with spinach.

Veal Ragout

PREPARATION TIME: 20 minutes

MICROWAVE COOKING TIME: 37-41 minutes, plus 5 minutes standing time

SERVES: 4 people

450g-900g/1½-2lbs veal shoulder or leg cut in 2.5cm/1 inch cubes
2 onions, sliced
225g/8oz mushrooms, quartered
60g/2oz/¼ cup butter or margarine
60g/2oz/¼ cup flour/plain flour
10ml/2 tsps thyme
1 bay leaf
1 clove garlic, minced
570ml/1 pint/2 cups beef stock
30ml/2 tbsps tomato paste/purée
Salt and pepper

ACCOMPANIMENT
225g/8oz/3 cups pasta
120g/4oz/1 cup grated cheese

Heat a browning dish 5 minutes on HIGH. Melt the butter 1 minute on HIGH. Brown the meat in 2 batches

Facing page: Liver Lyonnaise with Orange.

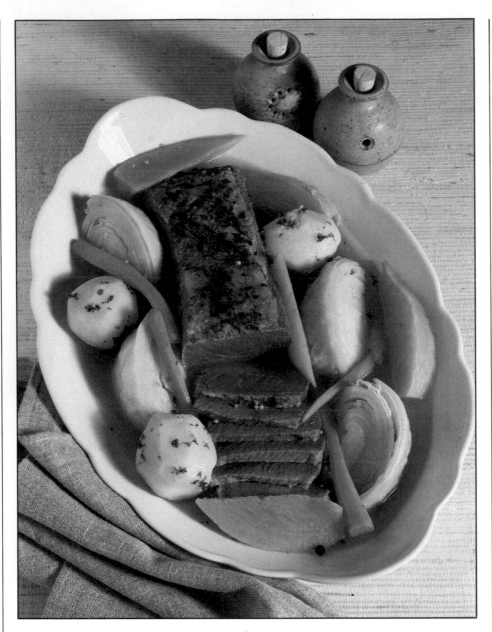

5ml/1 tsp coarsely crushed black peppercorns
10ml/2 tsps mustard seeds
2 crushed bay leaves
10ml/2 tsps dill
5ml/1 tsp crushed allspice berries
430ml/¾ pint/1½ cups water
6 carrots, peeled and quartered lengthwise
2 small rutabaga/swedes, peeled and cut into wedges
6-8 small potatoes, peeled and left whole
1 large head of white cabbage, cut into wedges

Put the corned/salt beef, water, herbs and spices into a large, deep casserole. Cover tightly and cook on HIGH for 8 minutes, or until the water boils. Reduce the setting to MEDIUM and cook 30 minutes, covered. Turn over the meat and add the carrots, potatoes and rutabaga/swedes. Re-cover the dish and cook a further 30-40 minutes on MEDIUM. Add the cabbage 15 minutes before the end of cooking. Leave to stand for 10 minutes before slicing the meat across the grain. Serve with the vegetables and some of the cooking liquid.

Veal Parmesan with Courgettes/Zucchini

PREPARATION TIME: 20 minutes

MICROWAVE COOKING TIME: 17-22 minutes

SERVES: 4 people

4 veal escalopes/cutlets
4 courgettes/zucchini

COATING
30g/1oz/2 tbsps seasoned breadcrumbs
45g/1½ oz/3 tbsps grated Parmesan cheese
1 egg, beaten
Salt and pepper

on HIGH for 3 minutes per batch. Cook the onions and mushrooms for 2 minutes on HIGH. Remove the meat and vegetables, and stir in the flour. Cook the flour for 3 minutes to brown slightly. Add the remaining ingredients and return the meat and the vegetables to the dish, or transfer to a casserole, cover and cook on MEDIUM 15 minutes. Put the pasta in water and partially cover with plastic wrap/cling film. Cook 6-10 minutes on HIGH, stirring occasionally. Leave to stand 5 minutes and drain and rinse in hot water. Remove the bay leaf from the ragout. Arrange the pasta in a serving dish and spoon the ragout into the middle. Sprinkle on grated cheese and heat 1 minute on HIGH to melt the cheese before serving.

New England Boiled Dinner

PREPARATION TIME: 20 minutes

MICROWAVE COOKING TIME: 1 hour 8 minutes to 1 hour 18 minutes

SERVES: 6-8 people

900g-1.5kg/2-3lbs corned/salt beef brisket

This page: New England Boiled Dinner. Facing page: Veal Parmesan with Courgettes/Zucchini.

SAUCE
1 400g/14oz can plum tomatoes
1 clove garlic, crushed
1 small onion, finely chopped
30ml/2 tbsps tomato purée/paste
Pinch oregano
Pinch basil
Pinch sugar
Pinch grated nutmeg
1 bay leaf
Salt and pepper

TOPPING
120g/4oz/1 cup mozzarella cheese
30g/2oz/¼ cup grated Parmesan cheese

Slice the zucchini/courgettes and cook 2 minutes on HIGH, with enough water to cover in a deep bowl. Mix the crumbs, Parmesan cheese, salt and pepper for the coating. Dip the veal in the egg and then in the breadcrumb coating. Put the veal into a shallow dish, cover loosely and cook 8-10 minutes. Do not turn the veal over, but rearrange once during cooking. Combine all the sauce ingredients in a deep bowl. Cook 3-4 minutes on HIGH. Arrange the courgette/zucchini slices in a serving dish, place the veal on top of the courgettes/zucchini and pour over the tomato sauce. Top with the mozzarella and Parmesan cheeses and cook 4-6 minutes on HIGH or Combination setting on a microwave convection oven. Serve immediately.

Beef Enchiladas

PREPARATION TIME: 20 minutes
MICROWAVE COOKING TIME: 12-14 minutes
SERVES: 4 people

225g/8oz package tortillas

SAUCE
1 onion, finely chopped
45ml/3 tbsps tomato purée/paste
1.2kg/1lb 10oz can tomatoes
1-2 small chili peppers, seeded and finely chopped
5ml/1 tsp ground coriander
1 bay leaf
Salt and pepper

FILLING
30ml/2 tbsps oil
225g/8oz minced/ground beef
1 clove garlic, finely minced
10ml/2 tsps ground cumin
1 green pepper, roughly chopped
12 black olives, stoned and chopped
Salt and pepper

GARNISH
1 avocado, sliced
120g/4oz/1 cup grated Cheddar or
    Monterey Jack cheese

If the tortillas are dry, brush them with water, cover in paper towels and heat 2 minutes on HIGH before rolling up. Combine all the sauce

This page: Risotto Stuffed Peppers (top) and Beef Enchiladas (bottom). Facing page: Chicken Livers and Walnut Pasta (top) and Kidney and Bacon Kebabs with Red Pepper Sauce (bottom).

ingredients in a deep bowl, cover the bowl loosely and cook 3 minutes on HIGH. Stir the sauce frequently to break up the tomatoes. If desired, blend the sauce until smooth in a food processor. Heat a browning dish for 3 minutes on HIGH. Pour in the oil and add the meat, breaking it up with a fork. Add the garlic and cumin and cook on HIGH for 3 minutes, breaking up the meat frequently. Add the green pepper and cook a further

minute on HIGH. Add the olives, salt and pepper. Roll up the filling in the tortillas and lay them in a shallow casserole, seam side down. Pour over the sauce and cook, uncovered, 1 minute on HIGH to heat through. Top with the avocado slices and cheese and heat 1 minute further on HIGH to melt the cheese.

Pepper Steak

PREPARATION TIME: 20 minutes

MICROWAVE COOKING TIME: 14 minutes

SERVES: 4 people

1 green pepper, sliced
1 red pepper, sliced
1 yellow pepper, sliced
900g/2lbs rump steak, cut in thin strips
30ml/2 tbsps oil
1 large onion, finely sliced
1 clove garlic
30ml/2 tbsps cornstarch/cornflour
30ml/2 tbsps soy sauce
30ml/2 tbsps dry sherry
430ml/¾ pint/1½ cups beef stock
1 small piece ginger root, grated
Salt and pepper

Heat a browning dish for 5 minutes on HIGH. Pour in the oil and add the strips of steak. Cook 2 minutes on HIGH. Add the onion, garlic and pepper slices. Mix the cornstarch/cornflour and the remaining ingredients and pour over the steak. Cook, uncovered, 7 minutes on HIGH or until the meat is cooked but the vegetables are still crisp. Serve with rice or chow mein noodles.

Filet Mignon with Mustard Peppercorn Hollandaise

PREPARATION TIME: 15 minutes

MICROWAVE COOKING TIME:
Steak 9 minutes rare
      10 minutes medium rare
      12 minutes medium
      14 minutes well done
Sauce 2 minutes

SERVES: 4 people

4 filet mignon/fillet steaks cut 7.5cms/ 1½ inches thick, brushed with oil on both sides

SAUCE
3 egg yolks
5ml/1 tbsp white wine vinegar
120g/4oz/½ cup butter
15ml/1 tbsp Dijon mustard
5ml/1 tsp green peppercorns
5ml/1 tsp chopped parsley
Salt and pepper

Heat a browning dish 5 minutes on HIGH. Cook the steak 2 minutes on one side and 2½ on the other for rare. For medium rare – 2 minutes on one side and 3½ minutes on the other. For medium – 3 minutes on one side and 4½ minutes on the other. For well done – 3 minutes on one side and 6 minutes on the other. Melt the butter 1 minute on HIGH. Mix the egg yolks, vinegar, salt and pepper in a glass measuring cup/jug. Beat in the butter and cook 15 seconds on HIGH and stir. Continue until the sauce thickens, about 2 minutes. Stir in the mustard, parsley and peppercorns. Serve with the steaks.

Kidney and Bacon Kebabs with Red Pepper Sauce

PREPARATION TIME: 20 minutes

MICROWAVE COOKING TIME:
9 minutes, plus
1 minute standing time

SERVES: 4 people

16 kidneys
8 strips bacon/streaky bacon
1 green pepper
60g/2oz/¼ cup butter or margarine

SAUCE
30ml/2 tbsps dry mustard
30ml/2 tbsps Worcestershire sauce
30ml/2 tbsps brown sauce/steak sauce
2 large caps pimento
Salt and pepper

Pierce the kidneys 2 or 3 times. Cut the kidneys in half through the middle and remove the cores with scissors. Wrap the kidneys in bacon and thread onto wooden skewers with the green pepper. Melt the butter for 1 minute on HIGH and brush over the kebabs. Blend the sauce ingredients together with any remaining butter in a food processor until smooth. Cook the sauce 2 minutes on HIGH. Put the kebabs on a roasting rack and cook 5 minutes on HIGH, turning once. Leave to stand 1 minute before serving. Brush with the cooking juices before serving with the sauce. Saffron rice may also be served.

Risotto Stuffed Peppers

PREPARATION TIME: 20 minutes

MICROWAVE COOKING TIME: 20 minutes

SERVES: 4 people

2 large or 4 small red, green or yellow peppers
30ml/2 tbsps oil
1 small onion, chopped
1 clove garlic, minced
120g/4oz/1 cup Italian risotto rice
60g/2oz/½ cup mushrooms
120g/4oz/1 cup roughly chopped salami
60g/2oz/¼ cup chopped black olives
225g/8oz canned tomatoes
1.25ml/¼ tsp basil
1.25ml/¼ tsp oregano
120g/4oz/1 cup mozzarella cheese, grated
Paprika
Salt and pepper

In a large casserole, cook the garlic, onion and mushrooms in the oil for 2 minutes on HIGH. Stir in the tomatoes, rice, herbs, salt and pepper. Cover the dish and cook on HIGH for 5 minutes. Stir in the meat and olives and leave to stand 5 minutes for the rice to continue cooking. If the peppers are small, cut 2.5cm/ 1 inch off the top to form a lid. Remove the core and seeds. If the peppers are large, cut in half lengthwise and remove the core and

Facing page: Filet Mignon with Mustard Peppercorn Hollandaise (top) and Pepper Steak (bottom).

seeds. Fill the peppers and place them in the casserole. Cover with plastic wrap/cling film and cook 8 minutes on HIGH, until the peppers are just tender. Top with the cheese and cook 2 minutes on MEDIUM to melt.

Veal Kidneys in Mustard Sauce

PREPARATION TIME: 20 minutes

MICROWAVE COOKING TIME: 12 minutes

SERVES: 4 people

2 veal kidneys
2 shallots, chopped
45g/1½ oz/3 tbsps butter or margarine
45g/1½ oz/3 tbsps flour
30ml/2 tbsps Dijon mustard
140ml/¼ pint/½ cup stock
140ml/¼ pint/½ cup light/single cream
140ml/¼ pint/½ cup dry white wine
15ml/1 tbsp capers
15ml/1 tbsp chopped chives
Salt and pepper

Remove the core from the kidneys and cut them into small pieces. Heat a browning dish for 5 minutes on HIGH. Melt the butter for 1 minute on HIGH and add the kidneys and the shallots. Cook 2 minutes on HIGH, stirring frequently. Add the flour, wine, stock, salt and pepper and cook a further 3 minutes on HIGH. Add the remaining ingredients and cook 2 minutes on HIGH. Serve immediately.

Sherried Sweetbreads

PREPARATION TIME: 20 minutes

MICROWAVE COOKING TIME: 17 minutes

SERVES: 4 people

450g/1lb lamb or veal sweetbreads, soaked in cold water
140ml/¼ pint/½ cup stock
60ml/4 tbsps/¼ cup dry sherry
120g/4oz mushrooms, sliced
220g/8oz small onions, peeled
60ml/4 tbsps/¼ cup heavy/double cream

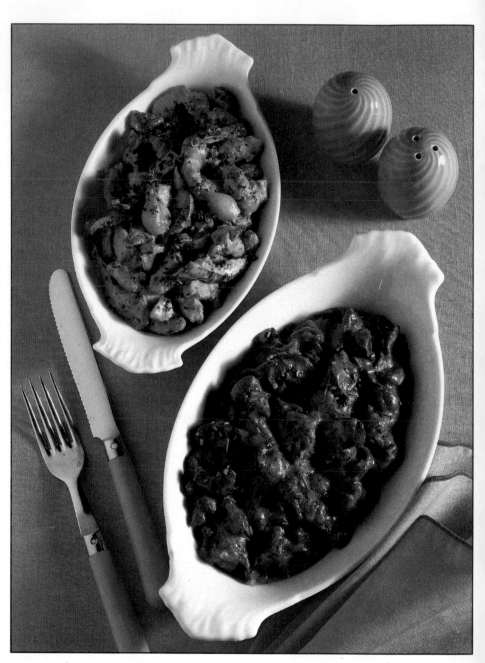

Grated nutmeg
15ml/1 tbsp tomato purée/paste
30ml/2 tbsps chopped parsley
Salt and pepper

Drain the sweetbreads and pierce several times. Cover with fresh water and cook 3 minutes on HIGH. Drain and allow to cool slightly. Peel the outer membrane off the sweetbreads. Cut the sweetbreads in half if they are large. Put the sweetbreads into a casserole with the onions, mushrooms, sherry, stock, salt, pepper and nutmeg. Cook 8 minutes

This page: Sherried Sweetbreads (top) and Veal Kidneys in Mustard Sauce (bottom). Facing page: Roast Beef with Stuffed Courgettes/Zucchini and Tomatoes (bottom).

on HIGH, or until tender. Remove the onions, mushrooms and sweetbreads. Cook the liquid until well reduced, about 5 minutes on HIGH. Add the cream and tomato purée/paste and cook 1 minute on HIGH. Mix all the ingredients together in the sauce. Serve with rice or in puff pastry shells.

Chicken Livers and Walnut Pasta

PREPARATION TIME: 15 minutes

MICROWAVE COOKING TIME: 13 minutes

SERVES: 4 people

450g/1lb chicken livers, trimmed and pierced
60g/2oz/¼ cup butter or margarine
1 clove garlic
120g/4oz/½ cup walnuts, roughly chopped
280ml/½ pint/1 cup stock
4 spring/green onions
30ml/2 tbsps chopped parsley
1 red pepper, chopped
30ml/2 tbsps sherry
Salt and pepper
225g/8oz pasta, cooked

Heat a browning dish for 5 minutes on HIGH. Melt the butter for 1 minute on HIGH and add the liver. Cook for 2 minutes on HIGH and add the garlic, salt and pepper and stock. Cook 3 minutes on HIGH. Remove the livers from the stock and pour the stock into a food processor. Add the walnuts and blend until smooth. Chop the green/spring onions and add to the sauce with the parsley, red peppers, and sherry. Pour over the livers and heat 2 minutes on HIGH. Pour over pasta to serve.

Roast Beef with Stuffed Courgettes/Zucchini and Tomatoes

PREPARATION TIME: 20 minutes

MICROWAVE COOKING TIME:
Beef 14-21 minutes – rare
     16-24 minutes – medium
     18-27 minutes – well done
plus 10 minutes standing time

COMBINATION MICROWAVE CONVECTION TIME:
Beef 10-12 minutes – rare
     11-13 minutes – medium
     12-14 minutes – well done
Vegetables 13 minutes

SERVES: 6-8 people

900g-1.5kg/2-3lbs boneless beef roast/ joint
6-8 tomatoes
6-8 courgettes/zucchini
60ml/4 tbsps chopped parsley
180g/6oz mushrooms, roughly chopped
60ml/4 tbsps chopped chives
60g/2oz/½ cup breadcrumbs
60g/2oz/1 cup grated cheese
Salt and pepper

Put the beef, fat side up, into a large casserole, cover loosely and cook for 14-21 minutes for rare, 16-24 minutes for medium, 18-27 minutes for well done on HIGH. Turn the beef over halfway through the cooking time. When cooked for the chosen amount of time cover with foil and leave to stand for 10 minutes before carving. The beef may also be cooked in a combination microwave and convection oven. Trim the ends of the courgettes/zucchini and cook, in enough water to cover, for 5 minutes on HIGH. Cut in half lengthwise and scoop out the flesh, leaving the shell intact. Chop the flesh roughly and mix with the chives, salt and pepper. Fill the shells and sprinkle on the grated cheese. Cut the tops from the round end of the tomatoes, scoop out the seeds and strain the juice. Mix the mushrooms, tomato juice, parsley, breadcrumbs, salt and pepper. Fill the tomatoes and replace the tops. Cook the courgettes/ zucchini 5 minutes on HIGH and the tomatoes 3 minutes on HIGH, or until the vegetables are tender. Serve with the beef.

Beef Bourguignonne

PREPARATION TIME: 20 minutes

MICROWAVE COOKING TIME:
53 minutes, plus
10 minutes standing time

SERVES: 4 people

2 thick-cut slices bacon cut in 1.25cm/ ½ inch strips
675g-900g/1½lbs-2lbs chuck/braising steak cut in 2.5cm/1 inch cubes
1 clove garlic, minced
225g/8oz small onions
60g/4 tbsps flour/plain flour
280ml/½ pint/1 cup Burgundy
280ml/½ pint/1 cup beef stock
5ml/1 tsp tomato paste/purée
225g/8oz mushrooms, left whole
1 bay leaf
5ml/1 tsp thyme or majoram
Salt and pepper

Heat a browning dish for 5 minutes on HIGH. Add the bacon and cook 3 minutes on HIGH, stirring frequently until brown. Remove the bacon and add the meat. Cook 3 minutes on HIGH to brown slightly. Remove the meat and add the onions. Cook 2 minutes on HIGH. Stir in the flour, stock, wine and tomato purée/paste. Add the bay leaf, salt and pepper. Return the bacon and meat to the casserole and add the mushrooms. Cover and cook 40 minutes on MEDIUM, or until the meat is tender. Stir occasionally. Leave to stand for 10 minutes before serving. Serve with parsley potatoes.

Steak and Mushroom Pudding

PREPARATION TIME: 25 minutes

MICROWAVE COOKING TIME:
51-52 minutes, plus
10 minutes standing time

SERVES: 4 people

PASTRY
225g/8oz/2 cups flour/plain flour
10ml/2 tsps baking powder
120g/4oz shredded suet or ¼ cup butter or margarine
5ml/1 tsp salt
140ml/¼ pint/½ cup water

FILLING
225g/8oz whole mushrooms
450g/1lb braising/chuck steak
30g/1oz/2 tbsps butter or margarine
30g/1oz/2 tbsps flour
1 small onion, finely chopped
280ml/½ pint/1 cup beef stock
10ml/2 tsps chopped parsley
5ml/1 tsp thyme
Salt and pepper

Facing page: Steak and Mushroom Pudding (top) and Beef Bourguignonne (bottom).

Melt the butter in a deep bowl for 30 seconds on HIGH. Stir in the flour and the stock and cook for 1-2 minutes on HIGH. Add the remaining ingredients for the filling and cover the bowl loosely. Cook for 35 minutes on MEDIUM. Meanwhile, make the pastry. Sift the flour and baking powder and salt into a mixing bowl. Cut in the butter or stir in the suet. Mix to a soft dough with the water. Roll out ⅔ of the dough and line a 1150ml/2 pint/ 4 cup glass bowl, spoon in the filling and dampen the edges of the pastry. Roll out the remaining pastry for the cover. Place it over the top of the filling, pressing down the edges to seal well. Make 2-3 cuts in the top to let out the steam. Cover loosely with plastic wrap/cling film and cook on LOW for 15 minutes, turning the bowl around several times. Leave to stand for 10 minutes before turning out.

Veal Escalopes with Vegetables

PREPARATION TIME: 20 minutes

MICROWAVE COOKING TIME: 20 minutes

SERVES: 4 people

4 veal escalopes/cutlets
30ml/2 tbsps oil
60g/2oz mangetout/peapods
2 carrots, peeled and thinly sliced
60g/2oz mushrooms, sliced
2 leeks, washed and thinly sliced
120g/4oz/1 cup low-fat soft cheese
140ml/¼ pint/½ cup dry white wine
15ml/1 tbsp lemon juice
15ml/1 tbsp chopped dill
Grated nutmeg
Salt and pepper

Heat a browning dish 3 minutes on HIGH. Add the oil and heat 1 minute on HIGH. Cook the veal for 8 minutes on HIGH. Add the mushrooms halfway through the cooking time. Combine the carrots and the leeks with the wine in a shallow dish and cook for 5 minutes on HIGH. Add the mangetout/peapods and cook a further 1 minute

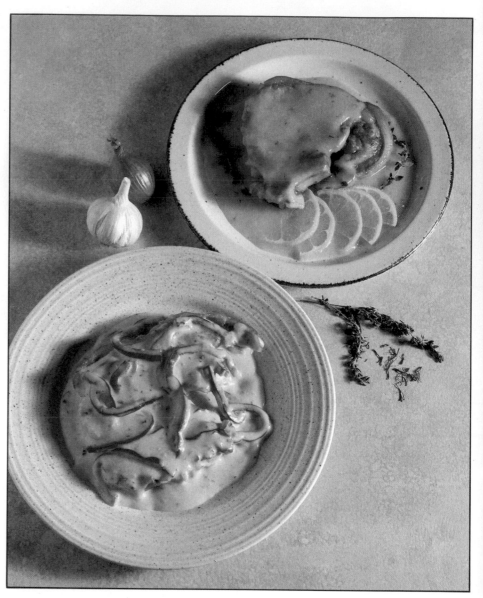

on HIGH. Drain the vegetables and reserve the liquid. Mix the cheese, vegetable cooking liquid, lemon juice, dill, nutmeg, salt and pepper in a deep bowl. Heat for 1 minute on HIGH, but do not allow the sauce to boil. Combine with the drained vegetables. Pour over the veal and heat through 1 minute on HIGH before serving.

Veal with Saffron Sauce

PREPARATION TIME: 20 minutes

MICROWAVE COOKING TIME: 26-27 minutes

SERVES: 4 people

4 veal chops
45g/1½ oz/3 tbsps butter or margarine
30g/1oz/2 tbsps flour/plain flour
2 shallots, finely chopped
1 red pepper, thinly sliced
140ml/¼ pint/½ cup white wine
140ml/¼ pint/½ cup light stock
140ml/¼ pint/½ cup light/single cream
Good pinch saffron
Salt and pepper

Heat a browning dish for 5 minutes on HIGH. Melt the butter for 1 minute on HIGH and put in the chops. Cook for 2 minutes on HIGH per side. Remove the chops from the dish and add the shallots. Cook for 1 minute on HIGH. Stir in the flour, wine, stock, salt, pepper and saffron.

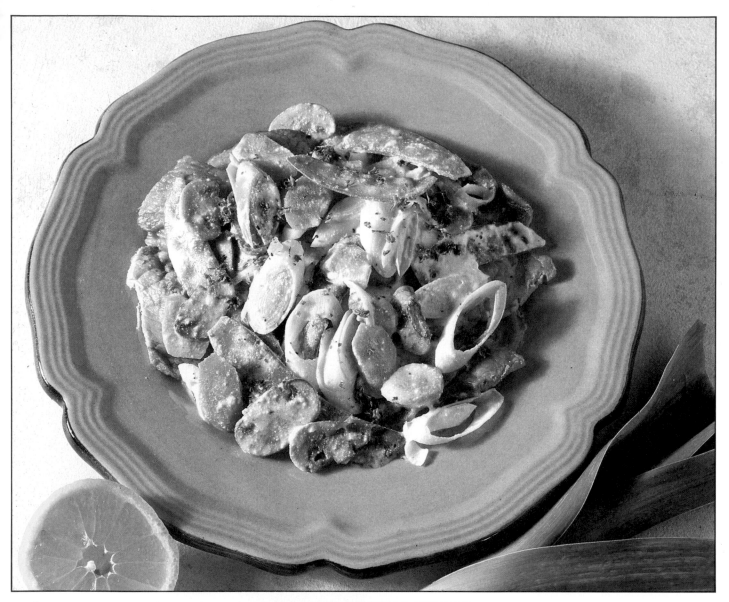

Cook 2-3 minutes on HIGH until thickened. Return the chops to the dish and add the sliced red pepper. Cover the dish or transfer to a covered casserole. Cook on MEDIUM for 15 minutes, or until the chops are tender. Remove the chops from the dish and stir in the cream. Pour the sauce over the chops to serve.

Veal Chops with Lemon and Thyme

PREPARATION TIME: 20 minutes

MICROWAVE COOKING TIME: 26-27 minutes

SERVES: 4 people

4 veal chops
60g/2oz/¼ cup butter or margarine
60g/2oz/¼ cup flour
1 clove garlic, minced
140ml/¼ pint/½ cup white wine
140ml/¼ pint/½ cup light stock
30ml/2 tbsps lemon juice
Salt and pepper

GARNISH
Sprigs of fresh thyme
Lemon slices

Heat a browning dish 5 minutes on HIGH. Melt the butter for 1 minute on HIGH. Put in the chops and cook 2 minutes on HIGH per side.

Facing page: Veal Chops with Lemon and Thyme (top) and Veal with Saffron Sauce (bottom). This page: Veal Escalopes with Vegetables.

Remove the chops from the dish and add the flour. Cook 1 minute to brown slightly. Stir in the wine, stock and lemon juice. Cook 2-3 minutes on HIGH until thickened. Season with salt and pepper and add a sprig of fresh thyme. Return the chops to the dish or transfer to a covered casserole. Cook on MEDIUM 15 minutes. Garnish with lemon slices and more fresh thyme.

POULTRY DISHES

Orange Glazed Duck

PREPARATION TIME: 15 minutes

MICROWAVE COOKING TIME: 40 minutes

SERVES: 3-4 people

2kg-2.5kg/4½-5lbs duckling
1 slice orange
1 slice onion
1 bay leaf
Salt

GLAZE
60ml/4 tbsps/¼ cup bitter orange
*   marmalade*
60ml/4 tbsps soy sauce
280ml/½ pint/1 cup chicken stock
10ml/2 tsps cornstarch/cornflour
Salt and pepper

GARNISH
Orange slices and watercress

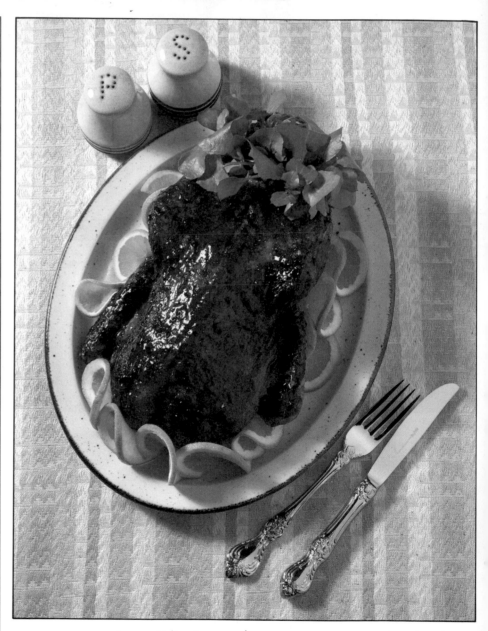

Prick the duck all over the skin with a fork, brush some of the soy sauce over both sides of the duck and sprinkle both sides lightly with salt. Place the duck breast side down in a roasting rack. Cook 10 minutes on HIGH and drain well. Return the duckling to the oven, reduce the power to MEDIUM and continue cooking a further 15 minutes. Combine remaining soy sauce with the orange marmalade. Turn the duck breast side up and brush with the glaze. Continue cooking for 15 minutes on MEDIUM, draining away the fat often and brushing with the glaze. Remove the duck from the roasting rack and leave to stand, loosely covered with foil, for 5 minutes before carving. Alternatively, cook 20-25 minutes on Combination in a microwave convection oven. Drain all the fat from the roasting tin, but leave the pan juices. Combine the chicken stock, cornstarch/cornflour, salt, pepper and remaining glaze with the

This page: Orange Glazed Duck. Facing page: Turkey with Broccoli (top) and Turkey Tetrazzini (bottom).

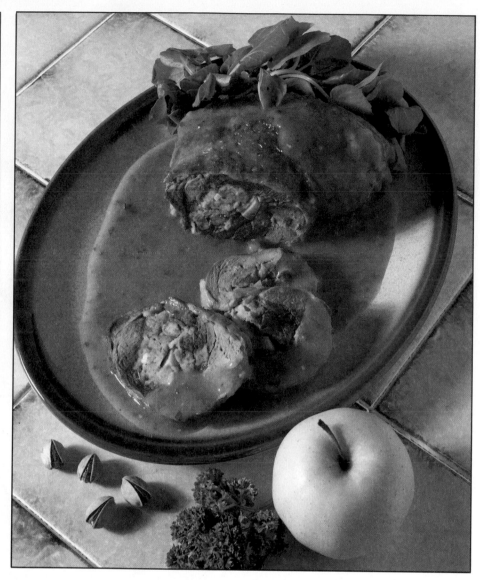

Stuffed Turkey Leg

PREPARATION TIME: 20 minutes

MICROWAVE COOKING TIME: 33-34 minutes

SERVES: 4 people

1 large turkey leg, bone removed

STUFFING
2 slices white bread made into crumbs
120g/4oz cooked ham, finely minced
60g/2oz/½ cup shelled pistachio nuts
1 apple, cored and chopped
2 sticks celery, finely chopped
1 shallot, finely chopped
Pinch thyme
1 egg, beaten
Salt and pepper

SAUCE
15ml/1 tbsp dripping from turkey
30g/2 tbsps flour/plain flour
Pan juices
280ml/½ pint/1 cup chicken stock
30ml/2 tbsps dry sherry
Salt and pepper

GARNISH
1 bunch watercress

Combine all the stuffing ingredients and push into the cavity of the turkey leg, but do not overstuff. Close any openings with wooden picks/cocktail sticks. Prick the turkey skin lightly all over and put the turkey leg on a roasting rack. Cover loosely with greaseproof/wax paper and cook for 15 minutes on MEDIUM. Turn the turkey leg over and continue cooking on MEDIUM a further 15 minutes. Alternatively, cook 20 minutes on Combination in a microwave convection oven. When the turkey is tender and no longer pink, remove from the roasting rack and keep warm. Remove all but 15ml/1 tbsp of the fat from the roasting dish. Stir in the flour and add the chicken stock, sherry, salt and pepper. Transfer to a deep bowl if

pan juices and pour into a small, deep bowl. Cook 2-3 minutes on HIGH until thickened. Remove the onion, orange slice and bay leaf from the cavity of the duck and put in a bouquet of watercress. Surround the duck with orange slices and serve the sauce separately.

Lemon Pepper Chicken

PREPARATION TIME: 20 minutes

MICROWAVE COOKING TIME: 10 minutes

SERVES: 4 people

4 chicken breasts
Juice of 1 lemon
15ml/1 tbsp coarsely ground black pepper

Paprika
Salt

GARNISH
Lemon slices
Watercress

Heat 2 metal skewers in a gas flame or on an electric burner/hob. Skin the chicken breasts. Make a criss-cross pattern on the chicken flesh with the hot skewers. Place the chicken in a casserole and sprinkle over the paprika, pepper, lemon juice and salt. Cover the dish tightly and cook 10 minutes on MEDIUM. Pour the juices back over the chicken to serve. Garnish with the lemon slices and watercress.

This page: Stuffed Turkey Leg. Facing page: Lemon Pepper Chicken (top) and Lime and Chili Chicken (bottom).

desired and cook 3-4 minutes on HIGH, stirring frequently until thickened. Slice the stuffed turkey leg and pour over some of the sauce. Garnish with watercress and serve the remaining sauce separately.

Chinese Wings

PREPARATION TIME: 15 minutes

MICROWAVE COOKING TIME: 17 minutes

SERVES: 4 people

1.5kg/3lbs chicken wings
280ml/½ pint/1 cup hoisin sauce
  (Chinese barbecue sauce)
45g/1½ oz/3 tbsps sesame seeds
30ml/2 tbsps vegetable oil
15ml/1 tbsp sesame seed oil
225g/8oz mangetout/peapods
225g/8oz bean sprouts
Small piece grated fresh ginger root
Salt and pepper

Brush the chicken wings with the hoisin sauce and cook for 10 minutes on HIGH on a roasting rack. Baste the chicken wings often with the sauce while cooking. When the wings are cooked and well coated with sauce, sprinkle with sesame seeds and set aside. Heat the oil in a browning dish for 5 minutes on HIGH. Add the mangetout/peapods, bean sprouts, ginger, salt and pepper. Cook for 2 minutes on HIGH and add the sesame seed oil after cooking. Serve the Chinese wings with the stir-fried vegetables.

Lime and Chili Chicken

PREPARATION TIME: 20 minutes

MICROWAVE COOKING TIME: 12 minutes

SERVES: 4 people

4 chicken breasts, boned
2 limes
1 green chili pepper
90ml/6 tbsps/½ cup heavy/double
  cream
Salt and pepper
Pinch sugar

Heat 2 metal skewers in a gas flame or on an electric hob/burner. Skin the chicken breasts and make a pattern on the chicken flesh with the hot skewers. Squeeze 1 lime for juice. Peel and slice the other lime thinly. Remove the seeds from the chili pepper and slice it very thinly. Put the chicken into a casserole. Sprinkle over a pinch of sugar, the sliced chili pepper, salt, pepper and lime juice. Cover and cook 10 minutes on MEDIUM. Remove the chicken and keep warm. Stir the cream into the juices in the casserole. Cook 2 minutes on HIGH, stirring frequently. Pour over the chicken and garnish with the sliced lime.

Tandoori Poussins

PREPARATION TIME: 20 minutes, plus 1 hour to marinate

MICROWAVE COOKING TIME: 15 minutes

SERVES: 4 people

4 poussins

MARINADE
120g/4oz/½ cup chopped onion
1 small piece fresh ginger, grated
10ml/2 tsps ground coriander
10ml/2 tsps ground cumin
10ml/2 tsps paprika
5ml/1 tsp turmeric
5ml/1 tsp chili powder
280ml/½ pint/1 cup plain yogurt
Juice of 1 lime
2 chopped green chili peppers
30ml/2 tbsps chopped chives
Salt and pepper

ACCOMPANIMENT
1 head of lettuce, broken into leaves
4 tomatoes, cut in wedges
1 lemon, cut in wedges

Combine all the marinade ingredients together. Skin the poussins and cut them in half. Prick the flesh and rub in the marinade. Leave for 1 hour. Cook on HIGH or a Combination setting for 15 minutes, basting frequently with the marinade. Leave to stand, loosely covered, for 5 minutes before serving. Heat any remaining marinade on MEDIUM for 1 minute, but do not allow to boil. Pour over the chicken and serve on a bed of lettuce with lemon and tomato wedges.

Turkey with Broccoli

PREPARATION TIME: 20 minutes

MICROWAVE COOKING TIME: 13-14 minutes

SERVES: 4 people

4 turkey escalopes/cutlets
12 broccoli spears
140ml/¼ pint/½ cup chicken stock
1 bay leaf
Salt and pepper

SAUCE
45g/3 tbsps butter or margarine
45g/3 tbsps flour/plain flour
430ml/¾ pint/1½ cups milk
60g/2oz/½ cup Colby/Red Leicester
  cheese
Pinch Cayenne pepper
Salt and pepper
Paprika

Trim the broccoli, and divide evenly among the turkey escalopes/cutlets. Roll the turkey around the broccoli and lay the rolls in a casserole, seam side down. Pour over the chicken stock, sprinkle on salt and pepper and add the bay leaf. Cover and cook 10 minutes on MEDIUM. Leave to stand while preparing the sauce. Melt the butter for 30 seconds in a deep bowl. Stir in the flour and the milk. Add the salt, pepper, mustard, Cayenne pepper and cook until thickened, about 3-4 minutes on HIGH. Add the cheese and stir to melt. Transfer the turkey and broccoli rolls to a serving dish and pour some of the sauce over each one. Sprinkle on paprika and serve the rest of the sauce separately.

Facing page: Chinese Wings (top) and Tandoori Poussins (bottom).

appears to be drying out at any time during cooking, baste with oil and cover loosely with wax paper/greaseproof paper. Reserve 1 tbsp fat from the roasting pan and skim off the rest and discard. Reserve the pan juices. Mix the reserved fat with the flour and stir into the pan juices. Add the stock, wine, salt and pepper and cook 2-3 minutes until thickened. Stir in the chopped herbs and serve with the carved chicken.

Duck with Peaches

PREPARATION TIME: 20 minutes

MICROWAVE COOKING TIME: 9 minutes

SERVES: 4 people

2 whole duck breasts
60g/4 tbsps/¼ cup butter
Salt and pepper

SAUCE
2 cans sliced peaches, drained and juice reserved
140ml/¼ pint/½ cup red wine
10ml/2 tsps cornstarch/cornflour
15ml/1 tbsp lime or lemon juice
1 bay leaf
Pinch cinnamon
Pinch nutmeg
15ml/1 tbsp whole allspice berries
60g/2oz/½ cup whole blanched almonds

Heat a browning dish for 5 minutes on HIGH. Melt the butter and put in the duck breasts. Brown the duck breasts 2 minutes on the skin side and 4 minutes on the other side. Remove from the dish and leave to stand while preparing the sauce. Mix the cornstarch/cornflour with the peach juice, red wine, lemon juice and the spices and bay leaf in a deep bowl. Cook on HIGH for 2-3 minutes until thickened. Remove the bay leaf and add the peaches. Slice the duck breast into thin slices. Pour the peach sauce over the duck breasts to serve.

This page: Herb Roasted Chicken. Facing page: Turkey Macadamia (top) and Duck with Peaches (bottom).

Herb Roasted Chicken

PREPARATION TIME: 25 minutes

MICROWAVE COOKING TIME: 26-33 minutes, plus 5-10 minutes standing time

SERVES: 4-6 people

1.5kg/3lbs roasting chicken
5ml/1 tsp each fresh thyme, basil, parsley, marjoram, chervil or tarragon
30ml/2 tbsps oil
Juice of 1 lemon
Salt and pepper

GRAVY
45g/1½ oz/3 tbsps flour/plain flour
Cooking juices from the chicken
430ml/¾ pint/1½ cups chicken stock
30ml/2 tbsps white wine
30ml/2 tbsps chopped mixed herbs as above
Salt and pepper

Chop the herbs finely. Loosen the skin of the chicken and stuff the herbs underneath. Prick the skin lightly and brush with the oil. Sprinkle over the lemon juice and pepper. Put onto a roasting rack breast-side down, and cook 30 minutes on MEDIUM, 25 minutes on HIGH and 30 minutes on a Combination setting. Turn the chicken halfway through cooking. Leave the chicken standing 5-10 minutes before carving. If the chicken

Spicy Tomato Chicken

PREPARATION TIME: 15 minutes

MICROWAVE COOKING TIME:
17 minutes, plus
5 minutes standing time

SERVES: 4 people

4 chicken breasts, skinned and boned
60ml/4 tbsps/¼ cup chicken stock or
  water
450g/1lb canned tomatoes
30ml/2 tbsps Worcestershire sauce
1 clove garlic, crushed
30ml/2 tbsps tomato purée/paste
30ml/2 tbsps cider vinegar
30g/1oz/2 tbsps light brown sugar or
  honey
1 small onion, finely chopped
1 bay leaf
Pinch allspice
Salt and pepper
GARNISH
4 tomatoes, skinned, seeded and cut into
  thin strips

Place the chicken in 1 layer in a large casserole with the stock or water. Cover tightly and cook on MEDIUM for 10 minutes. Leave to stand, covered, for at least 5 minutes while preparing the sauce. Combine all the sauce ingredients with the cooking liquid from the chicken in a deep bowl. Cook, uncovered, for 7 minutes on HIGH, until the sauce reduces and thickens. Remove the bay leaf and blend the sauce in a food processor until smooth. Arrange the chicken breasts on a serving plate and coat with the sauce. Add the tomato strips and reheat for 30 seconds on HIGH before serving.

Chicken with Watercress Sauce

PREPARATION TIME: 15 minutes

MICROWAVE COOKING TIME:
12 minutes, plus
5 minutes standing time

SERVES: 4 people

4 large chicken breasts, skinned and
  boned
30ml/2 tbsps water
60ml/4 tbsps/¼ cup lemon juice

SAUCE
120g/4oz/1 cup low fat soft cheese
140ml/¼ pint/½ cup light/single cream
  or milk
1 large bunch watercress, well washed
  and drained
Salt and pepper
GARNISH
Lemon slices
Watercress

Place the chicken in one layer in a large casserole. Pour over the water and the lemon juice. Cover tightly and cook 10 minutes on MEDIUM. Leave to stand, covered, at least 5 minutes while preparing the sauce. Combine the cheese and the cream or milk with the chicken cooking liquid and salt and pepper. Cook 1 minute on HIGH. Discard any tough stalks from the watercress and chop roughly. Add to the sauce and cook 1 minute on HIGH. Blend the sauce in a food processor until smooth and a delicate green colour. Coat over the chicken to serve. Garnish with lemon slices and watercress.

This page: Country Captain's Chicken. Facing page: Chicken with Watercress Sauce (top) and Spicy Tomato Chicken (bottom).

Country Captain's Chicken

PREPARATION TIME: 20 minutes

MICROWAVE COOKING TIME:
36 minutes

SERVES: 4 people

1.5kg/3lbs chicken pieces
60g/4 tbsps butter
30ml/2 tbsps curry powder
1 clove garlic, minced
1 large onion, sliced
60g/2oz/½ cup blanched whole almonds
60g/2oz/½ cup golden raisins/sultanas
2 apples, peeled and diced
1 450g/16oz can tomatoes
30ml/2 tbsps tomato purée/paste
1 bay leaf
30ml/2 tbsps chopped coriander
  (optional)
Pinch sugar
Salt and pepper

GARNISH
Desiccated coconut

Heat a browning dish for 5 minutes on HIGH. Melt the butter and add the chicken pieces. Cook 15 minutes on both sides or cook in 2 batches for 7½ minutes each batch if necessary. Remove the chicken and add the onion, garlic and curry powder. Cook 1 minute on HIGH. Replace the chicken, skin side down, and add the sultanas/raisins, apples and almonds. Mix the tomatoes, tomato purée/paste, lime juice, coriander, bay leaf, sugar, salt and pepper together and pour over the chicken. Cook 15 minutes on HIGH, or until the chicken is tender and no longer pink. Turn the chicken over halfway through cooking. Remove the bay leaf and serve with rice and garnish with desiccated coconut.

Piquant Duck

PREPARATION TIME: 25 minutes

MICROWAVE COOKING TIME: 27 minutes

SERVES: 4 people

8 duck portions/pieces
60g/2oz/¼ cup butter
4 large cloves garlic, minced

SAUCE
60ml/2 fl oz/¼ cup vinegar
280ml/½ pint/1 cup dry white wine
45ml/3 tbsps Dijon mustard
30ml/2 tbsps tomato purée/paste
30ml/2 tbsps chives
1 red pepper, very thinly sliced
140ml/¼ pint/½ cup heavy/double cream
Salt and pepper

Heat a browning dish for 5 minutes on HIGH, melt the butter and add the duck pieces skin side down. Brown the duck for 5 minutes per side. Add the garlic and cover the dish tightly. Cook until the duck is tender, about 15 minutes on HIGH. Pour off all the fat and leave the duck covered while preparing the sauce. Combine all the sauce ingredients except the red pepper and the cream

in a deep bowl. Add the garlic and any juices from the duck. Cook for 10 minutes on HIGH until well reduced. Add the cream and the red pepper and cook a further 2 minutes on HIGH. Trim the duck pieces neatly and pour over the sauce to serve.

Turkey Macadamia

PREPARATION TIME: 20 minutes

MICROWAVE COOKING TIME: 18 minutes

SERVES: 4 people

4 turkey breast escalopes/cutlets
1 225g (8oz) can pineapple chunks/ pieces, juice reserved
4 spring/green onions, sliced
4 tomatoes, peeled, seeded and quartered
125g/4oz/1 cup macadamia nuts

SAUCE
30ml/2 tbsps soy sauce
280ml/½ pint/1 cup stock
30ml/2 tbsps vinegar
30ml/2 tbsps brown sugar
15ml/3 tsps cornstarch/cornflour
Reserved pineapple juice

Place the turkey breasts in a casserole dish and pour over the pineapple juice. Cover the dish tightly and cook 10-15 minutes on MEDIUM. Leave to stand while preparing the sauce. Drain the pineapple juice from the turkey and combine it in a deep bowl with the remaining sauce ingredients. Add the pineapple pieces and the macadamia nuts. Cook, uncovered, for 2-3 minutes on HIGH, stirring frequently until thickened. Immediately add the tomatoes and the onions to the hot sauce and pour over the turkey to serve.

Turkey Tetrazzini

PREPARATION TIME: 20 minutes

MICROWAVE COOKING TIME: 6-8 minutes

SERVES: 4-6 people

60g/2oz/¼ cup butter or margarine
60g/2oz flour/plain flour

120g/4oz mushrooms, sliced
1 clove garlic, crushed
2 sticks celery, sliced
280ml/½ pint/1 cup chicken stock
280ml/½ pint/1 cup milk
140ml/¼ pint/½ cup double/heavy cream
30ml/2 tbsps dry white wine or sherry
12 black olives, pitted and roughly chopped
225g/8oz cooked turkey, cut in cubes
225g/8oz spaghetti
Salt and pepper
60g/4 tbsps/¼ cup each seasoned breadcrumbs and Parmesan cheese

Cook spaghetti in enough water to cover for 12 minutes on HIGH. Stir frequently. Drain and set aside. Melt the butter 30 seconds on HIGH, and add mushrooms, garlic and celery. Cook 1 minute on HIGH. Stir in the flour and add milk, stock and wine or sherry. Cook, uncovered, until thickened, about 5 minutes on HIGH. Add the cream and the olives. Combine with the turkey and spaghetti and pour into a casserole. Sprinkle cheese and crumbs on top and cook 8-10 minutes on HIGH. Serve immediately.

Duck with Cherries

PREPARATION TIME: 20 minutes

MICROWAVE COOKING TIME: 9 minutes

SERVES: 4 people

2 whole duck breasts
60g/4 tbsps/¼ cup butter or margarine
Salt and pepper

SAUCE
2 cans dark, pitted cherries, drained and juice reserved
140ml/¼ pint/½ cup red wine
30ml/2 tbsps red wine vinegar
Grated rind and juice of 1 orange
10ml/2 tsps cornstarch/cornflour
1 bay leaf
1 sprig thyme
Pinch salt

Facing page: Duck with Cherries (top) and Piquant Duck (bottom).

Heat a browning dish 5 minutes on HIGH. Add the butter and put in the duck breasts. Brown the duck breasts 2 minutes on the skin side and 4 minutes on the other side. Remove the duck from the dish and keep warm. Mix the reserved cherry juice with the wine, vinegar, orange rind and juice, cornstarch/cornflour, bay leaf and thyme in a small bowl. Cook for 3 minutes on HIGH until thickened, stirring frequently. Add a pinch of salt and remove the bay leaf and thyme. Add the cherries to the sauce and slice the duck breasts into thin slices. Pour over the cherry sauce to serve.

Pecan Poussins

PREPARATION TIME: 25 minutes

MICROWAVE COOKING TIME:
35 minutes

SERVES: 4 people

4 poussins or Cornish game hens
60ml/4 tbsps/¼ cup Worcestershire
*   sauce*

STUFFING
6 slices white bread made into crumbs
225g/8oz cooked ham
4 green/spring onions, chopped
5ml/1 tsp thyme
1 egg, beaten
Salt and pepper

SAUCE
430ml/¾ pint/1½ cups brown stock
180g/6oz/⅔ cup light brown sugar
90ml/6 tbsps/⅓ cup cider vinegar
120g/4oz/1 cup chopped pecans

GARNISH
Watercress

Process the ham and bread in a food processor until finely chopped. Add the egg, salt, pepper and thyme and process once or twice to mix thoroughly. Stir in the onion by hand. Stuff the poussins and tie the legs together with string. Brush each poussin with Worcestershire sauce. Cook 15-20 minutes on HIGH or 20 minutes on a Combination setting. Leave to stand 5 minutes

before serving. Mix the sauce ingredients together and cook on HIGH, uncovered, for 10-15 minutes. The sauce should be reduced and of syrupy consistency. Pour over the poussins to serve and garnish with watercress.

Chicken Paprika

PREPARATION TIME: 20 minutes

MICROWAVE COOKING TIME:
32 minutes, plus
5 minutes standing time

SERVES: 4-6 people

1.5kg/3lbs chicken pieces
30g/1oz/2 tbsps butter
2 onions, sliced
30ml/2 tbsps paprika
1 clove garlic, finely minced
30ml/2 tbsps tomato purée/paste
1 450g/1lb can tomatoes
120g/4oz mushrooms
1 green pepper, thinly sliced
1 bay leaf
Salt and pepper

This page: Chicken Paprika.
Facing page: Pecan Poussins.

GARNISH
Sour cream

Melt the butter for 30 seconds on HIGH in a large casserole. Add the paprika, onions and garlic. Cook, uncovered, 2 minutes on HIGH. Lay the chicken pieces into the casserole skin-side down with the thickest portions to the outside of the dish. Combine the tomato paste/purée with the tomatoes, bay leaf, salt and pepper. Pour the tomato sauce over the chicken and cover the casserole tightly. Cook for 15 minutes on HIGH. Turn over the chicken pieces and scatter the mushrooms and the pepper slices on top. Cook a further 15 minutes, or until the chicken is tender and no longer pink. Leave to stand, covered, for 5 minutes. Top with sour cream before serving with pasta or potatoes.

Microwave
MEAT & POULTRY

GAME DISHES

Quail with Artichokes and Vegetable Julienne

PREPARATION TIME: 25 minutes

MICROWAVE COOKING TIME: 19-21 minutes

SERVES: 4 people

8 quail
60g/4 tbsps/¼ cup butter or margarine
2 large artichokes, cooked
2 carrots, peeled
2 potatoes, peeled
2 leeks, washed

SAUCE
15ml/1 tbsps flour/plain flour
140ml/¼ pint/½ cup white wine
280ml/½ pint/1 cup double/heavy cream
30ml/2 tbsps Dijon mustard
Salt and pepper

GARNISH
Reserved artichoke leaves

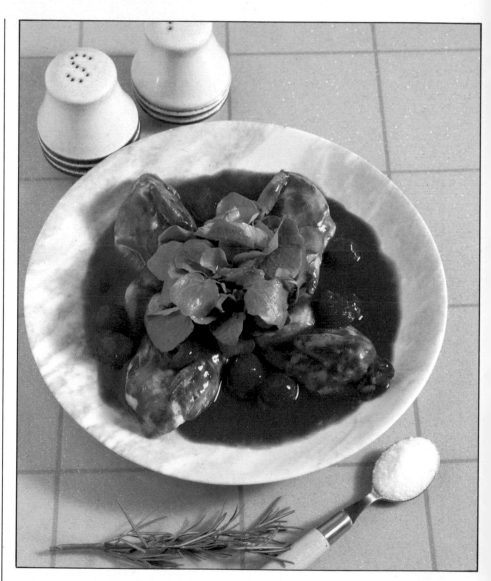

Peel the leaves from the artichokes and remove the chokes. Set the leaves aside and cut the artichoke bottoms into thin slices. Cut the carrots, potatoes and leeks into julienne strips. Heat a browning dish for 5 minutes on HIGH. Melt the butter and add the carrots and potatoes. Cook on HIGH for 2 minutes. Add the leeks and artichoke bottoms and cook for a further 1 minute on HIGH. Remove the vegetables and set them aside. Add the quail to the butter in a dish and cook for 4-6 minutes on HIGH, turning frequently to brown lightly. Remove the quail from the dish and add the flour, white wine and Dijon mustard. Return the quail to the dish, cover tightly and cook for 5 minutes on HIGH. Set the quail aside to keep warm. Add the cream and salt and pepper to the dish and stir well. Cook for 1 minute on HIGH to thicken slightly. Add the vegetables to the sauce and cook a further 1 minute on HIGH to heat

This page: Quail with Raspberries. Facing page: Quail with Apples and Calvados (top) and Quail with Artichokes and Vegetable Julienne (bottom).

through. Pour the sauce over the quail to serve and surround with the artichoke leaves.

Juniper Venison

PREPARATION TIME: 25 minutes

MICROWAVE COOKING TIME:
55 minutes, plus
10 minutes standing time

SERVES: 4 people

900g/2lbs venison, cut in 2.5cm/1 inch
    cubes
60g/2oz/¼ cup butter or margarine
60g/2oz/¼ cup flour/plain flour
570ml/1 pint/2 cups beef stock
60ml/4 tbsps/¼ cup red wine
1 shallot, finely chopped
1 sprig rosemary
15ml/1 tbsp juniper berries
1 bay leaf
Salt and pepper

ACCOMPANIMENT
450g/1lb potatoes, peeled and cut into
    small pieces
15g/1 tbsp butter or margarine
1 egg, beaten
Salt and pepper
Rowanberry jelly, redcurrant jelly or whole
    cranberry sauce

Cook the potatoes in enough water to cover for 15 minutes on HIGH. Leave to stand for 5 minutes before draining and mashing. Season the potatoes with salt and pepper and add the butter. Beat in half the egg and pipe the mixture out into small baskets on a plate or a microwave baking sheet. Cook for 1 minute on HIGH and then brush with the remaining beaten egg and sprinkle with paprika. Cook a further 2 minutes on HIGH and set aside. Heat a browning dish for 5 minutes on HIGH. Melt the butter and brown the meat and the shallot for 4-6 minutes on HIGH. Remove the meat and shallot and stir in the flour, stock, red wine, salt, pepper, juniper berries, rosemary and bay leaf. Return the meat to the dish or transfer to a casserole. Cover and cook for 30 minutes on MEDIUM, stirring frequently. Remove the bay leaf and the sprig of rosemary before serving. Reheat the potato baskets for 30 seconds on HIGH and fill each with a spoonful of the jelly or cranberry sauce. Serve the potato

baskets with the venison. Garnish with fresh rosemary if desired.

Marmalade Venison

PREPARATION TIME: 15 minutes

MICROWAVE COOKING TIME:
40 minutes, plus
10 minutes standing time

SERVES: 4 people

900g/2lbs venison, cut in 2.5cm/1 inch
    cubes
225g/8oz small onions, peeled and left
    whole

This page: **Juniper Venison (top)** **and Marmalade Venison (bottom).** **Facing page: Pheasant Alsacienne.**

60g/2oz/¼ cup butter or margarine
60g/2oz/¼ cup flour
570ml/1 pint/2 cups beef stock
60ml/4 tbsps/¼ cup orange marmalade

GARNISH
Orange slices
Chopped parsley

Heat a browning dish for 5 minutes on HIGH. Melt the butter and add

the venison. Cook 4-6 minutes on HIGH, stirring frequently. Remove the meat and add the onions. Cook 1-2 minutes on HIGH to brown slightly. Remove the onions and add the flour, stock and marmalade. Return the meat and the onions to the casserole, cover and cook 30 minutes on MEDIUM. Leave to stand 10 minutes before serving. Garnish with orange slices and sprinkle with chopped parsley before serving.

Garlic Roast Pigeon

PREPARATION TIME: 20 minutes

MICROWAVE COOKING TIME:
15 minutes, plus
5 minutes standing time

SERVES: 4 people

4 pigeons
60g/2oz/4 tbsps butter or margarine
12 cloves garlic, peeled
60ml/2 fl oz/¼ cup white wine
280ml/½ pint/1 cup chicken stock
1 bay leaf
1 sprig thyme
Salt and pepper

ACCOMPANIMENT
4 heads Belgian endive/chicory
280ml/½ pint/1 cup water and white
  wine mixed
Pinch sugar
Salt and pepper

Spread the butter on the pigeons and place them breast side up on a roasting rack with the cloves of garlic. Cook on HIGH or a Combination setting for 10 minutes. Leave the pigeons to stand for 5 minutes before serving. They may be served slightly pink. Meanwhile, mash the cloves of garlic and mix with the stock, wine, bay leaf and salt and pepper. Cook, uncovered, for 3 minutes to reduce the liquid. Purée the sauce until smooth. Cut the endive/chicory in half lengthwise and remove the cores. Put into a casserole dish with the wine and water mixed, sugar, salt and pepper. Cover loosely and cook for 2 minutes on HIGH. Drain and serve

around the pigeons. Pour the sauce over the pigeons and the endive to serve.

Pigeon Kebabs with Walnut Grape Pilaf

PREPARATION TIME: 20 minutes

MICROWAVE COOKING TIME:
14 minutes

SERVES: 4 people

3-4 pigeons, depending on size
8 strips of bacon/streaky bacon
30g/2 tbsps butter or margarine, melted

WALNUT GRAPE PILAF
180g/6oz/1½ cups brown rice
570ml/1 pint/2 cups stock and wine
  mixed
10ml/2 tsps thyme
120g/4oz/1 cup walnuts, chopped
1 small bunch purple or red grapes
Salt and pepper

Combine the rice with the stock and wine, salt, pepper and thyme in a large casserole. Cover loosely and cook for 10 minutes on HIGH. Cover completely and leave to stand 10 minutes for the rice to absorb the liquid. Add the chopped walnuts, cut the grapes in half and remove the seeds and add to the pilaf. Remove the breast meat from the pigeons and cut each breast half into 3 pieces. Thread onto skewers with the bacon. Brush each kebab with the melted butter or margarine and place on a roasting rack. Cook the kebabs 2 minutes per side. Set them aside, loosely covered, for 5 minutes before serving. Brush the kebabs with the cooking juices and serve on top of the pilaf.

Quail with Apples and Calvados

PREPARATION TIME: 20 minutes

MICROWAVE COOKING TIME:
17-19 minutes

SERVES: 4 people

8 quail
2 large apples, peeled and thinly sliced
60g/4 tbsps/¼ cup butter or margarine

SAUCE
15ml/1 tbsp flour/plain flour
140ml/¼ pint/½ cup white wine or cider
280ml/½ pint/1 cup double/heavy
  cream
60ml/4 tbsps/¼ cup Calvados or brandy
30ml/2 tbsps chopped parsley
Salt and butter

Heat a browning dish for 5 minutes on HIGH. Melt the butter and brown the quail for 4-6 minutes, turning often to brown evenly. Remove the quail and set aside. Add the sliced apples to the browning dish and cook for 2 minutes, turning over often to brown on both sides. If the apples are not browning sprinkle lightly with sugar. Remove the apples and set them aside. Stir the flour into the juices in the dish and add the white wine and the Calvados. Return the quail to the dish or transfer to a casserole. Cover the dish tightly and cook for 5 minutes on HIGH. Remove the quail and keep warm. Add the cream and the parsley to the dish with salt and pepper. Cook for 1 minute on HIGH. Add the apples to the sauce and pour over the quail to serve.

Pheasant Alsacienne

PREPARATION TIME: 20 minutes

MICROWAVE COOKING TIME:
28-30 minutes

SERVES: 4 people

2 pheasants, dressed
2 onion slices
2 sprigs thyme
30ml/2 tbsps oil

ACCOMPANIMENT
45g/3 tbsps butter
45g/3 tbsps flour
1 head white cabbage, shredded

Facing page: Pigeon Kebabs with Walnut Grape Pilaf (top) and Garlic Roast Pigeon (bottom).

2 apples, peeled and grated
30ml/2 tbsps caraway seeds
225g/8oz smoked sausage, sliced
280ml/½ pint/1 cup white wine
1 bay leaf
Salt and pepper

Prick the pheasants lightly all over the skin and brush with oil. Place the pheasants breast side down on a roasting rack, one at a time if necessary. Cook for 10 minutes on MEDIUM. Turn over and cook for a further 10 minutes on MEDIUM. Cook for 15 minutes on the Combination setting of a microwave convection oven, turning once. Cover and leave to stand while preparing the cabbage. Melt the butter in a large casserole for 30 seconds on HIGH. Add the flour and the wine and combine with the remaining ingredients. Cook for 8-10 minutes on HIGH, stirring frequently. Serve with the pheasants.

Wild Duck with Limes and Onions

PREPARATION TIME: 20 minutes

MICROWAVE COOKING TIME: 25 minutes

SERVES: 4 people

2 wild ducks
2 slices onion
2 bay leaves
60g/2oz/¼ cup butter or margarine

SAUCE
45g/1½ oz/3 tbsps flour/plain flour
Cooking juices from the duck
280ml/½ pint/1 cup stock
2 onions, finely sliced
Grated rind and juice of 1 lime
Pinch of sugar
Salt and pepper

GARNISH
Lime wedges

Prick the skin of the duck all over and rub with half of the butter. Put an onion slice and a bay leaf inside each duck. Put onto a roasting rack breast side down and cook for 5 minutes on MEDIUM. Turn the

ducks over and cook for 10 minutes further on MEDIUM. Cook on the Combination setting of a microwave convection oven for 16 minutes. Turn over after 8 minutes. Cover loosely and leave to stand for 5 minutes. Combine the pan juices with the remaining butter in a small bowl, and cook 30 seconds on HIGH to melt. Add the sliced onions, cover the dish loosely, and cook for 2 minutes on HIGH. Stir in the flour, stock, lime juice and grated rind. Add a pinch sugar, salt and pepper and cook a further 5 minutes on HIGH, or until thickened. Pour over the ducks to serve and surround with lime wedges.

Wild Duck with Blackcurrants and Port

PREPARATION TIME: 15 minutes

MICROWAVE COOKING TIME: 20-25 minutes

SERVES: 4 people

2 wild ducks
2 onion slices
2 sprigs thyme
30g/2 tbsps butter or margarine
450g/1lb can blackcurrants (if unavailable substitute other red berries or dark cherries)
15ml/1 tbsp red wine vinegar
140ml/¼ pint/½ cup port
15ml/1 tbsp cornstarch/cornflour
Pinch of salt and pepper

Prick the duck skin all over and rub each duck with the butter. Put a slice of onion and a sprig of thyme inside each duck and place them breast side down on a roasting rack. Cook on MEDIUM for 5 minutes. Turn over the ducks and cook a further 10 minutes on MEDIUM. Cook for 16 minutes on the Combination setting of a microwave convection oven. Turn halfway through the cooking time. Cover loosely and set aside for 5 minutes. Combine the blackcurrants with the port, vinegar, cornstarch/cornflour, pan juices from the duck, salt and pepper in a deep bowl. Cook, uncovered, for 5 minutes on HIGH or until thickened, stirring

frequently. Remove the onion and the thyme from the ducks and pour over the blackcurrant sauce to serve.

Quail with Raspberries

PREPARATION TIME: 15 minutes

MICROWAVE COOKING TIME: 9-11 minutes

SERVES: 4 people

8 quail
225g/8oz frozen raspberries
280ml/½ pint/1 cup red wine
15ml/1 tbsp red wine vinegar or raspberry vinegar
15g/1 tbsp sugar
1 sprig rosemary
15g/1 tbsp cornflour/cornstarch

GARNISH
Whole raspberries and watercress

Prick the quail lightly all over with a fork and rub with a bit of butter. Put the quail breast side down on a roasting rack in a circle with the thicker part of the quail pointing to the outside of the dish. Cook for 2 minutes on HIGH. Turn the quail over and cook for a further 3 minutes on HIGH. Cook for 6 minutes on the Combination setting of a microwave convection oven without turning. Cover loosely and set aside while preparing the sauce. Reserve 16 raspberries for garnish and combine the raspberries with the remaining sauce ingredients in a deep bowl. Cook for 4-6 minutes on HIGH, stirring frequently to break up the raspberries. When thickened, purée in a food processor until smooth. Strain to remove the raspberry seeds. Cut the quail in half and coat with the raspberry sauce. Garnish with the reserved whole raspberries and watercress to serve.

Dijon Rabbit with Capers

PREPARATION TIME: 15 minutes

MICROWAVE COOKING TIME: 34 minutes

SERVES: 4 people

8 rabbit quarters
45g/3 tbsps butter or margarine
45g/3 tbsps flour/plain flour
280ml/½ pint/1 cup stock
140ml/¼ pint/½ cup white wine
140ml/¼ pint/½ cup double/heavy
 cream
30ml/2 tbsps Dijon mustard
30ml/2 tbsps capers
15ml/1 tbsp chopped chives
Salt and pepper

Heat a browning dish for 5 minutes
on HIGH. Melt the butter and
brown the rabbit for 2 minutes on
each side. Remove the rabbit and add
the flour, stock, wine, salt, pepper
and mustard. Return the rabbit to
the dish or transfer to a casserole.
Cook, covered, for 25 minutes on
MEDIUM. Remove the rabbit from
the dish and add the capers, chives
and cream. Cook a further 2 minutes

on HIGH and pour over the rabbit
to serve. Serve with French/green
beans.

Pepper Rabbit and Mushrooms

PREPARATION TIME: 15 minutes	
MICROWAVE COOKING TIME: 34 minutes	
SERVES: 4 people	

8 rabbit quarters
45g/3 tbsps butter or margarine
45g/3 tbsps flour/plain flour
2 shallots, finely chopped
280ml/½ pint/1 cup stock
140ml/¼ pint/½ cup white wine
225g/½ lb mushrooms, sliced
140ml/¼ pint/½ cup heavy/double
 cream

**Left: Pepper Rabbit and
Mushrooms (top) and Dijon
Rabbit with Capers (bottom).
Right: Wild Duck with Limes and
Onions (top) and Wild Duck with
Blackcurrants and Port (bottom).**

5ml/1 tsp coarsely ground black pepper
15ml/1 tbsp chopped parsley
Salt

Heat a browning dish for 5 minutes
on HIGH. Melt the butter and
brown the rabbit pieces and the
shallots for 1 minute per side on
HIGH. Add the stock, wine, pepper
and salt. Cook, covered, for
25 minutes on MEDIUM. Add the
mushrooms and cook a further
2 minutes on HIGH. Remove the
rabbit from the casserole and stir in
the cream and parsley. Pour the sauce
over the rabbit to serve.

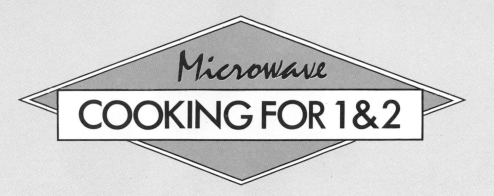

Microwave
COOKING FOR 1 & 2

Microwave
COOKING FOR 1&2

Do meals for singles or couples have to be uninspiring? Do people on their own have to rely on pre-prepared food for speed and convenience? Not when there is a microwave around. Small portions cook beautifully in practically the time it takes to open the package and read the cooking instructions. With a microwave oven there is no need to sacrifice variety for convenience.

Small packages of fresh vegetables and meat are readily available in supermarkets and specialty food stores. Even turkey and duck are available in manageable sizes for the small household. Cooking a dinner party for one special guest can be cheaper than dinner out. It can also be an occasion for experimenting with more elaborate preparations than you might want to attempt for large numbers.

However, leftovers come in handy, so don't shy away from cooking a whole turkey or a large piece of meat. Leftovers can be frozen and used as a basis for completely different meals later on. Small portions, well covered, will defrost in 2-3 minutes on a LOW or DEFROST setting. Soups can be kept refrigerated for up to two days and reheated on MEDIUM in about 2-5 minutes. Vegetable and flour-thickened soups can also be frozen, and then defrosted and reheated in about 10 minutes on a LOW or DEFROST setting, with frequent stirring. Meat, poultry and game stews and braises can be reheated as well, usually on MEDIUM for about 4-6 minutes. If frozen, they can be defrosted and reheated in about 12-15 minutes on LOW or DEFROST. Individual portions should be frozen in bags or containers that are suitable for reheating in microwave ovens or in individual serving dishes of the freezer-to-table variety.

All the recipes in this book were tested in an oven with a maximum power of 700 watts. Certain recipes were cooked in a combination microwave-convection oven, which combines the speed of microwave cooking with browning ability. However, any dish that requires browning can be placed under a preheated broiler or grill for a minute or two before serving. Also, toppings such as breadcrumbs, crushed cereals or cheeses can give an eye-pleasing finish to your very own brand of 'convenience' food.

Microwave

COOKING FOR 1 & 2

SOUPS AND APPETIZERS

Confetti Spread and Sesame Crackers

PREPARATION TIME: 15 minutes

MICROWAVE COOKING TIME:
10-12 minutes

SERVES: 2 people

SPREAD
225g/8oz/1 cup cream cheese
2 strips bacon, diced
15g/1 tbsp chopped chives
Red pepper flakes
4 chopped black olives
Crushed garlic
60g/2oz/¼ cup chopped green and red
    peppers, mixed
30g/1oz/2 tbsps frozen corn
Salt and pepper

CRACKERS/BISCUITS
60g/2oz/¼ cup all-purpose flour/plain
    flour
60g/2oz/¼ cup wholewheat flour/
    wholemeal flour
45g/1½ oz/1½ tbsps butter
10ml/2 tsps sesame seeds
15-30ml/1-2 tbsps cold water
1 egg, beaten with a pinch of salt
Salt and pepper

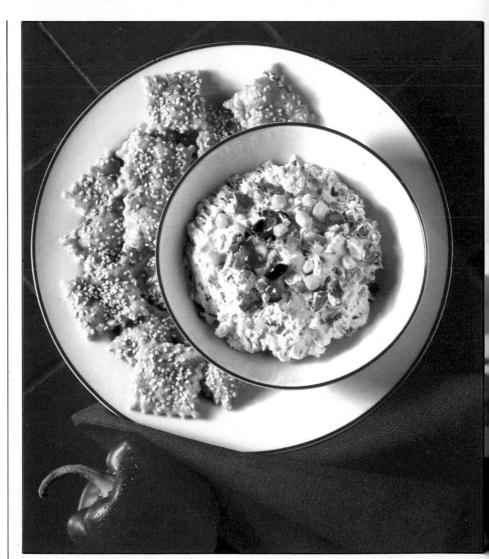

Put the flours, salt and pepper into the bowl of a food processor. Cut the butter into small pieces and add to the flour. Process until the mixture looks like fine breadcrumbs. Add 1 tbsp sesame seeds and add the water with the machine running until the mixture forms a dough. Roll out thinly on a floured board and brush with the egg. Sprinkle on the remaining sesame seeds and cut into 2.5cm (1″) squares. Arrange into a circle on a large plate and cook on HIGH for 3-6 minutes until crisp.

Cool on a wire rack. Makes 12 crackers.
Heat a browning dish for 3 minutes and cook the diced bacon on HIGH for 1-2 minutes or until crisp. Drain on paper towels and allow to cool. Put the chopped peppers and corn into a small bowl and cover with water. Cover the bowl with pierced

This page: Confetti Spread with Sesame Crackers. Facing page: Oriental Kebabs.

plastic wrap and cook on HIGH for 2 minutes. Rinse with cold water and leave to drain dry. Put the cream cheese into a small bowl and heat for

30-40 seconds on MEDIUM to soften. Add the bacon, peppers and the remaining ingredients, and mix well. Serve with the sesame seed crackers. Unused peppers can be frozen.

Marinated Shrimp and Sour Cream Sauce

PREPARATION TIME: 15 minutes

MICROWAVE COOKING TIME: 5 minutes

SERVES: 2 people

225g/½ lb fresh large shrimp, shelled and cleaned

MARINADE
140ml/¼ pint/½ cup white wine
30ml/1oz/2 tbsps white wine vinegar
1 bay leaf
2 black peppercorns
1 whole allspice berry
2 whole cloves
2.5ml/½ tsp dill seeds
½ small onion, sliced
Salt

SAUCE
140ml/¼ pint/½ cup sour cream
30-45ml/2-3 tbsps strained reserved
   marinade
2.5ml/½ tsp chopped dill, fresh or dried
2.5ml/½ tsp grated horseradish
Salt and pepper

GARNISH
Lettuce leaves
Sprigs of fresh dill

Combine all the marinade ingredients in a 570ml/1 pint casserole and cover. Cook for 2-3 minutes on HIGH until boiling. Stir in the shrimp, cover, and cook on MEDIUM for 2 minutes. Allow to cool in the marinade. If using fresh dill, reserve 2 small sprigs for garnish and chop 2.5ml/½ tsp. Drain the marinade and mix with the sour cream, dill, horseradish, and salt and pepper. Arrange lettuce on serving plates, and place on the shrimp. Top with some of the sauce and the reserved dill. Serve remaining sauce separately.

Scallop Parcels with Curry Sauce

PREPARATION TIME: 15 minutes

MICROWAVE COOKING TIME: 3-4 minutes

SERVES: 2 people

6 large or 8 small scallops
1 small sweet red pepper
2 large mushrooms
30ml/1oz/2 tbsps white wine
5ml/1 tsp black pepper
1.5ml/¼ tsp salt
1.5ml/¼ tsp ground ginger
Garlic powder
15ml/1 tbsp oil
Whole fresh chives

SAUCE
15g/1 tbsp curry powder
140ml/¼ pint/½ cup plain yogurt
Juice of ½ a lime
2.5ml/½ tsp mango chutney
Salt and pepper

Mix the wine, salt, pepper, oil, ginger, and a pinch of garlic powder together well. Put in the scallops and turn them to coat evenly. Cut the pepper into pieces the size of the scallops. Cut the mushrooms into 5mm (¼") slices. Layer the pepper, mushrooms and scallops, and tie each parcel with 2 whole chives. Put the parcels on their sides onto a microwave roasting rack and cook on HIGH for 30 seconds. Turn every 30 seconds, ending with the parcels scallop-sides up. Cook for a total of 2-3 minutes, brushing frequently with the ginger basting liquid. Serve hot or cold, with the curry sauce.
Put the curry powder for the sauce onto a small plate and cook for 1 minute on HIGH. Allow to cool, and combine with the other ingredients. Serve with the scallops.

Oriental Kebabs

PREPARATION TIME: 20 minutes

MICROWAVE COOKING TIME: 5-6 minutes

SERVES: 2 people

90g/3oz ground/minced pork or beef
30g/1oz/2 tbsp breadcrumbs
5ml/1 tsp chopped onion
1 small can pineapple chunks
6 cherry tomatoes

BASTING MIXTURE
60ml/2oz/¼ cup honey
60ml/2oz/¼ cup soy sauce
60ml/2oz/¼ cup rice wine
15ml/1 tbsp sesame seed oil
5ml/1 tsp ground ginger
Pepper

SWEET AND SOUR SAUCE
Remaining basting mixture
15ml/1 tbsp ketchup
5ml/1 tsp cornstarch/cornflour
Reserved pineapple juice
15ml/1 tbsp cider vinegar
2.5ml/½ tsp garlic powder

Mix together the basting ingredients. Mix the meat, breadcrumbs, chopped onion and 1 tbsp of the basting mixture. Shape into 8 meatballs. Drain the can of pineapple and reserve the juice. Thread the meatballs onto wooden skewers, alternating with the pineapple chunks and tomatoes. Place the kebabs on a roasting rack and brush with the baste. Cook on HIGH for 3 minutes, turning and basting each minute. Combine the ingredients for the sauce, and cook on HIGH for 2-3 minutes until thickened. Stir every 30 seconds. Serve with the kebabs. For one person only, use half the amount of all the ingredients. Cook the kebabs for 2 minutes, and the sauce for 1-2 minutes.

Tomato and Basil Soup

PREPARATION TIME: 15 minutes

MICROWAVE COOKING TIME: 5 minutes

SERVES: 2 people

Facing page: Scallop Parcels with Curry Sauce (top) and Marinated Shrimp and Sour Cream Sauce (bottom).

the vegetables lengthwise into thin strips. Add the carrot noodles to the consommé, cover with pierced plastic wrap, and cook on HIGH for 3 minutes. Add the zucchini/courgette and cook for an additional 1 minute on HIGH. Stir in the sherry before serving.

Cheesy Spinach Soup

PREPARATION TIME: 15 minutes

MICROWAVE COOKING TIME: 5 minutes

SERVES: 1 person

120g/4oz/½ cup frozen spinach
60g/2oz/½ cup shredded Red Leicester/ Colby cheese
30ml/1oz/2 tbsps hot water
15g/½ oz/1 tbsp butter
15g/½ oz/1 tbsp flour/plain flour
½ a chicken bouillon/stock cube
15ml/1 tbsp chopped onion
280ml/½ pint/1 cup milk
Pinch of thyme
Pinch of nutmeg
Salt and pepper

Put the spinach, onion and water into a small bowl and cover with pierced plastic wrap. Cook for 1 minute on HIGH and set aside. Put the butter into another bowl and cook for 30 seconds on HIGH or until melted. Add the flour, bouillon cube, nutmeg, thyme, milk, and salt and pepper. Cook on MEDIUM for 4 minutes or until thickened. Stir frequently. Add the spinach and its cooking liquid to the soup, and purée in a food processor until smooth. Stir in the cheese, reserving 1 tbsp. Re-heat on MEDIUM for 1 minute. Sprinkle the reserved cheese on top to serve.
To serve 2 people, double the ingredients and cook the soup for 5-6 minutes on MEDIUM.

700ml/1¼ pints/2 cups tomato sauce/ tinned tomatoes, liquidized and sieved
280ml/½ pint/1 cup hot water
½ a beef bouillon stock cube, or 5ml/1 tsp instant beef bouillon granules
30ml/1oz/2 tbsps cream
30ml/1oz/2 tbsps red wine
1.25ml/¼ tsp cornstarch/cornflour
Pinch sugar
2 tbsps fresh basil leaves
2 tbsps parsley
½ clove garlic
30ml/1oz/2 tbsps olive oil
Salt and pepper

Mix the tomato sauce, water, beef bouillon, sugar, and salt and pepper together in a 1150ml/2 pint, 1 quart casserole. Cover and cook for 2 minutes on HIGH. Mix the cornstarch and wine together and stir into the soup. Heat for 2 minutes on HIGH, stirring every 30 seconds. Put the basil leaves, parsley and garlic into a blender and purée. Add the oil in a thin, steady stream with the machine running. Re-heat the soup for 1 minute on HIGH, and stir in the cream just before serving. Add the

basil mixture, and stir through the soup.
To serve one person only, use half of all the ingredients, and cook the soup for a total of 2 minutes.

Consommé with Vegetable Noodles

PREPARATION TIME: 15 minutes

MICROWAVE COOKING TIME: 5 minutes

SERVES: 2 people

300g/10½ oz can condensed beef or chicken consommé
430ml/¾ pint/1½ cups water
1 bay leaf
15ml/½ oz/1 tbsp sherry
1 small zucchini/courgette
1 small carrot, peeled

Combine the consommé and the water. Add the bay leaf and heat through for 1 minute on HIGH. Cut ends off the zucchini/courgette and carrot, and using a swivel peeler, pare

This page: Consommé with Vegetable Noodles. Facing page: Cheesy Spinach Soup (top) and Tomato and Basil Soup (bottom).

SNACKS

Italian Ham Sandwiches

PREPARATION TIME: 10 minutes

MICROWAVE COOKING TIME:
4 minutes

SERVES: 2 people

120g/¼ lb Parma, or other Italian ham
60g/2oz sliced Mozzarella cheese
4 mild Italian peppers
15g/½ oz/1 tbsp butter or margarine
Pinch garlic powder
Pinch of oregano
2 French rolls

Mix the butter, garlic and oregano. Split the rolls and spread the butter thinly on each of the cut sides. Layer the ham, peppers and cheese on the bottom half of the roll. Place the top on and press down. Place the sandwiches on a paper towel in the oven. Cook on MEDIUM for 4-5 minutes or until the cheese melts. Serve immediately.

Sloppy Joes

PREPARATION TIME: 15 minutes

MICROWAVE COOKING TIME:
14 minutes

SERVES: 2 people

225g/½ lb ground/minced beef or pork
1 small onion, finely chopped
60g/2oz/¼ cup chopped green pepper
280ml/½ pint/1 cup tomato sauce/
* canned tomatoes*

**This page: Italian Ham
Sandwiches (top) and Cheese and
Mushroom Croissants (bottom).
Facing page: Sausage and
Sauerkraut Sandwiches (top) and
Sloppy Joes (bottom).**

2 tsps Worcestershire sauce
½ tsp dry mustard
1½ tsps cider vinegar
1 tsp brown sugar
Salt and pepper
2 Kaiser rolls or hamburger buns

Mix the meat and onion in a casserole and cook, uncovered, for 7 minutes on HIGH. Mash the meat with a fork several times while cooking, to break it up into small pieces. Strain off any fat. Add the remaining ingredients and stir well. Cover and cook for a further 5 minutes on HIGH, stirring occasionally. Wrap the rolls in paper towels and heat for 1-2 minutes on MEDIUM. Split and fill with the Sloppy Joe filling. Mixture freezes well.

Tacos

PREPARATION TIME: 15 minutes

MICROWAVE COOKING TIME: 6 minutes

SERVES: 2 people

4 taco shells
120g/¼ lb ground/minced beef
60g/2oz/¼ cup chopped onion
15g/½ oz/1 tbsp raisins
15g/½ oz/1 tbsp pine nuts
15g/½ oz/1 tbsp corn/sweetcorn
5ml/1 tsp chili powder
60ml/2oz/¼ cup tomato sauce/canned
    tomatoes
Salt and pepper

TOPPINGS
60g/2oz/½ cup grated cheese
140ml/¼ pint/½ cup sour cream
120g/4oz/½ cup chopped tomatoes
60g/2oz/1 cup shredded lettuce
1 chopped avocado

Put the beef and onion into a 1150ml/2 pint/1 quart casserole. Break the meat up well with a fork. Cover and cook for 2 minutes on HIGH, stirring occasionally to break into small pieces. Drain any fat from the meat and add salt and pepper, chili powder, corn, nuts, raisins and tomato sauce. Cover and cook on MEDIUM for 4 minutes. Spoon into the taco shells and serve with the various toppings.

Sausage and Sauerkraut Sandwiches

PREPARATION TIME: 10 minutes

MICROWAVE COOKING TIME: 1½ minutes

SERVES: 2 people

4 slices rye bread, light or dark
120g/¼ lb smoked sausage (kielbasa or
    bratwurst), thinly sliced
4 slices Muenster or Tilsit cheese
90g/3oz/½ cup drained sauerkraut
30g/1oz/2 tbsps butter or margarine

DRESSING
15ml/1 tbsp spicy brown mustard
2 tbsps mayonnaise
7.5ml/1½ tsps chopped dill pickle

Melt the butter for 30 seconds on HIGH in a small bowl. Mix dressing and spread on both sides of the bread slices. Layer on the sauerkraut, sausage and cheese. Heat a browning dish for 5 minutes on HIGH. Brush 1 side of the bread with melted butter and place the sandwich in the dish. Cook for 15 seconds, or until golden brown. Turn over and brush the other side with butter and cook that side for 20-30 seconds or until the bread is browned and the cheese melted. Serve hot.

Cheese and Mushroom Croissants

PREPARATION TIME: 15 minutes

MICROWAVE COOKING TIME: 3 minutes

SERVES: 1 person

1 croissant or crescent roll
5ml/1 tsp butter
2.5ml/½ tsp flour/plain flour
2 mushrooms, sliced
60g/2oz/¼ cup Gruyère cheese
60ml/2oz/¼ cup milk
15ml/½ oz/1 tbsp white wine
2.5ml/½ tsp Dijon mustard
Nutmeg
Salt and pepper

Split the top of the croissant, taking care not to cut through to the bottom or the ends. Melt 2.5ml/½ tsp butter in a small bowl for 15 seconds on HIGH. Add the mushrooms and cook for 30 seconds on HIGH and set aside. Melt the remaining butter in a 570ml/1 pint measure. Stir in the flour and add the milk and wine gradually. Add a pinch of nutmeg, mustard and salt and pepper. Cook on HIGH for 1 minute or until thick. Stir in the cheese and spoon into the croissant. Top with the mushrooms and heat through for 1 minute on MEDIUM. Serve immediately.

Pizza Muffins

PREPARATION TIME: 10 minutes

MICROWAVE COOKING TIME: 2 minutes

SERVES: 1 person

1 English muffin, split
30ml/2 tbsps tomato paste
30ml/1oz/2 tbsps water
1 green/spring onion, sliced
1.25ml/¼ tsp oregano
Pinch garlic powder
60g/2oz/¼ cup pepperoni or Italian
    salami, chopped, or 4 anchovies
2-3 Italian olives, stoned and halved
5ml/1 tsp capers
45g/1½ oz/⅓ cup grated Mozzarella
    cheese
15g/½ oz/1 tbsp Parmesan cheese
Salt and pepper

Mix the tomato paste with the water, salt and pepper, onion, oregano and garlic powder, and spread on the muffin halves. Arrange the sausage or a cross of anchovies on top. Add the olives and capers and sprinkle on the Mozzarella cheese. Sprinkle on the Parmesan cheese last and put the pizzas on a paper towel, then cook for 1½-2 minutes on HIGH. Turn the pizzas once or twice during cooking. For 2 people, double the ingredients and cook for 4-4½ minutes on HIGH.

Facing page: Tacos.

Vegetable Pockets

PREPARATION TIME: 10 minutes

MICROWAVE COOKING TIME:
4-5 minutes

SERVES: 2 people

1 piece wholewheat pitta bread
15ml/½ oz/1 tbsp olive oil
5ml/1 tsp lemon juice
1 tomato, roughly chopped
1 red onion, thinly sliced or 2 green/spring
    onions, sliced
1 green pepper, thinly sliced
60g/2oz/1 cup fresh spinach leaves
2.5ml/½ tsp chives
15ml/1 tbsp fresh basil leaves, if available
1 small zucchini/courgette, thinly sliced
6 black olives, stoned
30g/1oz/¼ cup crumbled feta cheese
Salt and pepper

Cut the pitta bread in half and open
out the pockets. Mix the lemon juice
and oil together with the salt and
pepper. Toss the cheese, tomato,
vegetables, herbs and olives together
in the dressing. Fill the pockets with
the vegetables and heat for 4-5
minutes on MEDIUM. Serve
immediately.

Tuna Melt

PREPARATION TIME: 10 minutes

MICROWAVE COOKING TIME:
2 minutes

SERVES: 1 person

1 English muffin, split
1 small can white tuna
30ml/2 tbsps cottage cheese
30ml/2 tbsps mayonnaise
1 stick celery, chopped
5ml/1 tsp chopped parsley
10ml/2 tsps chopped chives
2.5ml/½ tsp lemon juice
Alfalfa sprouts
30g/1oz/¼ cup grated Colby/Red
    Leicester cheese
Salt and pepper

Mix together the tuna, cottage
cheese, mayonnaise, celery, parsley,
chives, and salt and pepper. Taste and
add lemon juice if desired. Put alfalfa
sprouts on the muffin halves and

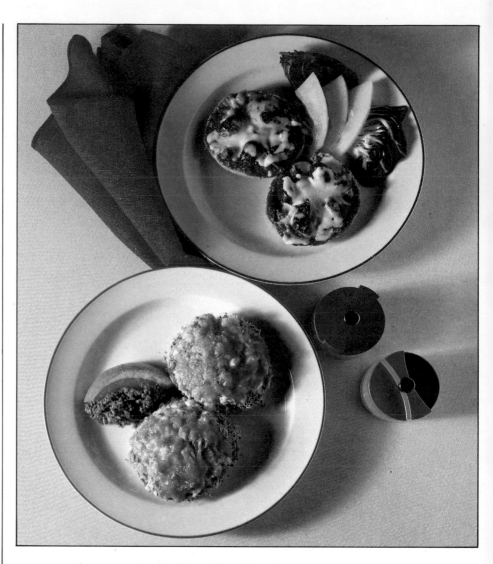

spoon on the tuna mixture. Top with
the cheese and heat for 1 minute on
MEDIUM. Increase the heat to
HIGH and heat for 1 minute further,
turning once or twice during cooking.
Serve immediately.

Pocketful of Shrimp

PREPARATION TIME: 10 minutes

MICROWAVE COOKING TIME:
2-4 minutes

SERVES: 2 people

1 piece pitta bread, cut in half
60g/2oz/½ cup bean sprouts
120g/4oz/½ cup cooked shrimp, peeled
    and de-veined
15ml/1 tbsp chili sauce
30ml/1oz/2 tbsps mayonnaise
2.5ml/½ tsp horseradish

**This page: Pizza Muffins (top) and
Tuna Melt (bottom). Facing page:
Pocketful of Shrimp (top) and
Vegetable Pockets (bottom).**

1 stick celery, chopped
1 ripe avocado, peeled and thickly sliced
15ml/1 tbsp lemon juice
Salt and pepper

Cut the pitta bread in half and open
a pocket in each half. Toss the
avocado slices in lemon juice and
place them in the sides of the
pockets. Fill each pocket with bean
sprouts. Mix the shrimp, chili sauce,
mayonnaise, horseradish, salt, pepper
and chopped celery together. Put on
top of the bean sprouts and heat
through for 2-4 minutes on
MEDIUM. Serve immediately.

EGG AND CHEESE

Piperade

PREPARATION TIME: 10 minutes

MICROWAVE COOKING TIME:
6 minutes, plus 1 minute standing time

SERVES: 1 person

30ml/1 tbsp finely chopped onion
7.5gm/¼ oz/½ tbsp butter
½ cap pimento, finely chopped
1 tomato
Pinch garlic powder
2 eggs
Pinch oregano
Salt and pepper

Put 570ml/1 pint/2 cups water into a bowl and cover with pierced plastic wrap. Heat for 3 minutes on HIGH or until boiling. Put in the tomato and leave for 30 seconds. Peel and seed the tomato, and chop roughly. Put the butter into a medium-sized bowl with the garlic powder and onion. Cook on HIGH for 3 minutes. Add the pimento, tomato and oregano. Cook on HIGH for 1 minute. Beat the eggs, salt and pepper together, and add to the bowl. Cook on HIGH for about 2 minutes, stirring every 30 seconds, or until the eggs are softly scrambled. Leave to stand for 1 minute before serving. Serve on buttered toast or English muffins, or with French bread.

Sunrise Scramble

PREPARATION TIME: 15 minutes

MICROWAVE COOKING TIME:
5 minutes, plus 1 minute standing time

SERVES: 1 person

30g/1oz/2 tbsps ham, finely chopped
2 eggs
15g/½ oz/1 tbsp butter
15g/½ oz/1 tbsp grated cheese
30g/1oz/¼ cup mushrooms, sliced
1 tomato
15ml/1 tbsp chopped parsley
Salt and pepper

Put the butter into a small bowl, add the mushrooms, and cook for 2 minutes on HIGH or until soft. Drain away any excess liquid. Add the ham, and cook for 1 minute on HIGH. Cut the tomato in quarters, but leave attached at the base. Heat for 1 minute on HIGH, and keep warm. Beat the eggs and add the cheese, parsley, and salt and pepper. Add the eggs to the bowl with the ham and mushrooms, and cook for 2 minutes on HIGH, stirring every 30 seconds until softly scrambled. Leave to stand for 1 minute. Fill the tomato with the egg mixture and serve.

Spinach and Cheese Layered Quiche

PREPARATION TIME: 20 minutes

MICROWAVE COOKING TIME:
11-14 minutes, plus 6 minutes standing time

SERVES: 2 people

PASTRY
60g/2oz/⅓ cup all-purpose flour
60g/2oz/⅓ cup wholewheat/wholemeal flour
60g/2oz/¼ cup margarine
30g/1oz/2 tbsps shortening
60ml/2oz/¼ cup ice cold water
Pinch of salt

FILLING
60g/2oz/½ cup shredded Gruyère or Swiss cheese
3 eggs
60ml/2oz/¼ cup half and half/single cream
60g/2oz/¼ cup chopped frozen spinach, well drained
Nutmeg
Cayenne pepper or Tabasco
Salt and pepper

Put the flours, salt, margarine and shortening into the bowl of a food processor and work until the mixture resembles fine breadcrumbs. With the machine running, add the water gradually until the dough holds together. It may not be necessary to add all the water. Roll out the pastry on a floured board to 3mm (⅛″) thick, and put into an 18cm (7″) pie plate. Trim the edge and flute. Refrigerate for 10 minutes. Mix the eggs, cheese, half and half/cream and salt and pepper together well. Divide the mixture in half: add the spinach and pinch of nutmeg to one half, and a pinch of Cayenne pepper or a dash of Tabasco to the other. Prick the base of the pastry with a fork and cook on HIGH for 2-3 minutes or until it starts to crisp. Pour in the cheese mixture and cook for 4 minutes on MEDIUM, or until softly set. Leave to stand for 1 minute. Pour on the spinach mixture and cook for a further 7-10 minutes or until the center is softly set. Leave to stand for 6 minutes before serving.

Facing page: Sunrise Scramble (top) and Piperade (bottom).

Niçoise Eggs

PREPARATION TIME: 10 minutes

MICROWAVE COOKING TIME:
9 minutes

SERVES: 2 person

2 eggs
4 tomatoes, peeled, seeded and chopped
5ml/1 tsp butter
2 mushrooms, chopped
30ml/1oz/2 tbsps white wine
15ml/1 tbsp capers
4 black olives, stoned and sliced
2 anchovies, chopped
15ml/1 tbsp tarragon
Pinch of paprika
Salt and pepper
30g/1oz/¼ cup Gruyère or Swiss cheese, grated

This page: Italian Fondue (left) and Niçoise Eggs (right). Facing page: Tuna and Tomato Quiche (top) and Spinach and Cheese Layered Quiche (bottom).

Put the butter into a small casserole and melt for 30 seconds on HIGH. Add the chopped mushrooms, tarragon and half the wine, and cook for 2 minutes on HIGH. Add the remaining ingredients except the cheese, eggs and paprika, and cook for 1-2 minutes on HIGH. Divide the tomato mixture into 2 custard cups/ramekin dishes and make a well in the center. Put an egg into the center of the mixture in each cup. Pierce the yolk with a sharp knife. Pour over the remaining wine. Cook for 3 minutes

on HIGH or until the white is set and yolk is still soft. Sprinkle on the cheese and paprika and cook for 1 minute on LOW to melt the cheese.

Italian Fondue

PREPARATION TIME: 10 minutes

MICROWAVE COOKING TIME:
5 minutes

SERVES: 1 person

120g/4oz/1 cup shredded Mozzarella cheese
60g/2oz/½ cup shredded mild Cheddar cheese
5ml/1 tsp cornstarch/cornflour
90ml/3oz/⅓ cup red wine

15ml/1 tbsp tomato paste
5ml/1 tsp dry vermouth
½ clove garlic, crushed
2.5ml/½ tsp basil
2.5ml/½ tsp oregano
1 French roll, cut into cubes, or broccoli
flowerets, carrot sticks and celery sticks

Toss the cheese and cornstarch to mix. Put the wine into a deep bowl and cook on MEDIUM for 1-2 minutes, or until it begins to bubble – do not allow it to boil. Add the remaining ingredients except the bread (or vegetables), and stir well to blend completely. Cook for a further 2-3 minutes on MEDIUM, or until the cheese melts. Stir every few seconds. If the mixture begins to boil, reduce the setting to LOW. Serve with the bread cubes or vegetables. Re-heat on LOW if necessary. Serve as an appetizer/starter or as an entrée with a tossed salad.
To serve 2 people, double the ingredients. Cook the wine for 2-3 minutes on MEDIUM, and the cheese and other ingredients for 3-4 minutes on MEDIUM.

Tuna and Tomato Quiche

PREPARATION TIME: 20 minutes

MICROWAVE COOKING TIME:
18 minutes, plus 6 minutes standing time

SERVES: 2 people

PASTRY
120g/4oz/⅔ cup all-purpose/plain flour
60g/2oz/¼ cup margarine
30g/1oz/2 tbsps shortening
30ml/1 tbsp paprika
Pinch of salt
60ml/2oz/¼ cup ice cold water

FILLING
1 can (about 180g/6oz) white tuna,
drained and flaked
3 eggs
2 tomatoes, peeled
60g/2oz/½ cup shredded Cheddar
cheese
60ml/2oz/¼ cup half and half/single
cream
15ml/1 tbsp chopped green/spring onion
Salt and pepper

TOPPING
15ml/1 tbsp dry, seasoned breadcrumbs
30g/1oz/2 tbsps grated Parmesan cheese

Put the flour, salt, paprika, margarine and shortening into the bowl of a food processor and work until the mixture resembles fine breadcrumbs. With the machine running, add the water gradually until the dough holds together. It may not be necessary to add all the water. Roll out the pastry on a floured board to 3mm (⅛") thick and put into an 18cm (7") pie plate. Trim the edge and flute. Refrigerate for 10 minutes. Beat the eggs with the salt, pepper and half and half/single cream. Add the cheese, onion and tuna. Cut the tomatoes into quarters and take out the seeds. Prick the base of the pastry and cook on HIGH for 2-3 minutes,

or until starting to crisp. Pour the filling into the pastry shell and decorate the top with the tomatoes. Cook on MEDIUM for 10-15 minutes. Mix the topping ingredients and sprinkle over the top of the quiche 5 minutes before the end of baking. Left-over quiche can be refrigerated for up to 2 days. Eat cold or re-heat on MEDIUM for 2 minutes.

Ham, Broccoli and Pineapple au Gratin

PREPARATION TIME: 15 minutes

MICROWAVE COOKING TIME:
10-12 minutes

SERVES: 2 people

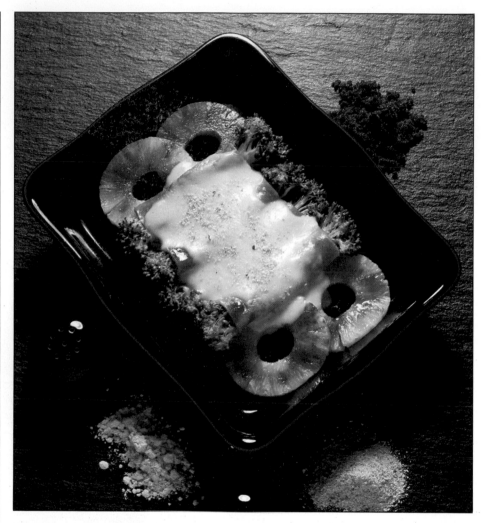

To serve 1 person, make full quantity sauce and cut all other ingredients to half quantity. Cook the mushrooms for 30 seconds on HIGH and the broccoli for 3 minutes on HIGH. Once assembled, cook for 2-3 minutes on MEDIUM. Left-over cheese sauce can be frozen, or kept in the refrigerator for 2 days. Bring to room temperature, re-heat on MEDIUM for 1-2 minutes to serve the sauce.

Asparagus and Tomato Omelette

PREPARATION TIME: 15 minutes
MICROWAVE COOKING TIME: 15 minutes
SERVES: 2 people

4 eggs, separated
120g/4oz/½ cup chopped asparagus, fresh or frozen
30ml/1oz/2 tbsps water
2 tomatoes, peeled, seeded and chopped
45g/1½ oz/⅓ cup Gruyère cheese, grated
90ml/3oz/⅓ cup milk
15g/½ oz/1 tbsp butter or margarine
5ml/1 tsp flour/plain flour
Salt and pepper

Put the asparagus and water into a 570ml/1 pint casserole. Cover and cook for 5-6 minutes on HIGH. Beat the egg yolks, milk, flour, and salt and pepper together. Beat the egg whites until stiff but not dry and fold into the yolks. Melt the butter in a 23cm (9″) pie plate for 30 seconds on HIGH. Pour the omelette mixture onto the plate and cook on MEDIUM for 7 minutes or until set. Lift the edges of the omelette to allow the uncooked mixture to spread evenly. Sprinkle with the cheese, and spread on the asparagus and chopped tomato. Fold over and cook for 1 minute on LOW to melt the cheese. Serve immediately.

4 slices cooked ham
8 broccoli spears
30g/1oz/¼ cup sliced mushrooms
15g/½ oz/1 tbsp butter
4 pineapple rings, drained
30ml/1oz/2 tbsps water
Pinch of salt
5ml/1 tsp dark brown sugar

SAUCE
15g/½ oz/1 tbsp flour/plain flour
15g/½ oz/1 tbsp butter
1.25ml/¼ tsp dry mustard
140ml/¼ pint/½ cup milk
30g/1oz/2 tbsps shredded Cheddar cheese
Salt and pepper

TOPPING
30g/1oz/¼ cup dry seasoned breadcrumbs

Put 15g/½ oz/1 tbsp butter in a small bowl and cook for 30 seconds on HIGH. Add the mushrooms and cook for 1 minute on HIGH and set aside. Put the broccoli spears into a casserole with the water and a pinch of salt. Cover and cook for 4 minutes on HIGH. Leave covered while preparing the sauce. In a 570ml/1 pint/2 cup measure, melt 15g/1oz/1 tbsp butter for 30 seconds on HIGH. Stir in the flour, mustard, salt and pepper. Add the milk gradually and cook on HIGH for 1-2 minutes, stirring frequently until thick. Stir in the cheese. Put 2 broccoli spears on each ham slice, stalks towards the middle, and top each with the mushrooms. Roll up and put seam-side down in a baking dish. Arrange pineapple rings on each side and sprinkle with the dark brown sugar. Coat the cheese sauce over the broccoli and ham rolls and top with the crumbs. Cook on MEDIUM for 3-4 minutes or until hot. Serve immediately.

This page: Ham, Broccoli, and Pineapple au Gratin. Facing page: Asparagus and Tomato Omelette.

Egg Foo Yung

PREPARATION TIME: 15 minutes

MICROWAVE COOKING TIME:
10 minutes

SERVES: 2 people

CRAB PATTIES
120g/4oz/½ cup frozen crabmeat,
   defrosted
15ml/1 tbsp chopped green pepper
15ml/1 tbsp chopped green onion/spring
   onion

30g/1oz/¼ cup chopped mushrooms
1 small clove garlic, crushed
60g/2oz/½ cup beansprouts
2 eggs, beaten
1.25ml/¼ tsp ground ginger
Salt and pepper

SAUCE
140ml/¼ pint/½ cup chicken bouillon
5ml/1 tsp sherry
15ml/1 tbsp soy sauce
5ml/1 tsp oyster sauce (optional)
2.5ml/½ tsp brown sugar
10ml/2 tsps cornstarch/cornflour

Beat the eggs in a medium-sized bowl and stir in the remaining ingredients for the patties. Cook on HIGH for 2 minutes, stirring frequently, until softly set. Heat a browning dish on HIGH for 5 minutes. Pour the mixture into the hot dish in 140ml/¼ pint/½ cup amounts, and cook for about 30 seconds per side on HIGH. Cover and keep warm. Combine the sauce ingredients in a 570ml/1 pint/2 cup measure and cook for 1-2 minutes, stirring frequently until clear and thickened. Pour over the patties and serve immediately.

Microwave
COOKING FOR 1 & 2

RICE, PASTA AND GRAINS

Bulgur and Spicy Lamb

PREPARATION TIME: 20 minutes

MICROWAVE COOKING TIME:
26 minutes

SERVES: 2 people

120g/4oz/1 cup bulgur wheat
280ml/½ pint/1 cup water
1 small onion, finely chopped
120g/4oz/¼ lb ground/minced lamb
2.5ml/¼ tsp oil
225g/8oz/1 cup canned plum tomatoes
5ml/1 tsp cumin
1.25ml/¼ tsp cinnamon
5ml/1 tsp chopped mint
30g/1oz/2 tbsps raisins
30g/1oz/2 tbsps almonds, chopped
60ml/2oz/¼ cup yogurt
1 egg
Salt and pepper
1 bay leaf

Put the bulgur and water into a 2 quart casserole with a pinch of salt. Cover and cook on HIGH for 5 minutes, and leave covered while preparing the rest of the ingredients. Heat a browning dish for 5 minutes on HIGH. Put in the oil, add the onion and lamb, breaking the latter up into small pieces with a fork. Add the cumin, cinnamon, and salt and pepper. Return the dish to the oven and cook for 5 minutes on HIGH, stirring frequently. Add the tomatoes, mint, bay leaf, and salt and pepper. Cover and cook for 5 minutes on HIGH. Add the raisins and almonds, and leave to stand. Drain the bulgur wheat well, pressing to remove excess moisture. Mix with the egg and yogurt. Add salt and pepper and put half the bulgur in the bottom of a baking dish. Spread with the lamb filling and cover with another layer of bulgur. Cook uncovered for 5-6 minutes on MEDIUM. Leave to stand, to firm up, for 5 minutes before serving. Serve with a cucumber and yogurt salad.

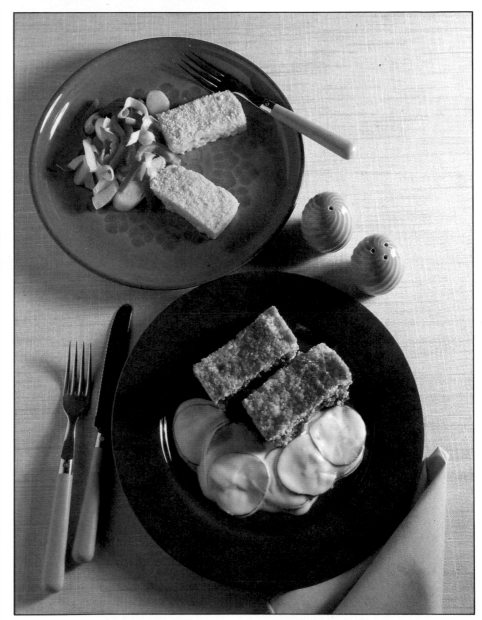

Facing page: Egg Foo Yung. This page: Polenta with Pepper and Leek Salad (top) and Bulgur and Spicy Lamb (bottom).

To serve 1 person, prepare the full quantity casserole and divide into two. One of the casseroles may be frozen.

Sausage Risotto

PREPARATION TIME: 15 minutes

MICROWAVE COOKING TIME: 29 minutes

SERVES: 2 people

60g/2oz/½ cup Italian rice, uncooked
30g/1oz/¼ cup broken, uncooked
   spaghetti
1 Italian sausage, mild or hot
15ml/1 tbsp oil
1 small onion, finely sliced
½ clove garlic, crushed
60g/2oz/½ cup quartered mushrooms
2 tomatoes, peeled and seeded
7.5ml/1½ tsps chopped parsley
2.5ml/½ tsp basil
280ml/½ pint/1 cup beef bouillon
60g/2oz/¼ cup Parmesan cheese
Salt and pepper

Remove sausage meat from casing. Heat a browning dish for 5 minutes on HIGH. Add the oil and sausage. Cook for 4 minutes on HIGH, breaking up the sausage meat with the fork. Add the onion, garlic and mushrooms, and cook for 2 minutes more on HIGH, stirring frequently. Put the contents of the browning dish into a 1150ml/2 pint/1 quart casserole and add the rice, spaghetti, basil, salt and pepper, and beef bouillon. Cover and cook for 15 minutes on HIGH. Stir in the parsley and chopped tomatoes, and leave to stand 3 minutes before serving. Sprinkle with Parmesan cheese.

Tri-colored Tagliatelle and Vegetables

PREPARATION TIME: 10 minutes

MICROWAVE COOKING TIME: 12 minutes, plus 2 minutes standing time

SERVES: 1 person

60g/2oz tagliatelle or fettucini (mixture
   of red, green and plain)
½ a small sweet red pepper, cut into 5mm
   (¼") strips
½ a small onion, thinly sliced
60g/2oz/½ cup broccoli flowerets
30g/1oz/2 tbsps butter
1 small clove garlic, crushed
7.5ml/1½ tsps dried rosemary (or 1 sprig
   fresh)
Grated Parmesan cheese
Salt and pepper

Put the pasta into a large bowl and cover with water. Cook for 6 minutes on HIGH. Leave to stand for 2 minutes. Rinse in hot water and leave to drain. If using fresh pasta, cut the cooking time in half. Put 15g/½ oz/1 tbsp butter into a medium-sized

This page: Sausage Risotto. Facing page: Tri-colored Tagliatelle and Vegetables.

bowl and add the broccoli, onion and red pepper strips. Cover with pierced plastic wrap and cook for 1-2 minutes on HIGH. Toss with the pasta and keep warm. Melt the remaining butter with the crushed garlic and rosemary for 30 seconds on HIGH in a small bowl or custard cup/ramekin dish. Strain the butter onto the pasta and vegetables and discard the rosemary and garlic. Season with salt and pepper. Heat the pasta through on MEDIUM for 2 minutes. Toss with

Parmesan cheese and serve. For 2 people, double all the ingredients. Cook the pasta for 10 minutes on HIGH if using dried, and 5 minutes on HIGH if using fresh. Cook the broccoli, onion and red pepper for 2-3 minutes on HIGH.

Polenta with Pepper and Leek Salad

PREPARATION TIME: 15 minutes

MICROWAVE COOKING TIME: 12 minutes, plus 5 minutes standing time

SERVES: 2 people

120g/4oz/½ cup yellow cornmeal
420ml/¾ pint/1½ cups water
15ml/1 tbsp finely chopped onion
30g/1oz/¼ cup shredded Mozzarella cheese
60g/2oz/¼ cup Parmesan cheese
Salt and pepper

SALAD
1 red pepper
1 large or 2 small leeks

DRESSING
15ml/1 tbsp vinegar
30ml/2 tbsps oil
2.5ml/½ tsp dry mustard
1.25ml/¼ tsp sugar
1.25ml/¼ tsp fennel seeds, crushed
1.25ml/¼ tsp marjoram

Mix the cornmeal, salt and pepper, onion and water in a large bowl. Cook for 6 minutes on HIGH. Add the Mozzarella, cover and leave to stand for 5 minutes. Spread into a square pan and sprinkle the top with the Parmesan cheese. Refrigerate, and when ready to use, cut into squares and heat for 1 minute on HIGH before serving. Slice the pepper into 5mm (¼") strips. Trim off the dark green tops of the leeks and slice the white part into quarters. Mix the dressing ingredients together and put the vegetables into a 1 pint casserole. Pour over the dressing and mix together well. Cover and cook for 5 minutes on MEDIUM. Serve warm with the polenta.

Barley Ring with Turkey Filling

PREPARATION TIME: 20 minutes

MICROWAVE COOKING TIME: 31 minutes, plus 5 minutes standing time

SERVES: 2 people

120g/4oz/1 cup pearl barley
850ml/1½ pints/3 cups water
1 egg, beaten
60g/2oz/½ cup whole cranberries
2.5ml/½ tsp sugar
Grated rind and juice of half an orange
60g/2oz/½ cup chopped walnuts
30g/1oz/2 tbsps butter or margarine
1 shallot
90g/3oz/¾ cup mushrooms, sliced
225g/8oz/½ lb uncooked boned turkey, cut into 2.5cm (1") pieces
15g/½ oz/1 tbsp flour/plain flour
140ml/¼ pint/½ cup chicken bouillon/stock
30ml/2 tbsps parsley
140ml/¼ pint/½ cup cream
Salt and pepper

Put the barley into a large bowl with the water and a pinch of salt. Cover with pierced plastic wrap and cook for 20 minutes on HIGH, stirring once. Leave to stand, covered, for at least 5 minutes. Combine the cranberries, sugar and orange juice in a small bowl. Cook uncovered for 1-2 minutes on HIGH. Drain the barley well, and fold in the parsley, cranberries, walnuts, orange rind and beaten egg. Press into a 570ml/1 pint/2 cup microwave ring-mold. Put the butter into a 570ml/1 pint/2 cup casserole and cook for 30 seconds on HIGH to melt. Add the turkey, shallot and mushrooms. Cover and cook for 2 minutes on HIGH, stirring every 30 seconds. Sprinkle on the flour and stir in well. Add the stock and cream and blend well. Season, cover and cook for an additional 3 minutes on HIGH, stirring every 30 seconds until thickened. Keep warm. Re-heat the barley ring covered with pierced plastic wrap for 3 minutes on HIGH. Turn it out and fill the center with the turkey.
To serve one person, cut all the

ingredients to half quantity, and omit the egg. Serve the barley as a pilaff topped with the turkey filling.

Indian Pilaff

PREPARATION TIME: 15 minutes

MICROWAVE COOKING TIME: 30 minutes

SERVES: 2 people

60g/2oz/½ cup long-grain rice (basmati, if available)
30g/1oz/¼ cup almonds, toasted
1 small onion, sliced
15ml/1 tbsp oil
30g/1oz/2 tbsps peas
2 okra, sliced
30g/1oz/2 tbsps coconut
30g/1oz/2 tbsps golden raisins
280ml/½ pint/1 cup chicken bouillon
15ml/1 tbsp lemon juice
15ml/1 tbsp curry powder
15ml/1 tbsp chopped parsley
2.5ml/½ tsp dried red pepper flakes
Salt and pepper

Heat a browning dish for 5 minutes on HIGH. Sprinkle on the almonds and return the dish to the oven. Cook on HIGH for 3 minutes, stirring the almonds every 30 seconds until golden brown. Remove the almonds from the dish and allow to cool. Add the oil to the browning dish and stir in the sliced onion. Return to the oven and cook for 2 minutes on HIGH or until golden brown. Add the curry powder and cook for 1 minute on HIGH. Put the onion into a casserole and add the rice, pepper flakes, coconut, chicken bouillon and lemon juice. Cover and cook on HIGH for 3 minutes until boiling. Reduce the setting to MEDIUM, add the raisins and cook for 12 minutes. Add the peas, okra and parsley 2 minutes before the end of the cooking time. Sprinkle with toasted almonds before serving. (One serving may be kept in the refrigerator for 2 days. Re-heat for 2-3 minutes on MEDIUM.)

Facing page: Barley Ring with Turkey Filling.

Fried Rice

PREPARATION TIME: 15 minutes

MICROWAVE COOKING TIME:
12 minutes

SERVES: 2 people

60g/2oz/½ cup quick-cooking rice
200ml/6oz/¾ cup water
3 dried Chinese mushrooms
2 green/spring onions, sliced
60g/2oz/¼ cup shrimp, peeled and de-
  veined
Small piece ginger root
Small can sliced bamboo shoots or lotus
  root
1 egg
7.5ml/1½ tsps soy sauce
2.5ml/½ tsp sesame oil
1 tbsp vegetable oil
Salt and pepper

Put the mushrooms into a bowl with
enough water to cover. Cover with
pierced plastic wrap and cook for
3 minutes on HIGH. Leave to stand
until softened. Put the rice, water and
a pinch of salt in a 150ml/2 pint/
1 quart casserole. Cover and cook on
HIGH for 2½ minutes. Leave to
stand while preparing the other
ingredients. Drain and slice the
mushrooms. Slice the ginger into thin
slivers. Beat the egg with the soy
sauce. Heat a browning dish for
5 minutes on HIGH, pour in the
vegetable oil and quickly add the
mushrooms, bamboo shoots, ginger,
and half the onion. Stir and return to
the oven, and cook for 1 minute on
HIGH. Mix the rice with the egg, soy
sauce and sesame oil, and stir into
the mixture in the browning dish.
Cook, uncovered, for 3 minutes on
HIGH, stirring every 30 seconds
until the egg sets. Add the shrimp
after 2 minutes. Serve garnished with
the remaining green onion.

Clam Shells in Saffron Sauce

PREPARATION TIME: 15 minutes

MICROWAVE COOKING TIME:
16 minutes, plus 5 minutes
standing time

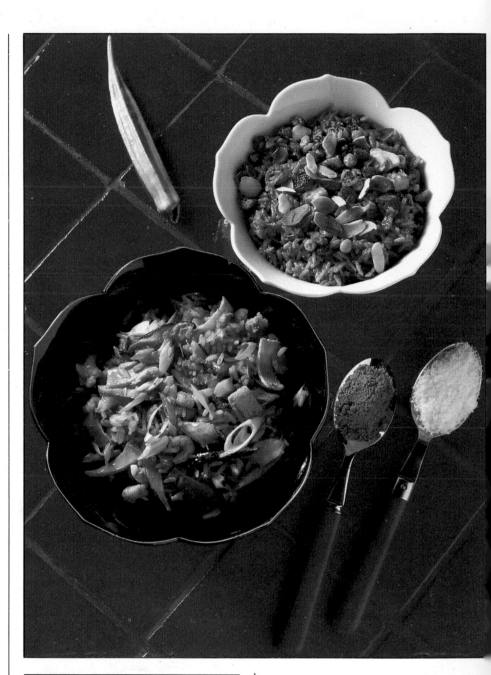

SERVES: 2 people

120g/4oz/1½ cups wholewheat
225g/8oz/1 cup canned whole clams,
  liquid reserved
30ml/2 tbsps chopped parsley
1-2 tomatoes, peeled, seeded and cut into
  5mm (¼") strips
1 shallot, finely chopped
15ml/1 tbsp saffron
15g/½ oz/1 tbsp butter
7ml/½ tbsp flour/plain flour
140ml/¼ pint/½ cup heavy/double
  cream
Reserved clam juice, made up to 140ml/
¼ pint/½ cup with water if necessary
30ml/1oz/2 tbsps white wine
Salt and pepper

Put the pasta shells into a large bowl
with enough hot water to cover.
Cook for 8 minutes on HIGH and
leave to stand for 5 minutes. Rinse
under hot water and leave in cold
water. Melt the butter in a small bowl
on HIGH for 30 seconds. Stir in the
flour and add the clam juice gradually. Add the wine, shallot and
saffron and cook, covered with

SAUCE

345g/12oz/1½ cups canned plum
   tomatoes
15ml/1 tbsp oil
60g/12oz/½ cup sliced mushrooms
½ clove garlic, crushed
1.25ml/¼ tsp basil
Pinch ground allspice
5ml/1 tsp tomato paste
1 bay leaf
Salt and pepper

FILLING

120g/4oz/½ cup frozen chopped spinach,
   defrosted
60g/2oz/¼ cup pepperoni sausage,
   skinned and chopped
120g/4oz/1 cup ricotta cheese
60g/2oz/¼ cup grated Parmesan cheese
   (plus extra for serving if desired)
Nutmeg
Salt and pepper

Put the cannelloni or large shell pasta
into a large, shallow casserole, and
pour over enough hot water to cover.
Cook for 8 minutes on HIGH. Leave
to stand for 5 minutes. Rinse in hot
water and leave standing in cold
water. Put the oil into a 1 quart
casserole and heat for 30 seconds on
HIGH. Add the mushrooms and
garlic and cook for 1 minute on
HIGH. Add the remaining sauce
ingredients, cover, and cook for
5 minutes on HIGH. Stir well and
mash the tomatoes to break them up.
Meanwhile drain the pasta well. Mix
the filling ingredients together and fill
the pasta. Put the pasta into a small
casserole dish and pour over the
tomato sauce. Cook on HIGH for
5 minutes to heat through. Serve
with additional Parmesan cheese.
To serve one person, halve the
quantity of each ingredient. Cook the
sauce for 3 minutes total in a smaller
casserole or bowl. Alternatively,
prepare this recipe in full and freeze
one half for later use.

**Facing page: Indian Pilaff (top)
and Fried Rice (bottom). This
page: Clam Shells in Saffron
Sauce (top) and Cannelloni Stuffed
with Spinach, Cheese and
Pepperoni (bottom).**

pierced plastic wrap, for 3 minutes
on HIGH until thickened. Stir every
30 seconds. Stir in the cream and
cook for 1 minute on HIGH. Mix in
the clams, parsley, and salt and
pepper. Cover and cook for 2
minutes on HIGH to heat through.
Add the tomato strips and cook for
1 minute on MEDIUM. Pour over
the pasta and serve immediately.
To serve 1 person, cut the quantity of
all the ingredients by half. Cook the
sauce for half of the recommended
time.

Cannelloni Stuffed with Spinach, Cheese and Pepperoni

PREPARATION TIME: 15 minutes

MICROWAVE COOKING TIME:
19 minutes, plus 5 minutes
standing time

SERVES: 2 people

6-8 (depending on size) cannelloni or
large shell pasta

Microwave
COOKING FOR 1 & 2

FISH AND SEAFOOD

Stuffed Trout

PREPARATION TIME: 15 minutes

MICROWAVE COOKING TIME: 5 minutes

SERVES: 1 person

1 whole rainbow trout, cleaned
1 shallot, finely chopped
120g/4oz/½ cup frozen chopped spinach, thawed
Pinch of nutmeg
90g/3oz/¼ cup flaked crabmeat
15g/½ oz/1 tbsp chopped hazelnuts
1 cap pimento, chopped
30ml/1oz/2 tbsps heavy/double cream
15ml/½ oz/1 tbsp lemon juice
Paprika
Salt and pepper

Put the spinach, nutmeg and shallot into a small bowl. Cover with pierced plastic wrap and cook for 1 minute on HIGH to soften the shallot. Stir in the crab, nuts, paprika, salt, pepper, pimento and cream. Trim the tail and fins of the trout, and spoon the stuffing into the cavity. Sprinkle with lemon juice and cook in a shallow baking dish covered with pierced plastic wrap for 4 minutes on HIGH. Peel the skin off the body of the trout, but leave on the head and tail. Garnish with lemon if desired.

Salmon Steaks Bernaise

PREPARATION TIME: 10 minutes

MICROWAVE COOKING TIME: 4-5 minutes

SERVES: 1 person

1 salmon steak
15ml/½ oz/1 tbsp lemon juice
Salt and pepper
SAUCE
2 egg yolks
5ml/1 tsp tarragon or white wine vinegar
5ml/1 tsp lemon juice
5ml/1 tsp chopped tarragon
5ml/1 tsp chopped parsley
Cayenne pepper
60g/2oz/¼ cup butter, melted

This page: Portuguese Seafood Stew. Facing page: Salmon Steaks Bernaise (top) and Stuffed Trout (bottom).

Have a bowl of ice water ready. Combine the egg yolks, vinegar, lemon juice and herbs in a 570ml/1 pint glass measure. In a small bowl, melt the butter for 1 minute on HIGH until very hot. Whisk it into the egg yolks. Cook on HIGH for 15

seconds and whisk again. Repeat the process until the sauce is thick: this usually takes about 2 minutes. Put immediately into the bowl of ice water to stop the cooking. Add the Cayenne pepper, and salt if necessary. If the sauce begins to curdle, put the measure immediately into ice water and beat vigorously. Put the fish into a small baking dish with salt and pepper and lemon juice. Cover with pierced plastic wrap and cook on MEDIUM for 2-3 minutes. Leave to stand, covered, while making the sauce.

Flounder with Avocado

PREPARATION TIME: 15 minutes

MICROWAVE COOKING TIME: 8 minutes

SERVES: 2 people

225g/½ lb flounder fillets, skinned
1 small ripe avocado
30ml/1oz/2 tbsps cream cheese
5ml/1 tsp chives
Juice of 1 lime (or of half a lemon)
15ml/½ oz/1 tbsp white wine
5ml/1 tsp butter
2.5ml/½ tsp flour/plain flour
140ml/¼ pint/½ cup heavy/double cream
Salt and pepper

GARNISH
Reserved chives
Reserved avocado slices

Reserve 2-4 thin slices of avocado and brush with the lemon or lime juice. Mash the rest of the avocado with the cream cheese, chives, salt and pepper, and 5ml/1 tsp lime or lemon juice. Spread the filling over the fish and fold each fillet in half. Put the fillets in a shallow casserole and pour over the wine and remaining juice. Cover with pierced plastic wrap and cook for 6 minutes on MEDIUM. Keep warm. In a small bowl, melt the butter for 30 seconds on HIGH and stir in the flour. Strain on the cooking liquid from the fish and add the cream. Cook, uncovered, for 2 minutes on HIGH until thickened. Remove the fish to

serve on plates and pour some of the sauce over each fillet. Garnish with the reserved avocado slices and chives.

Lemon and Almond Sole

PREPARATION TIME: 10 minutes

MICROWAVE COOKING TIME: 11 minutes

SERVES: 2 people

2 whole sole fillets
1 lemon
30g/1oz/2 tbsps butter
60g/2oz/½ cup almonds
30g/1oz/¼ cup cornflake crumbs
2-4 parsley sprigs
Salt and pepper

Cut 4 thin slices from the lemon and squeeze the rest for juice. Cut 2 circles of baking parchment/unwaxed paper and grease with 15g/½ oz/ 1 tbsp butter. Lay on the fillets of fish and sprinkle over the lemon juice, salt and pepper. Seal up the parcels by twisting the open edges of the paper together. Cook for 5 minutes on MEDIUM. Heat a browning dish on HIGH for 4 minutes and add the remaining butter. Stir in the almonds and cook for 2 minutes, stirring frequently until brown. Stir in the cornflake crumbs. Open the parcels to serve and spoon on the almond topping. Garnish with reserved lemon slices and parsley.

Portuguese Seafood Stew

PREPARATION TIME: 15 minutes

MICROWAVE COOKING TIME: 11 minutes

SERVES: 2 people

3 tomatoes, chopped
½ a green pepper, chopped
½ cup canned clams, in shells if possible, and liquid
1 cod fillet (about 120g/¼ lb), cut into 5cm (2") pieces
1 red snapper fillet (about 120g/¼ lb), cut into 5cm (2") pieces

4 large raw shrimp/prawns, peeled and de-veined, or 60g/2oz/½ cup small shrimp/prawns
½ a clove garlic, chopped
60g/2oz/¼ cup chopped onion
2 tbsps olive oil
5ml/1 tsp tomato paste
30ml/1 tbsp chopped parsley
6 chopped black olives
140ml/¼ pint/½ cup white wine
1 potato, cut into 2.5cm (1") pieces
Salt and pepper

Put the cod and snapper into a casserole. Put the olive oil into another casserole with the onion and garlic and heat for 1 minute on HIGH. Add the potatoes, liquid from the clams, and the wine. Cover and cook for 6 minutes on HIGH. Stir in the tomato paste, add the fish and peppers, and cook for 2 minutes on HIGH. Add the shrimp and cook a further minute on HIGH. Add the tomatoes, clams and olives and cook for another minute on HIGH. Season, and garnish with chopped parsley.

Macadamia Fillets

PREPARATION TIME: 10 minutes

MICROWAVE COOKING TIME: 5 minutes

SERVES: 2 people

2 sole or flounder fillets
1 small can pineapple chunks
¼ of a green pepper, cut into 5mm (¼") strips
1 green/spring onion, shredded
30g/1oz/⅓ cup Macadamia nuts, roughly chopped

SAUCE
Reserved pineapple juice
15ml/½ oz/1 tbsp honey
10ml/2 tsps soy sauce
15ml/½ oz/1 tbsp vinegar
1.25ml/¼ tsp dry mustard
1 tsp cornstarch/cornflour

Facing page: Flounder with Avocado (top) and Lemon and Almond Sole (bottom).

Drain the pineapple and set aside the chunks. Mix the juice and the other sauce ingredients together in a bowl. Add the green pepper and cook uncovered for 1-2 minutes on HIGH or until thickened, stirring every 30 seconds. Add the pineapple chunks, nuts and onions, and set aside. Put the fish into a shallow casserole, thinner portion towards the center of the dish. Cover with pierced plastic wrap, and cook for 2 minutes on HIGH. Allow to stand for 30 seconds. Remove carefully to serving dishes. Coat with the Macadamia sauce. Serve with fried rice or stir-fried vegetables.

This page: **Shrimp and Broccoli au Gratin.** Facing page: **Macadamia Fillets.**

Shrimp and Broccoli au Gratin

PREPARATION TIME: 10 minutes

MICROWAVE COOKING TIME: 6 minutes

SERVES: 2 people

120g/4oz/1 cup broccoli flowerets
225g/½ lb large cooked shrimp, peeled and de-veined
30g/1oz/2 tbsps Parmesan cheese
15g/½ oz/1 tbsp dry breadcrumbs
5ml/1 tsp paprika

SAUCE
30g/1oz/2 tbsps Cheddar cheese
15g/½ oz/1 tbsp butter
15g/½ oz/1 tbsp flour/plain flour
140ml/¼ pint/½ cup milk
Pinch of dry mustard
Pinch of Cayenne pepper
Salt and pepper

Melt 15g/1 tbsp butter in a small

140ml/¼ pint/½ cup heavy/double cream

Melt the butter in a 570ml/1 pint casserole for 30 seconds on HIGH and add the shallot. Cook for 1 minute on HIGH, add the flour, white wine and saffron, and stir well to mix. Add the scallops (cut in half if large) and cook for 1-2 minutes on HIGH. Stir in the cream, parsley and pepper, and cook for a further 2 minutes on HIGH. Serve on parsley rice.

Lobster in Sherry Cream

PREPARATION TIME: 20 minutes

MICROWAVE COOKING TIME: 4 minutes

SERVES: 2 people

1 whole large lobster, boiled; or 1 large lobster tail
60g/2oz/½ cup sliced mushrooms
2.5ml/½ tsp celery salt
140ml/¼ pint/½ cup heavy/double cream
30ml/1oz/2 tbsps sherry
2.5ml/½ tsp butter
2.5ml/½ tsp flour/plain flour
60g/2oz/½ cup Gruyère cheese
Paprika
Pepper

Crack the lobster claws and remove the meat. Remove the meat from the tail, and combine. Reserve the empty tail shell to cook in if desired. Melt the butter for 15 seconds on HIGH, and add the mushrooms. Cook for 1 minute on HIGH and add the flour, sherry, cream, celery salt, and pepper. Cook for 2 more minutes on HIGH until thick, stirring frequently. Add the lobster and spoon into the shell, or a baking dish. Sprinkle on the cheese and plenty of paprika. Cook for 2 minutes on HIGH. Serve immediately.

This page: Scallops in Saffron Cream (top) and Lobster in Sherry Cream (bottom). Facing page: Orange Glazed Lamb Chops with Glazed Vegetables.

bowl for 30 seconds on HIGH. Stir in the flour, mustard and Cayenne pepper. Add the milk gradually until smooth. Cook for 1-2 minutes on HIGH, stirring every 30 seconds. Add salt and pepper and stir in the Cheddar cheese. Cover and set aside. Put the broccoli in a small bowl with 30ml/1oz/2 tbsps water. Cover with pierced plastic wrap and cook for 3 minutes on HIGH until almost tender. In individual dishes or 1 large baking dish, scatter over the broccoli and shrimp. Coat over the sauce, and sprinkle on the Parmesan cheese, crumbs and paprika. Heat through for 1-2 minutes on HIGH before serving.

Scallops in Saffron Cream

PREPARATION TIME: 10 minutes

MICROWAVE COOKING TIME: 8 minutes

SERVES: 2 people

340g/12oz/2 cups uncooked scallops (or 180g/6oz/1 cup, if very large)
1 shallot, finely chopped
1 small red pepper cut into 5mm (¼″) strips
5ml/1 tsp parsley
5ml/1 tsp saffron
140ml/¼ pint/½ cup white wine
25g/¾ oz/1½ tbsps butter
25g/¾ oz/1½ tbsps flour/plain flour

MEAT, POULTRY AND GAME

Orange Glazed Lamb Chops with Glazed Vegetables

PREPARATION TIME: 20 minutes

MICROWAVE COOKING TIME:
14 minutes

SERVES: 2 people

2 lamb shoulder chops
140ml/¼ pint/½ cup orange juice
10ml/2 tsps dark corn syrup
2.5ml/½ tsp red wine vinegar or cider
    vinegar
2.5ml/½ tsp cornstarch/cornflour
15ml/½ oz/1 tbsp water
15ml/½ oz/1 tbsp oil
1 carrot, cut into thick barrel shapes
1 turnip, quartered
60g/2oz/½ cup small onions
1 small potato, quartered
15g/½ oz/1 tbsp butter
Salt and pepper

GARNISH
Orange slices

Heat a browning dish for 5 minutes on HIGH. Put in the oil and chops and cook for 2 minutes on HIGH, turning once, until lightly browned on both sides. Transfer the chops to a casserole dish. Melt the butter and add the vegetables. Cook for 5 minutes on HIGH, stirring frequently to brown evenly. Add to the casserole dish with the chops. De-glaze the browning dish with the orange juice and vinegar, scraping any sediment off the base of the dish. Stir in the corn syrup, salt and pepper, and pour over the chops and vegetables. Cover with pierced plastic wrap and cook on MEDIUM for 6 minutes, or until chops are cooked as much as desired. The chops may be served slightly pink. Remove the chops and vegetables from the casserole and dissolve the cornstarch/cornflour in the water. Stir into the liquid in the casserole and cook, uncovered, for 1 minute on HIGH or until boiling and clear. Pour over the chops and vegetables and garnish with orange slices.
To serve 1 person, reduce the quantity of each ingredient by half, but cook for the same length of time.

Pheasant in Gin

PREPARATION TIME: 15 minutes

MICROWAVE COOKING TIME:
22 minutes

SERVES: 2 people

1 small pheasant, dressed (about
   675-790g/1½-1¾ lbs)
1 apple, peeled and chopped
60ml/2oz/¼ cup gin
5ml/1 tsp juniper berries
2.5ml/½ tsp rosemary
30ml/1oz/2 tbsps chicken bouillon
15g/½ oz/1 tbsp butter
7.5g/1½ tsps flour/plain flour
225g/8oz/1½ cups shredded red cabbage

Heat a browning dish for 5 minutes on HIGH. Put in the butter and, when foaming, add the pheasant. Cook for 3 minutes to lightly brown all sides of the pheasant, turning four times while cooking. Transfer to a medium-sized deep casserole and set aside. Add flour to the dish and scrape up any sediment. Cook for 1 minute to lightly brown the flour. De-glaze the pan with chicken bouillon and add the casserole with the remaining ingredients except the cabbage. Cover and cook for 10 minutes or until the pheasant is tender. It may be served slightly pink. During the last 3 minutes, add the red cabbage. Can be served with the

warm vegetable salad instead of the red cabbage garnish.
To serve 1 person, prepare the complete recipe and use half. The other half will freeze well.

Spicy Steak Kebabs

PREPARATION TIME: 10 minutes, plus 1 hour to marinate meat

MICROWAVE COOKING TIME:
6 minutes

SERVES: 2 people

225g/8oz/½ lb sirloin steak, cut into 4cm
   (1½") cubes
1 leek, white part only
4 large mushrooms
4 cherry tomatoes
½ green pepper, sliced into 2.5cm
   (1") squares

MARINADE
30ml/1oz/2 tbsps oil
15ml/½ oz/1 tbsp lemon juice
½ clove garlic, crushed
1.25ml/¼ tsp ground cumin
1.25ml/¼ tsp ground coriander
1.25ml/¼ tsp gravy browning
Pinch Cayenne pepper
Salt and pepper

Mix the marinade ingredients together and put in the steak cubes, turning to coat evenly. Leave for 1 hour. Thread the meat and vegetables onto wooden skewers. Do not pack the ingredients too tightly together. Put on a roasting rack and cook on MEDIUM for about 6 minutes, turning and basting frequently until cooked as much as desired. Put remaining marinade into a smaller dish and cook for 2-3 minutes on HIGH until syrupy. Serve on a bed of rice. Pour the sauce over the cooked kebabs.
To serve one person, prepare only half of each ingredient, but cook for the same length of time.

**This page: Spicy Steak Kebabs.
Facing page: Pheasant in Gin.**

Stuffed Chicken Breasts in Lemon Tarragon Cream

PREPARATION TIME: 15 minutes

MICROWAVE COOKING TIME: 18 minutes

SERVES: 2 people

2 boned chicken breast halves, skinned
5g/1 tsp butter
60g/2oz/½ cup finely chopped
  mushrooms
90g/3oz package/carton cream cheese
30ml/1oz/2 tbsps white wine
15ml/½ oz/1 tbsp lemon juice
Salt and pepper

SAUCE
15g/½ oz/1 tbsp butter
7.5g/½ tbsp flour/plain flour
Juice of ½ lemon
140ml/¼ pint/½ cup chicken stock
60ml/2oz/¼ cup heavy/double cream
2.5ml/½ tsp chopped tarragon, fresh or
  dried
Salt and pepper

GARNISH
Lemon slices

Cut a pocket along the thicker side of each chicken breast half. Melt 15g/1 tbsp butter for 30 seconds on HIGH in a small bowl. Add the white wine, salt and pepper, and mushrooms. Cook, uncovered, for 2 minutes on HIGH to soften the mushrooms. Cook for an additional 1 minute to evaporate liquid if excessive. Mix with the cream cheese and fill the pockets of the chicken. Put the breasts into a small casserole and sprinkle over the lemon juice and about 15ml/½ oz/1 tbsp water. Cover and cook for about 12 minutes on MEDIUM or until white and firm. Keep warm. In a small bowl melt 1 tbsp butter for 30 seconds on HIGH. Stir in the flour and add the stock and lemon juice gradually. Pour in any cooking liquid from the chicken and add the cream and tarragon. Cook for 1-2 minutes on HIGH, stirring every 30 seconds until thickened. Add salt and pepper. Spoon over the chicken breasts to serve and garnish with lemon slices. Serve with French peas or zucchini/courgette rolls.

To serve one person, reduce the quantity of each ingredient by half. Cook the mushroom filling for the same length of time, and the filled chicken breasts for 10 minutes on MEDIUM. Cook the sauce for about 1 minute on HIGH.

Chicken, Ham and Cheese Rolls with Mustard Sauce

PREPARATION TIME: 15 minutes

MICROWAVE COOKING TIME: 9 minutes

SERVES: 1 person

1 chicken breast half, skinned and boned
1 thin slice cooked ham
1 thin slice Swiss cheese
5ml/1 tsp chopped capers
5ml/1 tsp butter
30g/1oz/2½ tbsps cornflake crumbs
1.25ml/¼ tsp paprika
Salt and pepper

SAUCE
15g/½ oz/1 tbsp butter or margarine
15g/½ oz/1 tbsp flour/plain flour
140ml/¼ pint/½ cup milk
45ml/1½ oz/3 tbsps dry white wine
5ml/1 tsp Dijon mustard
5ml/1 tsp salad mustard
Salt and pepper

Place the chicken breast between 2 pieces of waxed/greaseproof paper and flatten with a meat mallet to about 3mm (⅛"). Lay the cheese on top of the slice of ham. Sprinkle on the capers, and roll up, folding in the sides, and fasten with wooden picks/cocktail sticks. Melt 5ml/1 tsp butter for 30 seconds on HIGH. Combine the cornflake crumbs with the paprika and salt and pepper on a sheet of waxed/greaseproof paper. Brush the chicken with the melted butter and then roll in the crumbs to coat. Push the crumb coating into the surface of the chicken. Put the chicken seam side down into a small casserole dish and cook, uncovered, on MEDIUM for 2 minutes. Turn over, cook for a further 1 minute on MEDIUM, and keep warm while preparing the sauce. Melt 2.5ml/½ tbsp butter for 30 seconds on HIGH in a small bowl. Stir in the flour and add the milk and wine gradually. Stir in the mustards and salt and pepper. Cook, uncovered, for 1-2 minutes on HIGH, stirring every 30 seconds until thickened. Keep warm. Re-heat the chicken on HIGH for 2 minutes and serve with the sauce.
To serve 2 people, double all the ingredients. Cook the chicken for 4 minutes on MEDIUM and the sauce for 2-3 minutes on HIGH. Re-heat the chicken on HIGH for 2 minutes.

Rabbit with Olives

PREPARATION TIME: 15 minutes

MICROWAVE COOKING TIME: 23-28 minutes

SERVES: 2 people

2 rabbit pieces (hind- or fore-quarters)
30g/1oz/2 tbsps butter
10g/2 tsps flour/plain flour
1 shallot, chopped
60ml/2oz/¼ cup dry vermouth
60ml/2oz/¼ cup beef bouillon
60g/2oz/½ cup whole mushrooms
1.25ml/¼ tsp oregano
1.25ml/¼ tsp thyme
15ml/1 tbsp wholegrain mustard
12 stoned green olives, left whole
60ml/2oz/¼ cup heavy/double cream
Salt and pepper

Soak the rabbit overnight to whiten the meat, in enough water to cover, with a squeeze of lemon juice and a pinch of salt. Heat a browning dish for 5 minutes on HIGH. Melt the butter and cook the rabbit pieces for 2 minutes on HIGH, turning over after 1 minute to brown both sides. Remove from the dish to a 570ml/1 pint casserole. Add the mushrooms and shallot to the browning dish with the flour. Cook for 1 minute on HIGH to brown lightly. De-glaze the pan with the bouillon and pour the

Facing page: Chicken, Ham and Cheese Rolls with Mustard Sauce (top) and Stuffed Chicken Breasts in Lemon Tarragon Cream (bottom).

contents over the rabbit. Add the vermouth, herbs, mustard, and salt and pepper. Cover and cook on MEDIUM for 15-20 minutes, or until the rabbit is tender. After 10 minutes, add the olives and cream. Serve with rice or noodles.

To serve one person, half the complete recipe will freeze well.

Devilled Cornish Hen with Golden Rice Stuffing

PREPARATION TIME: 20 minutes

MICROWAVE COOKING TIME: 16 minutes

SERVES: 1 person

1 Cornish game hen/poussin (about 675g/1½ lbs)
30g/1oz/¼ cup quick-cooking rice
90ml/3oz/⅓ cup hot water
1 shallot, finely chopped
½ cap pimento, diced
15g/½ oz/1 tbsp chopped pecans
Pinch saffron
30ml/1oz/2 tbsps bottled steak sauce/ brown sauce
15g/½ oz/1 tbsp butter
2.5ml/½ tsp paprika
2.5ml/½ tsp dry mustard
2.5ml/½ tsp chili powder
5ml/1 tsp sugar
Pinch Cayenne pepper
60ml/2oz/¼ cup chicken bouillon
Salt and pepper

GARNISH
Small bunch watercress or parsley

Put the rice, saffron, shallot and hot water into a 570ml/1 pint casserole, cover, and cook on HIGH for 2 minutes or until the rice is tender and has absorbed all the color from the saffron. Add the pimento and pecans, and allow to cool slightly. Stuff the hen with rice. Mix together the spices, salt and pepper, and sugar. Melt 15g/½ oz/1 tbsp butter for 30 seconds on HIGH and brush it over the hen. Rub the spices over all surfaces of the hen. Close the cavity with wooden picks and place the hen, breast-side down, on a roasting rack. Combine remaining melted butter with the steak/brown sauce and any remaining spices. Cook the hen for 5 minutes on HIGH and baste with the steak/brown sauce mixture. Turn breast-side up, cook for 5 minutes on HIGH, and baste. Cook for 2 minutes more, or until the juices run clear. Leave to stand for 5 minutes before serving. Add the chicken bouillon to the remaining sauce mixture, re-heat for 1-2 minutes on HIGH and pour over the hen to serve. Garnish with watercress or parsley.

To serve 2 people, double all quantities. Add 5 minutes to the cooking time for the hens.

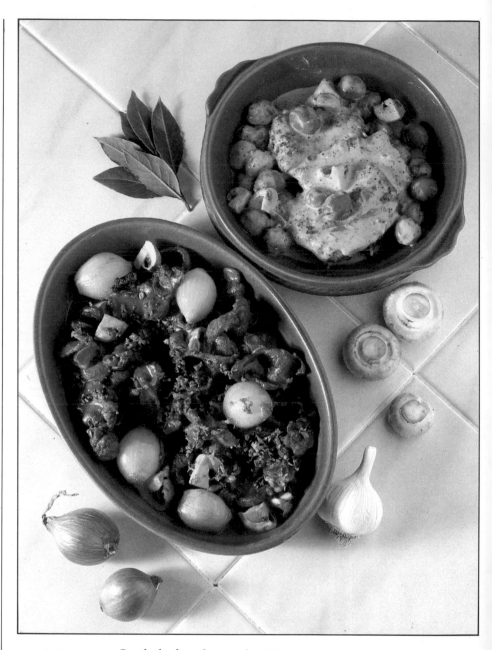

This page: **Rabbit with Olives (top) and Venison Bourguignonne (bottom). Facing page: Devilled Cornish Hen with Golden Rice Stuffing.**

Venison Bourguignonne

PREPARATION TIME: 15 minutes

MICROWAVE COOKING TIME: 36 minutes, plus 15 minutes standing time

SERVES: 2 people

225g/½ lb venison from the leg
1 thick-cut slice bacon, cut into 5mm (¼″) pieces
60g/2oz/½ cup small onions
30g/1oz/¼ cup mushrooms, quartered
½ clove garlic, crushed
15g/½ oz/1 tbsp butter
15g/½ oz/1 tbsp flour/plain flour
90ml/3oz/⅓ cup red wine
200ml/6oz/¾ cup beef bouillon
5ml/1 tsp tomato paste
1 bay leaf
5ml/¼ tsp thyme
Salt and pepper

Melt the butter for 30 seconds on HIGH in a large casserole. Add the onion, bacon, mushrooms and garlic, and cook for 1 minute on HIGH until slightly brown. Remove from the casserole and set aside. Add the venison and cook for 2-3 minutes on HIGH, stirring occasionally to brown slightly. Sprinkle on the flour, and cook for a further minute on HIGH. Stir in the wine, bouillon and tomato paste. Add the thyme and bay leaf and cover the casserole. Cook, stirring occasionally, for 15 minutes on MEDIUM. Add the remaining ingredients, re-cover the casserole, and cook for another 15 minutes on MEDIUM. Leave to stand for 15 minutes before serving. Serve with boiled potatoes or noodles. To serve one person, cook the full recipe, use half and the other half will freeze well.

Fiery Duck

PREPARATION TIME: 15-20 minutes, plus 30-60 minutes to marinate duck

MICROWAVE COOKING TIME: 8 minutes, plus 1 minute standing time

SERVES: 2 people

½ a duck breast, boned and skinned – about 225g/½ lb. If duck parts are unavailable, cut a whole duck into quarters and freeze the leg portions.
½ a small red pepper, sliced into 5mm (¼″) strips
2 sticks celery, thinly sliced
120g/4oz/1 cup beansprouts
2 green/spring onions, sliced
60g/2oz/½ cup roasted cashew nuts

2.5-5ml/½-1 tsp Szechuan pepper, or crushed dried chili peppers
2.5ml/½ tsp cornstarch/cornflour
60ml/2oz/¼ cup chicken bouillon

MARINADE
10ml/2 tsps rice or cider vinegar
10ml/2 tsps soy sauce
10ml/2 tsps sherry
10ml/2 tsps sesame seed oil
Pinch ground ginger
½ clove crushed garlic
Salt and pepper

Remove the skin and bone from the breast portions and cut the duck into thin strips. Combine the marinade ingredients in a medium-sized bowl and stir in the duck pieces. Cover the bowl and chill for 30-60 minutes. Drain the duck, reserving the marinade, and mix the cornstarch/cornflour, bouillon and Szechuan or chili pepper with the marinade. Put the duck into a large casserole and pour over sauce. Stir to mix, cover the dish and cook for 10 minutes on MEDIUM, stirring occasionally. Add the red pepper and celery to the casserole and cook for a further 2 minutes on HIGH. Stir in the cashews, onions and beansprouts. Serve with fried rice or crisp noodles. Best prepared for 2 people.

Turkey Korma (Mild Curry)

PREPARATION TIME: 15 minutes

MICROWAVE COOKING TIME: 10 minutes

SERVES: 1 person

1 turkey leg
30g/1oz/2 tbsps chopped onion
5ml/1 tsp oil
7.5g/1½ tsps butter or margarine
7.5ml/½ tbsp curry powder
5ml/1 tsp paprika
5ml/1 tsp ground coriander
25g/¾ oz/1½ tbsps flour/plain flour
140ml/¼ pint/½ cup chicken bouillon
15g/½ oz/1 tbsp golden raisins
15g/½ oz/1 tbsp roasted cashew nuts or shelled pistachio nuts
10ml/2 tsps unsweetened coconut

60ml/2oz/¼ cup plain yogurt
Salt and pepper

Skin and bone the turkey leg and cut the meat into 2.5cm (1″) pieces. Use half and freeze the other half for use later. Heat the oil in a large casserole for 30 seconds on HIGH. Add the butter and, when melted, add the onion, turkey and spices. Cook for 3 minutes on HIGH to cook the spices. Add the flour and bouillon and stir to mix well. Cover the casserole and cook for 5 minutes on HIGH, stirring frequently until the turkey is tender. Add the raisins, coconut, nuts, salt, pepper and yogurt. Leave to stand, covered, for 1 minute. Serve with rice and chutney.
To serve 2 people, use the whole turkey leg and double all other ingredients. Cook the casserole for 8 minutes on HIGH.

Ham Steaks with Mango Sauce

PREPARATION TIME: 10 minutes

MICROWAVE COOKING TIME: 13 minutes

SERVES: 2 people

2 fully cooked ham slices (about 120g/ ¼ lb each)
15g/½ oz/1 tbsp butter

SAUCE
1 ripe mango, peeled and thinly sliced
2.5ml/½ tsp ground ginger
Juice of half a lime
2.5ml/½ tsp soy sauce
Pinch Cayenne pepper
1.25ml/¼ tsp cornstarch/cornflour
90ml/3oz/⅓ cup orange juice

Cut the ham slices around the outside at 5cm (2″) intervals, 5mm (¼″) in from the edge, to stop them from curling. Reserve 4 thin slices of mango and purée the rest in a food processor with the remaining sauce ingredients. Heat a browning dish on

Facing page: Fiery Duck (top) and Turkey Korma (Mild Curry) (bottom).

HIGH for 5 minutes. Put in the butter and the ham steaks and cook for 1 minute on HIGH. Turn the ham steaks once to brown both sides. Remove the ham from the dish to a casserole and pour over the puréed sauce ingredients. Cook, uncovered, for about 5 minutes on MEDIUM, or until the sauce has thickened. If necessary, remove the ham and keep warm while cooking the sauce for a further 2 minutes on HIGH. Garnish with the reserved mango slices. Serve with sesame stir-fry.

To serve one person, use 1 ham slice and 7.5g/½ tbsp butter. Use full quantity sauce ingredients and cook for the same length of time as for 2 people.

Beef Roulades

PREPARATION TIME: 20 minutes

MICROWAVE COOKING TIME: 19 minutes

SERVES: 2 people

4 pieces rump steak, cut thin and flattened
1 dill pickle, cut into quarters lengthwise
2 green/spring onions, trimmed and cut in half lengthwise
15ml/1 tbsp oil

SAUCE
60g/2oz/½ cup mushrooms, quartered
7.5g/1½ tsp butter or margarine
10ml/2 tsps flour
1.25ml/¼ tsp thyme
1 bay leaf
180ml/5oz/⅔ cup beef bouillon
15ml/½ oz/1 tbsp red wine
Salt and pepper
Gravy browning (if necessary)

GARNISH
Buttered spinach pasta

Roll each of the beef slices around a quarter of the dill pickle and half a green/spring onion. Sprinkle with pepper and fasten with wooden picks/cocktail sticks. Heat a browning dish on HIGH for 5 minutes. Put in the oil and add the roulades. Cook for 8 minutes, turning frequently. Remove from the dish and set aside in a casserole dish.

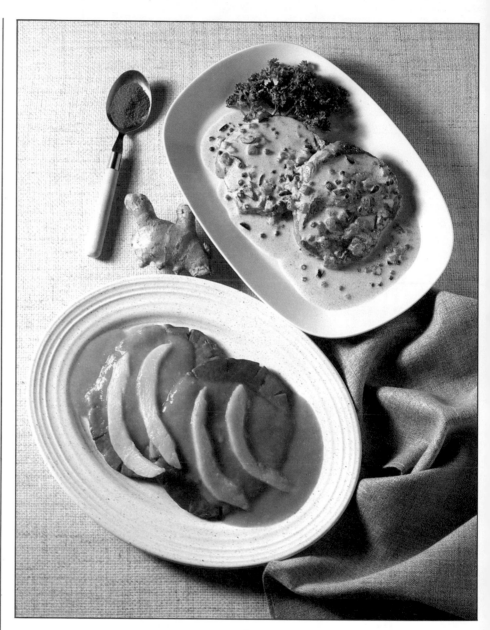

Add the butter to the dish and allow to melt. Add the mushrooms and cook for 1 minute on HIGH. Stir in the flour and cook for 2 minutes to brown lightly. Add the bouillon, wine, thyme and bay leaf, scraping any sediment off the surface of the browning dish. Add gravy browning for extra color if necessary. Season, and pour over the roulades. Cover the dish and cook for 12 minutes on MEDIUM. Test the meat with a knife and if not tender, cook for a further 3 minutes on HIGH. Serve with the pasta or French peas.

To serve one person, prepare only half the quantity of each ingredient and cook the roulades in the sauce for about 10 minutes on MEDIUM. Alternatively, the full quantity recipe freezes well.

Mexican Pork Casserole

PREPARATION TIME: 15 minutes

MICROWAVE COOKING TIME: 28 minutes

SERVES: 2 people

225g/8oz/½ lb boneless pork loin, cut into 2.5cm (1") cubes peppers, cover, and cook on MEDIUM for 17 minutes, or until the pork loses its pink color. Add the beans and heat for 2 minutes on MEDIUM. Serve with tortilla chips if desired.

To serve 1 person, prepare full quantity casserole, and freeze half.

Veal Chops in Peppercorn Cream Sauce

PREPARATION TIME: 15 minutes
MICROWAVE COOKING TIME: 25 minutes
SERVES: 2 people

2 loin veal chops
15g/½ oz/1 tbsp butter or margarine
140ml/¼ pint/½ cup heavy/ double cream
60ml/2oz/¼ cup chicken bouillon
30ml/½ oz/2 tbsps brandy
15ml/1 tbsp green peppercorns, dried (or packed in brine, drained and rinsed)
½ cap pimento, diced
2 black olives, stoned and sliced thinly
Salt and pepper

Remove some of the fat from the outside of the chops. Heat a browning dish on HIGH for 5 minutes. Put in the butter or margarine and the chops. Cook for 3 minutes on HIGH, turning once, until both sides are lightly browned. Remove the chops to a casserole. Deglaze the dish with the bouillon and add the brandy, salt and pepper. Pour the sauce over the chops, cover with pierced plastic wrap, and cook on MEDIUM for 15 minutes or until the chops are tender. Add the peppercorns, pimento and olives during the last 3 minutes of cooking time. If the chops are not tender after 15 minutes, cook for an additional 2 minutes on MEDIUM. Add the cream and cook 1 minute on HIGH. Serve with zucchini/courgette rolls, leeks Provençale, or French peas.

To serve 1 person, cut the quantities of each ingredient by half and cook for the same length of time.

0g/3oz/½ cup canned garbanzo beans/ chickpeas
0g/3oz/½ cup canned kidney beans
0g/1oz/¼ cup chopped sweet red pepper
0g/1oz/¼ cup chopped green pepper
½ small chili pepper, finely chopped
0g/1oz/¼ cup chopped onion
5g/½ oz/1 tbsp flour/plain flour
0ml/2 tsps oil
00ml/6oz/¾ cup beef bouillon/stock
5ml/1 tbsp instant coffee
½ clove garlic, crushed
.25ml/¼ tsp ground cumin
.25ml/¼ tsp ground coriander

GARNISH
Tortilla chips

Facing page: Veal Chops in Peppercorn Cream Sauce (top) and Ham Steaks with Mango Sauce (bottom). This page: Mexican Pork Casserole (top) and Beef Roulades (bottom).

Heat a browning dish for 5 minutes on HIGH. Put in the oil and add the pork cubes. Cook for 2 minutes on HIGH, stirring frequently, until slightly browned. Add the cumin, coriander, garlic, onion and flour, and cook for 1-2 minutes on HIGH. Dissolve the instant coffee in the bouillon/stock and add to the casserole, stirring well. Add the

VEGETABLES

Corn on the Cob with Flavored Butters

PREPARATION TIME: 10 minutes

MICROWAVE COOKING TIME: 8 minutes

SERVES: 2 people

2 ears of corn
45g/1½ oz/3 tbsps butter with a choice
    of:
2.5ml/½ tsp wholegrain mustard, or
2.5ml/½ tsp tomato purée and
    1.25ml/¼ tsp basil, or
2.5ml/½ tsp garlic powder and
    1.25ml/¼ tsp parsley, or
2.5ml/½ tsp chili powder

Clean the husks and silk from the ears/cobs of corn and wrap each in plastic wrap, or put into a roasting bag and seal tightly. Cook for about 8 minutes, turning once. Mix the butter with one or more of the flavoring choices and serve with the hot corn.

Leeks Provençale

PREPARATION TIME: 10 minutes

MICROWAVE COOKING TIME: 8 minutes

SERVES: 2 people

3 leeks, washed, trimmed and cut into
    5cm (2″) pieces
1 small clove garlic, finely chopped
2 tomatoes, chopped
15ml/1 tbsp oil
30ml/2 tbsps white wine
2.5ml/½ tsp thyme
15ml/1 tbsp chopped parsley
Salt and pepper

Put the oil into a 1150ml/2 pint/ 1 quart casserole, and add the leeks and garlic, tossing to coat. Cook, uncovered, for 3 minutes on HIGH, stirring occasionally. Add the herbs,

This page: Corn on the Cob with Flavored Butters. Facing page: French Peas (top) and Leeks Provençale (bottom).

white wine, salt and pepper, and cover and cook for a further 5 minutes on HIGH. Add the tomatoes and cook for 1 minute on HIGH. Serve immediately.

To serve one person, use 1 large or 2 small leeks and half of each of the other ingredients. Cook the leeks for 2 minutes on HIGH and after adding the other ingredients, cook for a further 3-4 minutes on HIGH. Add the tomatoes and cook for 1 minute on HIGH.

Eggplant/Aubergine Niramish

PREPARATION TIME: 20 minutes

MICROWAVE COOKING TIME: 17 minutes

SERVES: 2 people

1 eggplant/aubergine
30g/1oz/2 tbsps butter
1 clove garlic, finely chopped
1 small onion, chopped
1 small potato, diced
1 small carrot, diced
30g/1oz/¼ cup peas
225g/8oz/1 cup canned tomatoes,
   chopped and juice reserved
5ml/1 tsp flour/plain flour
30g/1oz/¼ cup raisins
30g/1oz/¼ cup pine nuts or chopped
   almonds
15ml/1 tbsp chopped coriander leaves or
   parsley
1.25ml/¼ tsp ground coriander
1.25ml/¼ tsp ground cumin
1.25ml/¼ tsp turmeric
1.25ml/¼ tsp fenugreek
1.25ml/¼ tsp ground ginger
Cayenne pepper
Paprika
Salt and pepper

GARNISH
60ml/2oz/¼ cup plain yogurt
Parsley or coriander leaves

Cut the eggplant/aubergine in half lengthwise and score the flesh lightly. Sprinkle with salt and leave to stand for 20 minutes. The salt will draw out any bitterness. Rinse the eggplant well and pat dry. Melt the butter for 30 seconds on HIGH in a large

casserole. Add the spices and cook for 2 minutes on HIGH. Add the onion, garlic, carrots and potatoes. Cover and cook for 3 minutes on HIGH. Stir in the flour and add the tomato juice and pulp and chopped coriander or parsley. Cover the bowl and cook on HIGH for a further 5 minutes or until vegetables are just tender. Add the raisins, nuts and peas. Put the eggplant in another casserole, cover, and cook for 5 minutes on HIGH. Scoop out the flesh and reserve the skins. Mix the eggplant with the vegetable filling and fill the skins. Sprinkle with paprika and cook for 3 minutes on HIGH. Serve immediately. Top with a spoonful of yogurt and garnish with sprigs of parsley or coriander.

To serve 1 person, prepare the full quantity, serve one half and freeze the other.

French Peas

PREPARATION TIME: 10 minutes

MICROWAVE COOKING TIME: 6-10 minutes

SERVES: 2 people

225g/8oz/1½ cups peas, fresh or frozen
4 leaves Romaine/cos lettuce
60g/2oz/½ cup parsley or chervil sprigs
120g/4oz/½ cup small onions, peeled
5ml/1 tsp sugar
15g/½ oz/1 tbsp butter
15g/½ oz/1 tbsp flour/plain flour
2 sticks celery, diced
140ml/¼ pint/½ cup chicken bouillon/
   stock
Salt and pepper

If using fresh peas, shell them and combine with the celery, onions, half the bouillon/stock, salt and pepper, and sugar in a 1150ml/2 pint/1 quart casserole. Cover and cook for 7 minutes on HIGH until almost tender. Add the lettuce and parsley (or chervil) and cook for a further 2 minutes on HIGH. Set aside. (If using frozen peas, combine the lettuce and parsley at the beginning and cook for a total of 5 minutes.) Melt the butter in a small bowl for 30 seconds on HIGH. Add the flour and remaining stock, and cook,

uncovered, for 1 minute on HIGH. Stir into the peas, and serve. Best cooked for 2 people.

Stuffed Potatoes

PREPARATION TIME: 15 minutes

MICROWAVE COOKING TIME: 18 minutes, plus 5 minutes standing time

SERVES: 1 person

1 large baking potato
10ml/2 tsps chopped chives
30ml/1oz/2 tbsps milk
2 strips bacon
30ml/1oz/2 tbsps sour cream
15g/½ oz/1 tbsp crumbled blue cheese
15g/½ oz/1 tbsp shredded/grated
   Cheddar cheese
15ml/1 tbsp dry seasoned breadcrumbs
Paprika
Salt and pepper

Heat a browning dish for 5 minutes on HIGH. Put in the bacon and cook for 2-3 minutes on HIGH, or until crisp. Crumble the bacon and set it aside. Pierce the potato skin several times with a fork. Put the potato on a plate and cook on HIGH for 5 minutes, or until soft. Turn over after 2 minutes. Cover it tightly in foil and leave it to stand for 5 minutes. Cut the potato in half lengthwise and scoop out the flesh, reserving the shells. Heat the milk for 30 seconds on HIGH, add to the potato with the sour cream and beat well. Add the chives, salt and pepper, bacon and blue cheese, and spoon into the potato shells. Sprinkle on the Cheddar cheese, crumbs and paprika. Cook on MEDIUM for 3 minutes and increase the setting to HIGH for 1 minute. Serve immediately.

For two people, use the full quantity recipe for a side dish, or double the quantity of each ingredient. Cook the potatoes for 7 minutes on HIGH, and the filled potato shells for 4 minutes on MEDIUM and 1 minute on HIGH.

Facing page: Eggplant/Aubergine Niramish (top) and Stuffed Potatoes (bottom).

CLB 1548
© 1986 Illustrations and text: Colour Library Books Ltd., Guildford, Surrey, England.
Text filmsetting by Focus Photoset Ltd., London, England.
Printed and bound in Barcelona, Spain by Cronión, S.A.
All rights reserved.
ISBN 0 86283 419 8